IN THE
FIRST LINE
OF
BATTLE

IN THE
FIRST LINE
OF
BATTLE
THE 12TH ILLINOIS CAVALRY
IN THE
CIVIL WAR

SAMUEL M. BLACKWELL, JR.

NORTHERN ILLINOIS UNIVERSITY PRESS, DEKALB

Library of Congress Cataloging-in-Publication Data

Blackwell, Samuel M.

In the first line of battle: the 12th Illinois Cavalry in the Civil War/

Samuel M. Blackwell, Jr.

p.   cm.

Includes bibliographical references (p.) and index.

ISBN 0-87580-279-6 (acid-free paper)

1. United States. Army. Illinois Cavalry Regiment, 12th (1862–1866)

2. Illinois–History–Civil War, 1861–1865–Regimental histories.

3. United States–History–Civil War, 1861–1865–Regimental histories. I. Title.

E505.6 12th .B58 2001

973.7'473–dc212001030469

To the officers and men of the

12th Illinois Volunteer Cavalry,

and to my mother,

Mrs. Bernice C. Blackwell

Contents

List of Maps

Acknowledgments

No one who ever completes a project like this can do it alone, and I am no exception. During the creation of this book many people offered their help and advice and lent considerable expertise to the preparation of the manuscript.

I would like to thank several of my colleagues at Northern Illinois University, particularly Otto H. Olsen, professor emeritus and former chair of the Department of History, for his patience and direction during the research and writing of this work. Few people have the pleasure of working with such an eminent historian and teacher. His support and his guidance were invaluable. Thanks also go to William Logue, professor emeritus of history, former assistant department chair, and director of graduate studies in the history department. His knowledge of military history and his patience in dealing with this project are greatly appreciated. Carl P. Parrini, professor emeritus of diplomatic history, was also of great help to me in his attention to detail regarding the French intervention in Mexico from 1863 until the end of the Civil War.

Several institutions generously contributed their resources and the services of their personnel to aid me in the completion of this project: the National Archives and Library of Congress in Washington, D.C.; the Institute of Military History at the U.S. Army War College, Carlisle Barracks, Pennsylvania; the Illinois State Archives and Illinois State Historical Library in Springfield, Illinois; the Chicago Historical Society; and the Founders Memorial Library at Northern Illinois University.

The Alderman Library at the University of Virginia supplied me not only with the letters of the William Henry Redman Collection but also with a number of photographs of the members of the 12th Illinois Cavalry. The Tennessee State Library and Archives in Nashville, Tennessee, supplied me with information on the role of the 12th Illinois during the final months of the war in 1865. The Mansfield State Commemorative Site in Mansfield, Louisiana, provided information on the performance of the 12th Illinois Cavalry during its year of service in that state. Donely Brice and Laura Sagert of the Texas State Library and Archives in Austin guided me through the papers of Andrew Jackson Hamilton, the first reconstruction governor of Texas. At the Institute of American History at the University of Texas, William Richter helped me sift through the Civil War newspaper collection there. Randy Gilbert of the Camp Ford Museum Project of Tyler, Texas, was also a great help in locating information about prisoners of war from the 12th Illinois who were interned at Camp Ford during the conflict.

Very special thanks go to many people in Virginia who assisted me often in their gracious way. Ludwell Harrison Johnson, professor emeritus of history at the College of William and Mary in Williamsburg; Robert K. Krick, chief historian at Fredericksburg, Chancellorsville, Spotsylvania National Military Park; and A. Wilson Greene, executive director at the Pamplin Civil War Site, deserve special thanks for helping me to narrow the focus of my research to the federal cavalry and for directing me toward cavalry organizations in Illinois.

Historians William Longacre, Clark B. Hall, Robert J. O'Neil, Dennis Frye, E. Skip Tyler, and Alan Tischler, as well as B. B. and Page Mitchell of the Brandy Station Association, unselfishly lent their time and expertise—at all hours of the day and night—to answering my many inquiries about the topography of the battlefields at Brandy Station.

I would like to thank Mark Whitlock, Captain, Ordinance, in the Illinois Army National Guard and assistant director of the Illinois Military Museum in Springfield, Illinois; and Dr. John Schmale of Mahomet, Illinois, who helped me with the information necessary to describe the regimental flag and company guidons that the 12th Illinois carried into war in 1861. Also thank you to Patricia Gardner Swanson and Diane Baker Orgler who gave me information about their families.

Finally, I would like to thank Barbara Sherman, Kevin Butterfield, and Mary Lincoln, my editors, who have shown uncommon expertise and patience in the preparation of this manuscript.

. . .

I chose the 12th Illinois Cavalry as a research topic after a trip to Camp Butler Military Cemetery on a cold blustery January day in the early 1990s.

I was looking for graves of another Illinois Cavalry regiment, the 8th, which is far better known than the 12th, included a larger number of famous persons, and came from a much more affluent area of northern Illinois. I had just heard a very informative presentation on the 8th Illinois by Marshall Krolick. Krolick, a past president of the Chicago Civil War Round Table, more than anyone else suggested I research the 12th. I thought I would begin my study by taking a look at some of the gravestones of the regiment's members to see if I could find names of men who had not lived through the training phase (there were usually a few in every regiment who perished from disease or exposure during the first weeks).

In my search I came across four gravestones of members of the 12th Illinois Cavalry Regiment. I asked Camp Butler foreman Michael Gavin if he knew anything about these four men, and he replied that he did not. He was aware that the 12th Illinois was known as the sister regiment of the 8th and had seen its share of combat, and that one of its colors was in the Hall of Flags in Springfield, but beyond that he knew very little. He added that he had never met anyone who knew much about the 12th. He was sure, however, that the records of the regiment were in the Illinois State Archives in Springfield if anyone would care to check them. After explaining this, he asked me to wait while he went inside his home, which is on the cemetery grounds, and he returned a moment later with a brief written history of Camp Butler.

The Civil War–era photo of Camp Butler appears to have been taken in the late winter or spring of 1862. It depicts a wooden stockade with walls that appear to be about ten feet high. There are a center gate, the usual guard towers, wooden buildings in which prisoners are housed, and what appears to be two formations of prisoners turned out for roll call. Outside the camp gates Union soldiers are going through close-order drill. A primitive road, which would later become Camp Butler Road (Illinois Rural Route 1), is in the foreground. The ground is dotted with patches of melting snow, and the trees are nearly bare. All in all, Camp Butler looks like what it was: a depressing, desolate military installation.

Camp Butler served two purposes during the Civil War. It was what today's U.S. Army would refer to as a Basic Combat Training Center, and it was also one of the prisoner-of-war camps that were so common during the Civil War. The prisoners who were interned at Camp Butler in 1862 were apparently Confederates who had been captured at Belmont, Missouri; Fort Donnelson, Tennessee; or Shiloh. The outcome of the war at that point was still very much in doubt, and I wondered about the attitudes of most of the prisoners housed in that central Illinois stockade. Mostly, however, I began to wonder about those four soldiers, the young men of the 12th Illinois who were buried here.

Mike Gavin bade me goodbye and wished me well in my hunt for the 12th Illinois. (He seemed to know I was going to write about the 12th Illinois before I did!) Then I drove to the Illinois State Archives in downtown Springfield.

At the Illinois State Archives I spoke with chief historian Wayne Temple, who is an acknowledged scholar on Abraham Lincoln and is one of the foremost experts on the history of the Illinois National Guard and the militia that preceded it. Wayne is a true gentlemen and is very patient with students of the Civil War who are trying to find their way through the maze of documents that tell the stories of the Illinois units that fought in the war. He directed me to the reports of the adjutant general, the chief administrative officer of the volunteer militia. The A.G., as he is informally called, published a roster that listed the members of each unit in the militia by name, age, date of birth, county or country of origin, occupation, and so on. The A.G.'s records included a brief history of each unit telling where it served during the war and which actions it participated in. One set of those A.G. records contains five volumes. After all, Illinois sent 157 infantry regiments, seventeen cavalry regiments, and four batteries of artillery to the U.S. Army during the war. When I looked up the adjutant general's records for the 12th Illinois, I discovered that the unit had served in three theaters of the war and had ended its tour in Texas during the first year of Reconstruction.

I returned to Northern Illinois University, where I was completing my doctorate in history. I ran a check and found that no other works existed on the 12th Illinois. I also checked in with the U.S. Army Institute of Military History at the U.S. Army War College at Carlisle Barracks, Pennsylvania. The institute holds the largest collection of unit histories in the United States. Its staff knows the whereabouts of every unit history that has been written and is aware of who is writing about which unit at any point in time.

The U.S. Army Institute of Military History is also the workplace of Richard Sommers. Dick is a superb historian, a true scholar of Grant's overland campaign of 1864, and a researcher with a near-encyclopedic mind. I asked him to do a search on the 12th Illinois and he agreed, but he could find nothing on the unit. (This was in the days before electronic search engines and Web sites. Since that time William Tubbs has written two articles for the *Illinois History Quarterly* that list all primary and secondary sources on every Illinois unit that served in the Civil War.) After talking with Dick Sommers I contacted Marshall Krolick in Chicago and told him what I had learned. He suggested that I contribute to the scholarship on Illinois mounted units by completing a history of the 12th Illinois Cavalry as a Ph.D. dissertation. Without his encouragement, I would never have undertaken this project.

Next I returned to the Illinois State Archives and met with senior archivists Lowell Voekel and Cody Wright one late-December morning. I put in a request for the files of the 12th Illinois Cavalry and was surprised when I was told that the "gurney" containing the records would be brought out shortly. The records of the 12th Illinois take up so much space that they must be rolled out on a six-foot-long hospital cart. They contain the original muster rolls and all official correspondence relating to the 12th Illinois during muster, training, and the first three years in service.

I remembered seeing Civil War–era sketches by artists like Alfred Waud that showed men enlisting in the army. Muster rolls were spread out on large tables under a tent awning or under a large tree. It seemed that each man must have stopped at least a dozen times to sign his name or write his initials. When I unfolded the first muster roll of the 12th Illinois, that of the regimental staff, I understood the drawings. The roll consumed two entire research tables.

Going through that first muster roll and those of the ten companies that followed was like taking a journey back in time to the spring of 1862. I began to feel that I was listening those men who were enlisting in the 12th Illinois. They were telling me who they were, where they lived, what they did for a living. They were even describing their physical appearance–their height, weight, age, eye color, and hair color. As I continued exploring the documents, I found letters from wives and mothers. Sometimes they were wondering about the whereabouts of their husbands and sons, and more often than not they were requesting the pension that was due mothers and widows of men who had fallen on the battlefield.

After I was finished perusing the records, I walked a few blocks to the old state capitol, where Lincoln had given his house-divided speech in 1858. I went downstairs to the manuscripts section of the Illinois State Historical Library. There I obtained the help of senior archivist Cheryl Schnirring, who like Richard Sommers and Wayne Temple is a superb researcher, and located most of my additional materials: letters, diaries, and other collections that relate to the 12th Illinois.

Finally, I returned to Northern Illinois University in DeKalb and presented my plan to Dr. Otto Olsen, chair of the Department of History and a noted scholar on the Civil War and Reconstruction. He listened, asked me where else I had checked for material on the 12th Illinois, then granted his approval of the topic. Dr. Olsen then urged me to check other cavalry-unit histories of both the Union and Confederate armies. When I did, I discovered that the bulk of the published histories on Illinois units were of the 6th and 7th Illinois Cavalry Regiments that had been with General Benjamin Grierson on his famous raid through Mississippi in the spring of

1863. And there was, of course, a history of the 8th Illinois by its surgeon Abner Hard, for which Marshall Krolick had written an introduction to the most recent edition.

As I read through a number of these regimental histories that were written in the decades after the war, I experienced the same feelings expressed by Warren Wilkenson in the preface to his marvelous volume, *Mother, May You Never See the Sights That I Have Seen.* Wilkenson writes of "flowery Victorian prose taking up space that would have been served better by facts." That made me want to explore the history of the 12th Illinois from the ground up. I was interested in the everyday life of the volunteer militiamen, in and out of combat. I was interested in what Emory Thomas calls the "mud and blood" of the soldiers' existence, from enlistment to muster to release from active duty.

The soldiers interested me. As I got to know them by reading their files, letters, and diaries, I began to realize that the 12th Illinois was similar to the other units I had read about in many ways, though also quite different. They participated in over twenty engagements and suffered around 250 casualties, and their enlistment was frozen for almost a year after the war was over.

To learn more about the men of the 12th Illinois and their experiences during the war, I needed their military records. I made numerous lengthy journeys to the National Archives and Records Administration in Washington, D.C., to obtain the records. Mike Musik and Bill Lynd were indispensable in helping me to search through the maze of the company muster rolls, the regimental order books, and the soldiers' individual military and pension records. They also directed me to the map divisions of the National Archives and the Library of Congress. There I was able to obtain duplicates of various Civil War maps that helped me to understand the terrain on which the men of the 12th Illinois fought.

Not only did I need to see a map of the terrain, particularly that of the battle locations in Virginia, but I also needed to walk through the areas where the 12th Illinois had fought and to see the small communities and road networks that still existed. I had to see the rivers and the fords, anything that would help me to get an idea of what the 12th Illinois had experienced during the four years they were in the service of the United States. These areas were not going to be easy to find. In the days before high-flying aircraft and satellites, cavalry units north and south were the eyes and the ears of the army. Therefore, they usually did not camp near the main body. They were always out in front, searching and probing enemy lines, trying to find out the strength and direction of the enemy force. Most of the locations where they fought are not on National Park Service maps or even on state or county maps. A scholar must have the help of local historians who know their towns and counties like the back of their hand. In this aspect of my research, I was indeed fortunate.

In Virginia Clark B. Hall, who has accomplished so much in the preservation of the battlefield at Brandy Station near Culpeper, Virginia, graciously gave took the time to show me around the battlefield of Fleetwood Heights. He also introduced me to Bob O'Neil, whose fine work on the cavalry battles of Aldie, Middleburg, and Upperville I quote often in this book. O'Neil directed me to places in northwestern Virginia where the 12th Illinois was involved in the opening actions of the Gettysburg campaign. When I visited Antietam, park historian Ted Alexander helped me to realize that although the road network around McCoy's Ford is no longer exactly the way it was when Stuart crossed there and opposed the 12th Illinois in October 1862. There have been some changes to the road network, and I discuss them in the manuscript. Don Stockton, who has created many maps for the Brandy Station Association and for a number of historical publications, Terry Sheahan, and H. E. Howard and Co. were of great help with the maps that appear in this book.

Allan Tischler, author of the *Harpers Ferry Cavalry Escape,* and Denis Frye, former chief historian at Harpers Ferry National Historic Park, spent many hours with me explaining the route of the 12th Illinois Cavalry as it escaped right under the guns of A. P. Hill's Confederate corps on that dark night in September of 1862. Robert J. Krick of the Chancellorsville, Fredericksburg, Spotsylvania National Military Park and A. Wilson Greene, now of Pamplin Park Civil War Site, Dinwiddie County, Virginia, gave of their time on a couple of hot Virginia afternoons to point me to sources of information about the combat record of the 12th Illinois that I had not thought of.

One of the most fascinating discoveries I made was a collection at the Alderman Library of the University of Virginia at Charlottesville of letters written by William Henry Redman. Robert Johnson, the curator for the Alderman Library, introduced me to the collection. Redman had risen from the rank of private to that of captain in the 12th Illinois. He was captured in the winter of 1862 and escaped, he participated in the Stoneman Raid, he was with the 12th Illinois on the first day at Gettysburg, and he survived the Third Battle of Brandy Station. Redman reenlisted as a veteran and finished the war as the regimental historian in May of 1866. He returned to his home in Lanark, Illinois, for a short while, then moved to Iowa City, where he graduated from the University of Iowa, became a lawyer, and for many years served in the Iowa legislature as the Speaker of the House of Representatives.

At Gettysburg National Military Park, historian D. Scott Hartwig gave unselfishly of his time and considerable expertise on the cavalry of Buford's division on the first day at Gettysburg. It was Scott who pointed me toward the manuscript room at the Chicago Historical Society, where I found a very informative letter written by Colonel William Gamble, who commanded Buford's 1st Brigade in the afternoon of 1 July. The letter traces the movements of his brigade all through that afternoon and confirms what Scott and I had suspected, that the 12th Illinois and three other regiments saved the Union army from certain destruction.

In Louisiana Sam Hyde of the Center for Regional Studies at Southeastern Louisiana University in Hammond, Louisiana, supplied me with bibliographic materials pertaining to the Civil War in that state. Steve Mayeaux provided me with material on the Red River campaign of 1864. John House of the Mansfield Louisiana Commemorative Historical Site pointed me toward with a great deal of material on the role of the 12th Illinois Cavalry in the Red River campaign.

In Tennessee, at the State Library and Archives, Marilyn Bell-Hughes lent her considerable expertise by helping me to track down reports in various Memphis newspapers about the 12th Illinois's conflict with bushwhackers during the final days of the Civil War. And finally, in Texas information on the last assignment of the 12th Illinois was provided by archivist and historian Donely Brice, who was particularly helpful in guiding me through the papers of Andrew Jackson Hamilton, the first Reconstruction governor of Texas. Donely put me in touch with Barry Crouch of the Gallaudet University in Washington, D.C. Barry is a fount of knowledge about the records of the Freedmen's Bureau and about the history of Texas during Reconstruction. Randy Gilbert, with his incredible database of the Confederate Military Prison at Camp Ford, Texas, supplied me with the names of the four members of the 12th Illinois Cavalry who were imprisoned there until the Trans-Mississippi Confederate government granted their final exchange over a month after the surrender of Lee's army at Gettysburg.

IN THE
FIRST LINE
OF
BATTLE

Introduction

In the months after war broke out in April 1861, 750 young Illinois men, mostly from the northern part of the state, volunteered for active duty and prepared to fight a war that threatened the security of the United States in a way that the young nation had never experienced. These men who formed the 12th Illinois Volunteer Cavalry have been left out of historical accounts of the conflict, but their story deserves telling.

The 12th Illinois Cavalry was the only mounted unit from Illinois that served in three different theaters of combat. It was one of only two Illinois mounted units that spent a great deal of time in the eastern theater of the war, serving primarily in Virginia, then under the Department of the Gulf and Eastern Louisiana. The 12th even operated out of Memphis, Tennessee, for a short time under the Department of the Mississippi.

The troops of the 12th Illinois began serving the Union in early 1862 and later were faced with a circumstance that is one of the greatest fears of all militia and reserve units—they were frozen in service after the end of the war. While the U.S. Army was undergoing a major reorganization in late 1865 and early 1866, the 12th Illinois was forced to remain in Federal service in the Trans-Mississippi and was sent to Texas. It remained in the east-central part of that state during the early days of Reconstruction and engaged in pacification duty until late June 1866, easing tensions between blacks and whites and maintaining order in an uneasy time. In the summer of 1866 the men returned to

Illinois and the unit was finally disbanded. After four long years, the men were at last to return to their homes.

What follows is a narrative history of an Illinois cavalry unit that is remarkable in many ways. It fought in three theaters, remained in uniform long after Lee's surrender, experienced a major disruption in unit harmony, suffered a high desertion rate, and yet came through the war with colors intact. The troops suffered through more than twenty conflicts over the course of their service, and their casualties were high—some two hundred. In spite of such crippling adversity, most of the original members of the 12th Illinois discharged honorably in June 1866.

No early or current academic study of the 12th Illinois exists in the National Archives and Records Administration or the Library of Congress in Washington, D.C.; the Institute of Military History at the U.S. Army War College in Carlisle Barracks, Pennsylvannia; the Illinois State Archives or the Illinois Historical Library in Springfield, Illinois. For whatever reason, the ordinary men of the 12th Illinois left their history to whoever was assigned the detail of compiling it and went their separate ways. Some of the men participated in a veteran's organization called the Grand Army of the Republic, and their reunions continued well into the twentieth century. A few of the commissioned officers of the 12th Illinois became members of the Military Order of the Loyal Legion of the United States. But most of the men of the 12th resumed their normal lives as much as possible after the war and faded away into history. These men from northern Illinois who rode off to war in the spring of 1862, and who remained away for more than four years with only one Christmas interlude, have been mostly forgotten.

In any war the front-line participants know little of the overall strategic planning that goes into a military operation. The men of the 12th Illinois were no different. What they knew was from their own experience as front-line soldiers or was gleaned from the rumor mill and local newspapers. This history will place the 12th Illinois within the larger conflict, but as much as possible the story will be told from its members' perspective. Many of the words and phrases describing the role of the 12th in camp life, furlough, and combat are from original source materials. They are the written words of men in 12th or in units that fought closely beside them. This is the story of ordinary men who were placed in extraordinary circumstances in a war that most of them supported and thought they understood.

The immediate provocation, as the young men from northern Illinois understood it, was the secession in 1861. Most of the members of the 12th Illinois were devoted to preserving the Union, and they were willing to leave their homes, wives, families, and sweethearts to risk their own lives to preserve America's unique experiment in representative government. So away they—the Headquarters Company along with Companies A, B, C, D, E, F, and G, approximately 480 men—went to war in the spring of 1862 with heads held high, and guidons, the swallow-tailed pennants that marked each squadron and company in the boots of the color sergeants, in the front ranks with the colonel and regimental staff. Companies H and I, originally known as Barker's and McClellan's Dragoons, joined the Regiment in the early fall of that year. The soldiers' horses pranced down the main streets of Springfield to the train station. Sabers and spurs were jingling, bugles were sounding, and bands were playing. The men were loaded on a government-chartered train, and they headed east, expecting to end the war in less than a year.

"Rally 'round the Flag"

When war broke out in April 1861, the president of the United States, in a somewhat belated effort to stem a six-month-long rebellion, placed the regular army on alert. Soldiers moved from their posts on the western frontier to the East, where the major battles would undoubtedly be fought. The problem was that the regular U.S. Army was a small organization of 1,108 officers and 15,529 enlisted men.[1]

Because there was no formal army reserve, and conscription was not yet on anyone's mind, Lincoln had no practical choice but to do what the Constitution says that a chief executive can do during a time of rebellion: call forth the state militias to put down the insurrection. He issued a call for seventy-five thousand militia troops to augment the regular army. The militia rolls were impressive: those in the North showed 2,471,377 men and those in the South about one million.[2]

The figures for both North and South, however, were misleading. Quite often, men whose names appeared on the rolls were old and infirm, and some had been dead for years. Michigan, for example, had 109,000 men on the muster rolls but could assemble only 1,241 men in twenty-eight companies on short notice. In Illinois, as in most other Midwestern states, it quickly became apparent that these few regiments of soldiers were not going to be enough and that all the state militias in the Union could not field the seventy-five thousand volunteers that Lincoln had asked for. So Illinois and other states began to organize volunteer militias.[3]

Entire regiments that had existed on paper were disbanded, and their officers and senior noncommissioned officers, known as "the cadre," were elevated in rank several grades above their pre-1861 position and sent out to recruit as many men as could be found. The more men a militia officer recruited, the higher rank he would hold in the volunteer militia. Thus, many militia sergeants became lieutenants or captains, and many captains and lieutenants became majors or lieutenant colonels. The result was an army of virtually untrained troops led by officers who knew little more than the rudiments of military drill and how to fire a musket.

Other military units were organized by prominent citizens who had high political connections with state government and were rewarded with command of the regiments that they raised. This system produced a very large volunteer army of more than two and a half million men, mostly infantry, before the conflict ended. Illinois furnished more than its share of soldiers, sending 156 regiments of infantry, seventeen regiments of cavalry, and five batteries of artillery to fight the War of the Rebellion between 1861 and 1865. The Illinois contribution amounted to fully one-tenth of the soldiers in the U.S. Army during the Civil War. The Illinois men fought in every theater of the war with, for the most part, impressive combat records.[4]

The majority of the men from Illinois who enlisted in the army went into the infantry. It was considered the place to be: where the action was and where the demand was. Some, however, preferred the cavalry, which was considered by many to be the *corps d'elite* of the Union army. Young men enlisted in the cavalry because they thought it glamorous, because they were familiar with horses, or because they just did not like the idea of walking. Most of them had either read or heard about Sir Walter Scott's character Charles O'Malley, the Irish Dragoon, and the thrill of being a cavalryman was undeniable.[5]

Everything about the cavalryman made him special. Even his clothing was different. Early in the war the Union cavalryman wore a short jacket trimmed in yellow, and around his waist was a gold or yellow sash. His pants were doubly reinforced—which made them look smarter as well as last longer—and sported yellow stripes down the side. He wore high riding boots with brass spurs on the heels that jingled when he rode or walked. Instead of gloves he wore gauntlets that stretched from his wrists halfway to his elbows. The saber that he wore at his side jingled in cadence with his spurs as he rode. The cavalryman carried the carbine rifle, which was lighter and easier to load and fire than the standard infantryman's weapon. If he was unfortunate enough to run out of ammunition for his carbine, there was always his Colt or Remington revolver, which he could fire six times.[6]

The cost of equipping a mounted unit was one reason the War Department was less than enamored with the cavalry. While it was relatively inexpensive to equip a regiment of infantry, the cost for a cavalry regiment was around six hundred thousand dollars, and Lincoln's first secretary of war, Simon Cameron, simply did not want to spend that much. Also, most officers of the old army believed that the uses of the cavalry were limited, that the cavalry was more for show than for real combat duty. Because they were products of the other branches of the combat arm—infantry, artillery, and engineers—they were not well informed about the proper use of cavalry. The United States Military Academy at West Point did not even have a course in cavalry tactics until 1847. Lieutenant James M. Hawse did initiate a West Point course in equestrian cavalry tactics in 1847, but because of discrimination by an in-fantry-biased high command, the army had no cavalry until 1832, when a battalion of mounted infantry was formed.[7]

Cavalry regiments had achieved fame in the Mexican-American War, among them the 3rd United States Regiment, which fought so well at Cha-pultepec and survived the war intact. But most of those regiments were dis-banded or demobilized and sent home after that conflict. In 1855 U.S. Secre-tary of War Jefferson Davis, a veteran of Mexico, began to reform the army and authorized two additional regiments of cavalry, the 1st and 2nd Dra-goons. This gave the United States three cavalry regiments and one mounted infantry regiment during the six years before the outbreak of the Civil War.[8]

At the end of the 1850s the army once again changed its Table of Organi-zation and Equipment (T.O.E.). The 1st and 2nd Dragoons became the 1st and 2nd Cavalry; the regiment of mounted rifles was combined with the 3rd Dragoons to become the 3rd Cavalry; the old 1st and 2nd Cavalry of the Mexican War were renumbered the 4th and 5th Cavalry; and a new regiment was added, the 6th Cavalry. At the onset of the Civil War the United States had fewer than four thousand mounted troops, most of whom were, at the sound the guns at Fort Sumter, making their way back to the East from their far-flung posts on the frontier. But not all regular cavalrymen returned to the East. A great many officers and some enlisted men resigned from the Federal service and joined the Confederacy. Still others remained at their frontier posts to help keep the Indian menace at bay while whites fought one another.[9]

Like it or not, the government was going to have to use the volunteer mounted units. There would be three major combat theaters and a host of minor departments, so it became clear that a large number of cavalry units would be needed. Simon Cameron, Lincoln's secretary of war, began to ac-cept volunteer cavalry regiments in the summer of 1861. By that time, Illinois had already begun to recruit its mounted units. The first seven Illinois cavalry regiments during the Civil War were designated for the West and the Trans-Mississippi. The 8th Illinois, from the counties of Cook, DuPage, Kane, and Kendall, was one of the first Illinois cavalry units to be organized to serve in the East. It arrived in the Virginia theater early in the conflict and remained there almost until the end of the war.[10]

The 12th Illinois Volunteer Cavalry would serve in three theaters of conflict, beginning in the East. It was organized by a special order from the U.S. Department of War as a two-battalion regiment comprising eight companies. The companies were lettered from A to K, and their muster bore the dates of 24 and 28 February 1862.[11]

While the companies were being organized, the regiment went into training at Camp Douglas near Chicago. The men did not stay there long. Like so many early Federal camps of instruction, Camp Douglas was part basic-training establishment and part prisoner-of-war facility.[12] There were seven thousand Confederate prisoners at Camp Douglas, so there was much guarding of POWs and little military drill. Because of the number of prisoners interned there and the close confines of the prison area, disease was a constant problem. Two men, from Companies D and G, died at the camp. The 12th Illinois was soon transferred to Camp Butler, six miles from Springfield, Illinois.[13]

Like Camp Douglas, Camp Butler housed many Confederate prisoners from the early battles in Tennessee and Missouri and even a few Rebels from the Virginia theater. It also had too many men in too close confinement, and disease, particularly pneumonia, was rampant. At Camp Butler there are graves of 847 Confederate soldiers who died during imprisonment during the Civil War, and there also are plenty of Union graves. Eight men from the 12th Illinois's Companies A, C, D, E, and F perished in the months of February, March, and April 1862 during the time of organization and initial training at Camp Butler, seven of them from disease.[14]

Camp Butler was located adjacent to a military cemetery in the rolling hills of central Illinois. It was one of the worst camps of instruction even by the standards of the time. Camp Butler was new, had been hastily constructed, was dirty and overcrowded, and was unprepared when members of the 12th Illinois began to arrive in large numbers to begin the instruction phase of the training that eventually would turn them into soldiers. Trooper Ashley Alexander of Company A wrote that many soldiers had to build their own barracks and set up stoves to keep themselves warm. He commented that it was rather cold but that he liked the "central climate" better than that of the northern counties where he was raised and that of Texas, which he had visited.[15]

Arms and horses had not yet been delivered when the regiment first arrived, so the men engaged in infantry drill: they marched; formed platoons, companies, and battalions; studied the arms manual; learned how to use the bayonet and how to salute (and who not to salute); received warnings about punishments they would receive if transgressions occurred, and so on. One of the great fears of volunteer cavalrymen in general, and of the 12th Illinois in particular, was that if they became too proficient in infantry drill, they might remain infantry. In a fit of rage, regiment commander Colonel Arno Voss proclaimed that he would disband the 12th Illinois if equipment and horses were not quickly furnished. "He did not bring us down here to guard prisoners," Trooper Alexander wrote.[16]

But the basic school of the soldier always has been the infantry, so they drilled, usually for four hours a day, whether they liked it or not. The training usually was conducted by sergeants and lieutenants. Major John Fonda, a veteran of the war with Mexico, was probably the only instructor of the 12th Illinois who had any combat experience. How much help Fonda was able to give the 12th Illinois in the early months of 1862 is open to speculation. As camp commandant he was responsible not only for basic infantry training (drill, ceremony, and firearms and bayonet instruction), but also for procurement of food (for men and horses), clothing, weapons, and ammunition. The inexperienced instructors, managed as well as they could. They read the drill manual, interpreted what had to be done, and applied it to the recruits.[17]

Soldiers at that time were drilled in what is known today as linear combat. Long parallel lines of soldiers would march toward each other, halt approximately fifty yards apart, fire their weapons into the enemy ranks, and then charge with the empty muskets and bayonets. The idea was to get as many men as possible to fire at the same time, thereby discharging a virtual wall of lead at their opponents.

While each company was being drilled, new recruits were constantly being registered on the muster rolls. The 12th Illinois, like most other volunteer units, had recruiters not only in the counties that fed the regiment but also in other parts of the state. Men were registering volunteers in such diverse places as Joliet, Springfield, Quincy, and Chicago. As each recruit arrived, he was issued what equipment and clothing were available, possibly a pair of woolen pants, some shoes, a greatcoat (not all of the men in the 12th Illinois had a greatcoat that winter—in fact, unless they had civilian outerwear, many had no overcoat at all), some gloves, and an old musket that had probably been in a militia armory since 1818, when Illinois became a state.[18]

In addition to the problems of close-order drill and limited clothing and equipment, there was the daily drill with a twelve-pound musket in the middle of winter. Trooper Winthrop S. G. Allen of Company F wrote in a letter to his family that all of the men in his company drilled except the captain, a man by the name of William Gilmore, who apparently had received his commission because of his friendship with an unnamed state official. Allen wrote that Captain Gilmore was "extremely impressed" with the fact that he was an officer and had total control over the lives of some sixty individuals. Criticisms of officers by enlisted men, spoken and unspoken, were common during training, but action was taken against Gilmore. The "hateful, mean, and incompetent" man was asked to resign by the executive officer of the regiment, Lieutenant Colonel Hasbrouck Davis, after several complaints were lodged. Released from the service, Gilmore became the "amiable sort of fellow" he apparently had been before the war and his leadership role changed him.[19]

As spring approached and the weather became more tolerable, the drill began to improve, and the troops of the 12th Cavalry began to receive equipment. As horses began to arrive, the morale of the men shot high. They would remain a mounted unit. Eventually each man was issued all of his equipment, which included one blue greatcoat with yellow facing, one dress jacket, one pair of cavalry boots, two blankets (one for the horse and one for the trooper), one pair of shoes, two shirts, two pairs of underdrawers, two pairs of socks (wool, double-footed), one kepi forage cap, and one stable hook. Each also received a pair of spurs, a canteen, a haversack, a saddle and saddlebags, a surcingle, a nose bag, a picket pin and a lariat, a curb bit and a bridle halter, a watering bridle, and a curry comb and brush. Each man was issued a saber and a saber belt, a carbine and a carbine sling, a revolver, holsters for the revolver and the carbine, gun tools, and two cartridge boxes. One Iowa cavalryman recalled:

> Fully equipped for the field, the green cavalryman was a fearful and wonderful object. Mounted upon his charger, in the midst of all the paraphernalia and adornments of war, a moving arsenal and military depot, he must have struck surprise if not terror, into the minds of his enemies. . . . This mass of furniture, with the saddle, would weigh in most cases seventy pounds. . . . When the rider was in the saddle, begirt with all his magazine, it was easy to imagine him protected from any ordinary assault. His properties rose before and behind him like fortifications, and those strung over his shoulders covered well his flanks. To the uninitiated it was a mystery how the rider got into the saddle.[20]

Horses were issued at the end of the spring. Like most mounts of volunteer units, they seem to have been largely unbroken and untrained. A cavalryman of the 7th Indiana described a cavalry review that probably was very similar to cavalry reviews of the 12th Illinois in its early days of mounted drill.

> The men were as green as their horses, some of them never having been on a horse's back. . . . Those who had wild steeds, had great difficulty in maintaining their positions in the saddle, and some in attempting to mount suddenly found themselves on the ground. However, after great effort, the horses were

sufficiently quieted, so as to stand in reasonable proximity to each other. . . . [The colonel] gave the command "Draw Sabres." The men obeyed the order. The sabres in being drawn made a great rattling and clatter, and waved over the horses' heads, the sight and sound of which greatly frightened them.[21]

Forty-two men of the 12th Illinois's Company A were dispatched to guard the Springfield armory during the June 1862 vote on the proposed new Illinois constitution. During a rainstorm the untrained horses reared and plunged, depositing their riders on the ground. "Some wheeled and dashed madly about," and it was a wonder, wrote Alexander, that no one was killed. "Unfortunate" enough to have been selected by Colonel Voss to guard the armory, Alexander complained about the untrained chargers issued to Company A and that because he was busy guarding the armory, he did not get to vote—"all because of Colonel Voss and the damned old Democrats."[22]

When the 12th Illinois was finally mounted and equipped with everything except their carbines and was going through ever more serious drill, the martial spirit seemed to fade a bit. Guarding the prisoners also was beginning to wear down the once-eager men. Alexander wrote that he would love to get out of the service and expressed a change in attitude toward the Confederate prisoners that was shared by some of his fellow recruits. They were "the worst looking wretches that the lord ever let exist as men. They are dressed in all colors and fashions. It is hard to tell an officer from a private. I would like to hang every one of them." With the arrival of spring the prisoners began to attempt escape. Winthrop Allen believed that the farmers around the area harbored the runaway Rebels, but a search party scoured a number of farms and found very few of them. The men of the 12th were pleased to hear rumors that all the prisoners would be sent north to Camp Douglas and that Camp Butler would be closed.[23]

Rebel prisoners would not long be a problem for the 12th Illinois, however. On 24 June 1862, approximately three months after mustering in, the regiment received orders to entrain for the front. The assignment was to the eastern theater of the war: the town of Martinsburg, Virginia, among the northern approaches to the Shenandoah Valley. The regiment that left Springfield, Illinois, three days later was an eight-company regiment of approximately seven hundred men. Three additional companies, known as Barker's and McClellan's Dragoons, awaited them in Virginia. The regimental commander was Colonel Arno Voss, a forty-two-year-old resident of Chicago who had seen some service in the 7th Illinois Volunteer Infantry earlier in the war. Like many Union cavalry commanders, Colonel Voss was of German descent, having been born in Prussia. Voss was not a very popular man, and his politics might have been the problem. He was a member of the loyal opposition. Lincoln referred to him as "a damned irreconcilable democrat" during one of his famous debates with Stephen Douglas.[24]

The second in command, executive officer Lieutenant Colonel Hasbrouck Davis, was a Chicago lawyer whose law firm, Davis and Nissen, had offices over the Hoffman and Gelpeke's Bank at 46 LaSalle Street. Third in command was Major Hamilton B. Dox, a Chicago banker whom Davis wanted in the regiment because "he was and had been a good friend." John Fonda, commandant at Camp Butler and a well-qualified officer of Dutch descent, was the second major. Jonathan Slade and Alexander Stewart were the battalion adjutants. Rounding out the commissioned staff was the chaplain, Abraham Joseph Warner, an Episcopal priest from Waterbury, Connecticut, who had lived in the Midwest for many years. He stayed with the regiment through its first enlistment, and his private diary survives to this day. By modern standards this was a small staff, but it probably was augmented by orderlies.[25]

As the 12th Illinois Volunteer Cavalry stood in the Springfield depot waiting to entrain for the eastern battlefields, the average age of its members was twenty-five years and five months. The youngest recruits were sixteen and the oldest forty-eight. One of the companies had an average age of twenty-eight, another twenty-three. One company had as many as twenty-five troopers under the age of twenty. Another company had thirteen men over forty years of age, while two companies had no one that old.[26] (See appendix for a table showing the makeup of the 12th.)

The average height of the men in the 12th Illinois was five feet, eight inches, a bit below what some people considered to be the ideal height for a cavalryman. The tallest man in the regiment was six feet, three inches, and the shortest was 4 feet, 8 inches; both of them were of unusual height for horse soldiers. Coincidentally, the company with the shortest recruit also could boast of having the most men over six feet, a total of thirteen.

About 50 percent of the men in the 12th listed Illinois as their place of birth. Those from outside the state were primarily from New York, Ohio, and Pennsylvania. Many of the men were foreign born, with the majority of the immigrants fairly evenly divided between Irishmen and Germans.

It is safe to say that the regiment was a mirror of its time as far as occupations of the recruits. The vast majority were farmers. Among those born across the Atlantic, the Irish were the common laborers and the Germans the skilled craftsmen. One of the companies was lucky enough to include a Russian cigar maker, another had a musician and a "gentleman." There were blacksmiths, shoemakers, saddlers, masons, and teamsters. The 12th could boast of several railroad men, engineers, gunsmiths, and coopers on its list of recruits.

The officer corps at the company level was typical. Most of the officers seem to have received their commissions because of political contacts or because of personal contacts with officers high in the regiment. Most were professional men, chiefly lawyers.[27]

It must have been a stirring sight to see the 12th Illinois Cavalry at the train station in Springfield on the morning of the 27 June 1862. The men would have been formed into companies, each with its own swallow-tailed guidon that it would carry all through the war. With the regimental commander would be the national colors and the regimental standard unfurled to catch the breeze. The regimental standard of the 12th Illinois Volunteer Cavalry depicted an eagle with wings spread on a blue field. The numerical designation of the unit appeared on a scroll at the bottom of the eagle's talons.[28]

As the men of the 12th Illinois boarded the train for the eastern theater, their thoughts were like those most American soldiers who have joined the colors in a conflict. They thought their tour would be filled with high adventure, thrilling mounted charges, and personal glory for all. Those who returned to Illinois for their first furlough eighteen months later described to their families a much different war, a war with neither glory nor thrill.

"Drop Carbines!...Draw Sabres!....Charge!"

When the 12th Illinois Volunteer Cavalry departed from Springfield on 27 June 1862, Private Ashley H. Alexander seemed glad enough to leave Camp Butler and commented that the command was in high spirits, eager to get to the East. The 12th Illinois would finally see some action.[1]

The original marching orders appear to have been well thought out. Colonel Arno Voss, commander of the 12th Illinois Cavalry, had arranged for only two troops, each equivalent to an infantry company of about sixty men and officers, to travel on the first of three trains. The horses and their forage were to be connected to the trains so everyone and everything would arrive in Virginia as a unit, ready to be offloaded and committed to action. This was not to be. The horses and the farriers who handled them left before the troops, and neither the "horses nor those who took care of them had anything to eat."[2]

By the morning of 28 June, the troop trains were at the crossing of the Illinois Central Railroad about eighty miles from Springfield and forty-three miles from the Illinois-Indiana state line, near the present site of Tolono, Illinois. Alexander wrote to his sister the following month that the country in that part of Illinois was flat, with many small farms dotting the landscape and only a few train stations with small towns around them. Only one town in Illinois "seemed to have any respect for soldiers." The women of Homer were waiting with baskets of pies and cakes when the train stopped there for water. The young ladies wished the troops well and joked that if the train stayed long enough, they might return "with horses and carry some of us to their respective homes."[3]

The chaplain noted that the people of Indiana seemed more patriotic than the people of Illinois. At Arnica Arno Voss came out of the officers' car and spoke to the crowd that had gathered at the railroad station. "He addressed them for some time giving an account of his regiment; whence they came, whither they were going, and that they had an arduous task to maintain the high position which the western troops had already gained for bravery and good conduct in the field."[4]

On the morning the troops prepared to leave Indianapolis, a soldier from Company B, drunk from the night before, was shot by Captain Stephen Bronson of Company C, who had been called upon to discipline the still-besotted enlisted man. The soldier "was left in the hospital in Indianapolis" to recuperate. Such internal conflict was not uncommon among Union regiments, but for the 12th Illinois and Captain Bronson this was only the beginning.[5]

Near Zanesville, Ohio, the troop train finally overtook the train containing the horses and farriers. The soldiers found it a welcome sight, for if the 12th arrived at its destination with no mounts, it would face the possibility of becoming an infantry regiment, a fate that no self-respecting cavalryman would have tolerated. After leaving Zanesville the military transport train was sidetracked at Spencer Station to permit a passenger train to pass and to await another engine to assist it in climbing a steep grade. There a citizen tossed a paper into the train that contained accounts of the Seven Days campaign then in progress around Richmond. The Federals taking a licking in Virginia, but the morale of the 12th Illinois remained high. All of the men were anxious to "see the elephant," their term for a unit's first experience in combat.[6]

From Spencer Station the train traveled to Cambridge, Ohio. After leaving Cambridge the 12th suffered its second casualty of the trip: a soldier standing on top of one of the cars was hit by a bridge and killed. The clearance of the bridges of early railroads was barely high enough to accommodate the rail cars, let alone an observer standing on top of one to get a better view.

After several delays the troop train was finally allowed to complete its journey into Wheeling, Virginia (now West Virginia), where it arrived at about midnight. The following day the men unloaded the trains and set up a semipermanent bivouac on an island in the middle of the Ohio River between Bridgeport, Ohio, and Wheeling. To the men of the 12th Illinois, Camp Carlisle had perfect scenery and security. One member of the unit described the camp as an old fairground nestled in a valley that would "compare with many a one in Switzerland."[7]

On the Fourth of July the members of the 12th Illinois Volunteer Cavalry became the center of attention as the vanguard of a parade through downtown Wheeling. Later that night there was a fireworks display at Camp Carlisle. Almost a full year before the formal secession of the western counties of Virginia from the Confederacy, intense pro-Union feeling was apparent in Wheeling, one of western Virginia's largest communities and its northernmost.

On 7 July the 12th Cavalry was ordered to proceed to Camp Wool, located on the Martinsburg-Winchester Turnpike near Martinsburg, Virginia. Martinsburg was a hotbed of secessionist feeling. The Confederate spy Belle Boyd had grown up there, and the Rebel raiders of Brigadier Turner Ashby had quartered there as houseguests of the townspeople earlier in the year. As the men of the 12th Illinois arrived and set up camp, they received the welcome news that their principal weapons had at last arrived.[8]

The men were to be equipped with the Burnside carbine, a first-class weapon purchased by the Federal government in larger numbers than any other. Patented on 25 March 1856 by Ambrose E. Burnside (later to be commander of the Army of the Potomac), it was produced in four types and was the first U.S. Army weapon to use a metallic cartridge. The 12th Illinois Cavalry used the type-3 Burnside carbine during most of the Civil War. It fired a .54-caliber round that was described by Sergeant Winthrop S. G. Allen as "a real man-stopper." The carbine was "convenient and pretty as well as destructive and a terrible weapon—they are about 2 1/2 [foot] long barrel 2 ft. breech loading, and rifled." Allen continued, "One can load and fire them 10 times per minute with care and take a very deliberate aim, in some target practice the other day a ball was shot 400 yards through a sheet iron car which is about 1/16 inch thick and almost cut through the other side."[9]

Throughout the months of July and August the men of the 12th Illinois familiarized themselves with their weapons and trained for what would later be called search-and-destroy missions. Rebel guerrilla bands were becoming a serious problem, and it was hoped that the 12th Illinois would help to keep them under control. Unbeknownst to the men of the 12th, their unit had become part of a loosely organized mounted force whose mission was to guard the northernmost approaches to the Shenandoah Valley against a Confederate invasion of the states of Ohio and Pennsylvania.

The Rebel guerrillas used the remote northern Virginia mountains as a lair from which to strike at the Federal-dominated railroads and garrisons in the region. Approaching the Union camps under cover of darkness, the Rebels would get close enough to the pickets to tell friend from foe then open fire into the faces of the Federal cavalrymen and gallop away. The raids were especially deadly because Confederate guerrilla bands favored the double-barreled shotgun, which at close range can do about as much damage to a human body as a small cannon.[10]

The Federals retaliated by stretching a rope attached to two trees across the road at night and placing a man on either side of the road. When the Rebels arrived, the two Union troopers hidden in the trees would raise the rope, "clotheslining" the Confederates. In the confusion Federal cavalrymen hidden in ambush would open fire and either kill or seriously wound most of the raiders. The tactic effectively checked many of the guerrilla attacks, but the raids had awakened the officers and men of the 12th Illinois to the fact that they no longer were in a secure, peaceful environment; they were indeed at war.[11]

The guerrilla attacks to which the members of the 12th Illinois Cavalry were subjected during the last weeks of the summer of 1862 were carried out by bands of Confederate partisans that were augmented by a few battalions of regulars sent into the Shenandoah Valley by the Richmond government. The partisan bands had no centralized structure, and what little organization there was appears to have been a holdover from the earlier activities of partisan leader Turner Ashby, who had a phenomenal reputation as both a guerrilla leader and a conventional cavalry commander in Stonewall Jackson's celebrated Shenandoah Valley campaign.

Ashby was a self-taught soldier who until the death of his brother at the hands of a Federal cavalry patrol had looked at the war as a kind of sport. He had ridden to war with a sense of adventure, a hunting horn, and a riding crop. Ashby's love of adventure and his habit of getting close to the enemy contributed to the myths and rumors about him. He was so successful that rumors circulated among several Union camps that Ashby had a lookalike or that he had been killed in a number of skirmishes but had somehow always managed to return from the dead to lead again.[12]

Ashby was killed leading an infantry charge near Harrisonburg, Virginia, on 6 June 1862. His death was kept under wraps for most of the summer. By the end of the second Manassas campaign in August 1862 members of many Federal cavalry organizations, including the 12th Illinois, were unaware of his death. Members of the 12th believed that the troops who constantly harassed their outpost were under Ashby's command.[13]

The guerrilla activity in front of the 12th began to increase sharply during the first week of September as Confederate forces prepared for what is now called the Antietam campaign (to contemporaries it was the Great Maryland campaign) of the fall of 1862. Robert E. Lee, commander of the Confederate Army of Northern Virginia since June, knew that the fate of the Confederacy hung in the balance that fall. After eighteen months of war the long casualty lists and the scores of walking wounded returning home to the small towns of the North and South had put a damper on patriotic fervor. If the South could win one shattering victory, the Lincoln government might have to sue for peace, and the South just might win the war.

Despite one-sided victories over Union General George B. McClellan on the Virginia peninsula and in the second Manassas campaign, the Confederacy desperately needed such a victory. The Confederate hope of European intervention, perhaps even formal military intervention, had not materialized. Moreover, the Confederacy's financial structure was tottering, and its war economy was beginning to groan and crack alarmingly under the pressure of the all-out struggle. West of the Allegheny Mountains things had gone very badly for the South. One by one the Confederate river forts of Henry, Donelson, and Island Number 10 had caved in under unrelenting Federal pressure. A Confederate near-victory at Shiloh was lost in the second day's fighting. Memphis, a key river port, had fallen on the same day as Ashby's death, and New Orleans, the Confederacy's largest port city, was in Union hands. Confederate General Braxton Bragg was supposed to be leading an army northward to bring Kentucky back into the Confederate fold and then to threaten the Ohio River Valley, but Lee and others had doubts about Bragg's capacity to maintain his supply line.[14]

The Confederacy was losing, Lee was aware of it, and the South was in need of a decisive victory. During the eighteen months before Antietam, the Confederacy had fought in sixteen major actions in the East and West, primarily on the offensive. In the Civil War the side that was on the offensive was at a decided disadvantage. The South's losses—fifty thousand casualties, the equivalent to two and a half army corps—were staggering. If there was to be another massive bloodletting, the South had to win, so the next fight had to be carefully planned to ensure a victory.[15]

Lee had four options, each with a disadvantage. He could drive eastward and attack Washington, D.C., as Lincoln and a great many alarmed Washingtonians feared he would, but the lack of adequate munitions and supplies dissuaded him. Lee's second option was to slip away into the ever-friendly Shenandoah Valley, where supplies and good rail and road networks awaited, but that would mean giving up the field at Manassas where he had lost nine thousand men, and the open field could give initiative to the enemy, something to which Lee would never consent. Another possibility was to withdraw to the South and leave northern Virginia to the Federals, who would further ravage it during the critical harvest season.[16]

The fourth possibility was by far the best, and that was to invade the North. If Lee could go into Maryland and then into Pennsylvania, he might spark a revolution in Maryland, and he could certainly provide for his troops in those states. Lee was not sure where the decisive battle would be fought, but he hoped that it would produce the long-awaited European intervention and recognition.[17]

On 3 September 1862, Lee began shifting his army north toward Lees-burg, near the shallow fords of the Potomac, to cross into Maryland. His plan was to send Major General James Longstreet's corps deep into Mary-land to a little town called Boonsboro about fifteen miles from the Pennsyl-vania line. Then he would dispatch Stonewall Jackson's corps to the north-east to force the evacuation of Winchester and the large arsenal at Harpers Ferry. This would win the much-needed supplies. Also, Jackson had learned through his guerrilla and spy networks that there was a sizable Federal cav-alry garrison in the Winchester-Harpers Ferry area. In the early fall of 1862 the Army of Northern Virginia was feeling the loss of the prime horse breeding states of Kentucky, Tennessee, and Maryland. The capture of a siz-able mounted garrison would help to make up for the loss of horseflesh suf-fered in the three campaigns of the spring and summer.[18]

Lee crossed into Maryland. In the vanguard were Major General Daniel Harvey Hill's newly formed corps of replacement recruits and other vol-unteers from all over the South. The size of the corps barely equaled the nine thousand men lost at the second battle at Manassas. While Lee and his immediate staff were planning the invasion and the Davis administra-tion was approving it, Jeb Stuart's superb Confederate cavalry was posi-tioning itself to the south, between Lee's three army corps and McClellan's Army of the Potomac.[19]

The officers and men of the 12th Illinois Cavalry, meanwhile, remained at Camp Wool on the outskirts of Martinsburg, a short distance to the west of Lee's planned invasion line. They were part of a command made up of the 65th Illinois Infantry, 125th New York Infantry, and Battery M of the 2nd Illinois Artillery—a combined infantry-cavalry force of near brigade-level strength under Brigadier General Julius White. According to White, "There were left in the valley by the enemy some unassigned cavalry, con-sisting of Ashby's regiment, the 17th Virginia Cavalry, and two or three companies of mounted men known as the Third Maryland Line—all under the general command of Colonel Ashby." (White evidently did not yet know about Ashby's death three months prior.)

The Confederates hoped these highly mobile independent commands would pin down the Federal cavalry, keeping it occupied while Major Gen-eral A. P. Hill's Confederate corps began to move northward toward the Federal garrison at Harpers Ferry. White relates that the Confederate com-mands "were not slow in making their appearance in front of our outposts, and there were frequent skirmishes at and near the opposing lines,"[20] mak-ing it difficult for the Federal mounted arm to ascertain the exact location or direction of the main body of the Army of Northern Virginia.

Lieutenant Colonel Hasbrouck Davis was commanding the 12th Illinois in the absence of Colonel Arno Voss, who had gone to Washington to see about procuring additional weapons, a mission that resulted in the receipt of several hundred Burnside carbines on 21 July. Davis was stationed with a force of about ninety-five men at an outpost about three miles south of Martinsburg on the Winchester Turnpike. The force was mainly distributed among pickets and vedettes in front and on either flank. Approximately twenty men, mostly from Companies F and G, remained at the principal outpost with Colonel Davis.[21]

The pickets were distributed around a road between Martinsburg and Winchester known as the Old Martinsburg-Winchester Turnpike. The turnpike runs for about ten miles south-southwest from Martinsburg, roughly parallel to the Baltimore and Ohio Railroad tracks, then continues south to Winchester, twisting and turning among the small hillocks between the Waffle and Bull Run mountains. There are several small towns along the road, and a stone bridge crosses it. The Opequon Creek transects the area.[22]

On the morning of 5 September 1862, at Bunker Hill in Virginia (now West Virginia), Confederate guerrillas who were conducting a recruiting drive held a meeting. During the height of a speech in which the Rebel captain was extolling the virtues of Southern independence, the party was surprised by a detachment of the 12th Illinois Cavalry. Shots were exchanged, and the Rebels began to advance toward the Federal pickets and vedettes, which, seeing themselves outnumbered, began to retreat toward Martinsburg. Lieutenant Thomas Logan of Company G attempted a counterattack with about eighteen men along the pike and suddenly found himself surrounded by Rebel cavalry. Logan sent a message to Lieutenant Colonel Davis, then attempted to dismount and fight. He was seriously wounded in the skirmish.[23]

After receiving Logan's report, Davis sent for reinforcements from Colonel Voss, now returned from Washington. Voss dispatched Company A. Two other companies of the 12th Illinois were also ordered to the site, along with four companies of the 65th Illinois Infantry and a three-gun section of Battery M of the 2nd Illinois Artillery, but only Company A would participate in the fighting. When Company A reported under the leadership of Captain Thomas W. Grosvenor, Colonel Davis found himself in command of fifty-eight men and officers who were ready for action. "Forming them in columns of fours . . . headed by Captain T. W. Grosvenor, with Lieutenant William M. Luff in charge of the leading platoon, a rapid march was begun, which, as the column neared the advanced picket post of the enemy, was increased to a gallop."[24]

Company A arrived on the scene of action so quickly that they killed one Rebel picket wounded another before the rest could mount and retreat toward the small town of Darkesville, about five miles south of Martinsburg.

When the Rebels' battle line was in the center of town on a street that intersected the pike, the men of Company A came thundering into town at a gallop. To their absolute horror they found the three hundred Rebels drawn up into three lines, carbines ready. The Union troopers had ridden into an ambush. Davis made a split-second decision and ordered his men out of columns and into a line formation. If he had not done so, the number of casualties would have been enormous.

While the men of the 12th Illinois were forming into a line, the Rebels delivered their first volley. Brigadier General Julius White, the commander of the men stationed at Martinsburg, described the confrontation:

> At this fire, Captain Grosvenor and Private Charles D. Clark, who had been unable to check the speed of their horses, fell in close proximity to the enemy's line, and were made targets for subsequent firing. Clark, being very near the enemy, held up his hand in token of surrender, but this was unheeded, and while lying on the ground asking quarter he was shot through the body. Lieutenant Luff, whose horse succumbed to the fourth bullet, being dismounted, addressed himself to the business of removing his captain, Grosvenor, to the rear, which he accomplished amidst a shower of bullets.
>
> For a short time the firing was rapid and destructive, the enemy suffering most, but it soon became evident to Colonel Davis that such a contest could ultimately end only in disaster to his command, because of the great preponderance in numbers of the enemy.[25]

Davis had outrun his support, and he had no artillery. He was in very real danger of being surrounded and cut off. In a near-hopeless situation that could lead to surrender and the horrors of a Confederate prison camp, he gave a new order: "Drop carbines! . . . Draw sabres! . . . Charge!" Brigadier General Julius White would later praise the charge: "The result fully justified the daring but deliberate act, and after desultory firing by the enemy, their line was ridden down and broken, the rapid and continuous cut of the sabre resounding upon the heads and arms of the resisting, while most of them were soon in rapid retreat."[26]

Confederate Captain George Baylor, commander of Company B of the 12th Virginia, reported that the Rebel units involved were Companies B and I of the 12th Virginia and a squadron of the 11th Virginia Cavalry. He described the encounter:

> On the 6th, our company drove in the enemy's pickets on the Martinsburg turnpike . . . capturing eight prisoners. Ascertaining that the force . . . was too strong for us, we began retiring, and had reached Darkesville, when suddenly the enemy charged our rear. Company B, covering the retreat, soon faced about, met

the enemy's charge and repulsed it, taking some dozen prisoners, killing the lieutenant colonel [Hasbrouck Davis] and 12 men of the Twelfth Illinois Cavalry.

Baylor's report fewer Federal losses than the enemy did. Baylor also wrote that "the colonel's saddle and bridle graced my horse the remainder of the war and was allowed me at the surrender." But the report of the death of Lieutenant Colonel Hasbrouck Davis was erroneous. His horse was shot out from under him, and he was pinned under it until he was rescued by his men, but he was not killed.[27]

The men of the 12th Illinois kept up their pursuit for ten or twelve miles and took many prisoners. Private Chris Ward captured three Confederates. He cornered them in a small lot surrounded by a high fence and demanded that they throw down their weapons. They did. Ward then loaded his empty carbine and marched the prisoners away.

Private Theron Hollenbeck of Company A made a close escape that day. A mounted Rebel officer charged Hollenbeck and fired at his head, but the bullet struck the stock of Hollenbeck's gun, sending splinters into the air and wounding Hollenbeck in the face. Hollenbeck turned and fired at the Rebel, dropping him from his horse. It was about eight in the morning, and various Union patrols were mounted. Some of the remainder of the 12th Illinois came on the scene. Companies B and E were ordered in the direction of Smithfield to the southeast and Winchester to the southwest to search for Rebel patrols. Captain Bronson was able to overtake a couple of small detachments of Rebels, and he took one prisoner.[28]

Colonel Voss states in his official report of the action south of Martinsburg that of the nearly seven hundred men in the Confederate's 17th Virginia Cavalry Regiment, forty-one were taken prisoner and twenty-five were killed. Eleven men of the 12th Illinois were wounded, two of them mortally. The casualties were normal for a cavalry company in combat for the first time. Two of the men wounded during the raid were officers. Captain Grosvenor received a pistol shot in the upper arm but survived to end the war as a major. Lieutenant Logan was wounded below the right shoulder blade. The rest of the wounds ranged from slight to severe. Privates Valentine Kinline and Noah Mitchell of Company F died of their wounds within days of the engagement. Kinline's wound was in the right lung, and the ball could not be extracted with the primitive surgical methods employed during the Civil War.[29]

Eleven members of the 12th Illinois were wounded at Darkesville and lived. The case of John McCarthy, assistant surgeon for the unit, provides gruesome evidence of the ferocity of a Civil War cavalry charge. Captain Thomas Grosvenor, who was commanding the lead element of the 12th Illinois that day, had decided to place a medical doctor in charge of the lead

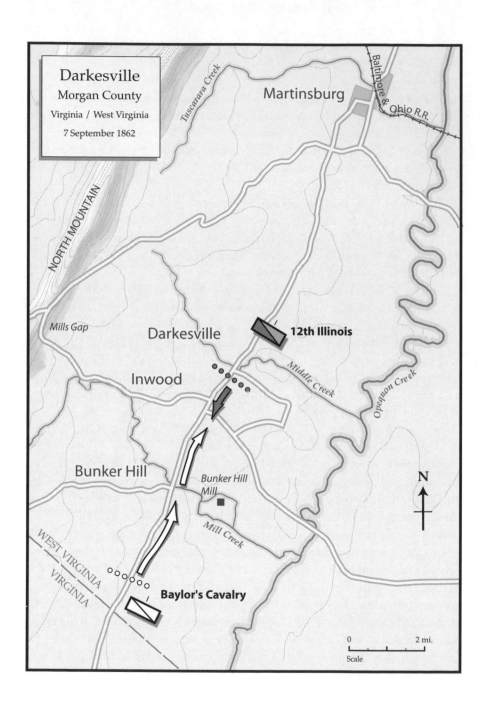

Darkesville
Morgan County
Virginia / West Virginia
7 September 1862

Martinsburg

Baltimore & Ohio R.R.

Tuscarara Creek

NORTH MOUNTAIN

Mills Gap

Darkesville

12th Illinois

Middle Creek

Opequon Creek

Inwood

Bunker Hill

Bunker Hill Mill

Mill Creek

WEST VIRGINIA

VIRGINIA

Baylor's Cavalry

N

0   2 mi.
Scale

element for the good of the men. McCarthy, a graduate of Rush Medical School in Chicago, was with the lead element when the order was given to charge the Confederates. Shot in the right knee, McCarthy was knocked from his horse and onto the ground. Many of the sixty men in the command rode over him, causing hemorrhaging in the lungs and a broken scapula. He was captured by the Confederates, held for one day, then released back to the Federals, whereupon he had to treat his own injury as well as those of several other troopers.[30]

Private Oren Higgins of Company C was also injured in the cavalry charge at Darkesville. When the 12th Illinois slammed into the Confederates at more than thirty miles per hour, Higgins was thrown forward onto the pommel of his saddle and suffered a hernia. Somehow Surgeon McCarthy, unmindful of his own wounds, cared for Higgins and started the paper trail that eventually resulted in Higgins's medical discharge from the army.[31]

Several weeks after the confrontation Chaplain Warner noted in his diary a conversation with a soldier who was taken prisoner at Martinsburg, a Private Swats of the 17th Virginia Cavalry Battalion. Swats asserted that the Rebel cavalry the 12th Illinois had encountered at Darkesville was part of a raid that had been planned by Stonewall Jackson. The Confederate force had consisted of seven companies of the 17th Virginia Cavalry Battalion and two companies of the 12th Virginia Calvary Regiment that were detached by Jackson for the skirmish. It appears that this force was acting almost as Jackson's extreme left flank as his army moved toward Harpers Ferry. The Rebels had left the battlefield at Manassas and had reached Martinsburg after a march of about two days. They had arrived south of Martinsburg at about nine o'clock in the evening on 6 September, encamped, and set up their ambush. The objective, according to Swats, was to draw the Federal cavalry out of its camp in Martinsburg and then surround the unit and either annihilate or capture it as the opportunity arose. At daylight on 7 September, the Rebels drove into the 12th Illinois pickets and drew up in line of battle. When they discovered Federal troops to their rear, the Rebels retreated to Darkesville, a retreat that probably cost them the victory. The Rebel prisoner also stated that from four to five hundred men were involved in the fight, but Chaplain Warner believed that that was a gross overestimation; he placed the number of Rebels at about seventy-five.[32]

The fight at Darkesville was the 12th Illinois Cavalry's first action, and the 12th got the better of its foe, which by the late summer of 1862 was a well-trained, well-led, and well-motivated military organization. According to all reports, the 12th Illinois was the only Union outfit in the fight. The companies from the 65th Illinois and from Battery M arrived too late to be of much service.[33]

The old Winchester Turnpike where Captain Grosvenor and Lieutenant Colonel Davis led their charging troopers against the gray-clad men of Jackson's advance guard is now West Virginia Route 11. Exit 16 on Interstate 81 leads to the old part of Martinsburg, which in many ways is unchanged since the Civil War. In the small community of Darkesville, one can gauge almost exactly where the Rebels were waiting for the Federals because the street names remain the same. South of Darkesville and about five or six miles north of Winchester is the little town of Bunker Hill. It was here that Hasbrouck Davis had his first outpost watch for the approaching Rebels. There are no signs or markers to commemorate the fight of 6 September 1862, nor are there any markers to show the final resting place of Valentine Kinline and Noah Mitchell.

If reflection on the quick victory at Darkesville was strong in the minds of the 12th Illinois troopers, it was also short-lived. After visiting the recuperating Captain Grosvenor on 12 September, Chaplain Warner returned to his quarters to rewrite his "diary for the purpose of Historical Accuracy." While he was working on the diary, he heard "heavy and fast tramping of horses and went outside to learn the cause." He was informed that the Confederates had crossed the Potomac at Boteler's Ford and were advancing on Williamsport. Men in the garrison at Camp Wool were ordered to pack or burn everything and to move as quickly as possible to Harpers Ferry. Late that night, the men of all the regiments boarded trains and were carried to their destination. They arrived at two o'clock in the morning on 13 September.[34]

Harpers Ferry is situated on a point of land at the confluence of the Shenandoah and Potomac Rivers in the Blue Ridge Mountains. Militarily it was an inviting place to attack and a very poor place to defend. Confederate Major General A. P. Hill, who under the command of Major General T. J. "Stonewall" Jackson was given the task of enveloping the ferry and forcing its surrender, stated, "I would rather attempt to take the place twenty times than to defend it once."[35]

Because Lee was moving his main army east of Harpers Ferry on its route toward Hagerstown, Maryland, he had decided to force the Federals out of Harpers Ferry to ensure that no Union troops would harass the Confederates' left flank or rear. Lee placed such importance on the task that he detailed fully one-third of his army under the command of Stonewall Jackson to secure Confederate control of the town. Union General George McClellan had also long seen the importance of Harpers Ferry. He understood the threat it offered to Lee's invasion, and he had worded his orders to assure its place of importance in the minds of the commanders of the garrison, Brigadier General Julius White and Colonel Dixon Standsbury Miles, who was actually in command even though White outranked him.

The North lost the battle for Harpers Ferry, and the loss was a crucial one. After the Union surrendered its garrison, A. P. Hill's corps was able to march across the Virginia hills and arrive on the Antietam battlefield in time to secure Lee's right flank during the final stages of that on 17 September. People would later argue in a court of inquiry—and historians would later contend—that if Colonel Miles had been able to hold Hill at Harpers Ferry for just a few hours longer, Lee's right flank would have collapsed under the constant Union pressure. The majority of Lee's army would have been forced to capitulate, and the Civil War would have ended in the East. There were, however, some bright spots in the Union defeat at Harpers Ferry. The 12th Illinois Cavalry's dramatic escape from the besieged garrison is one of the most interesting exploits of any mounted unit in the war.

By 1862 Harpers Ferry, where the 12th Illinois detrained in the early morning hours of 13 September, already bore the scars of war. Over the years it had grown from a tiny village into an industrialized town. The growth of Harpers Ferry had received its first real impetus in the 1790s when President George Washington urged Congress to establish a national armory there on the Potomac. The armory supported the economy of the town and encouraged the establishment of small industries on adjacent Virginius Island. The arrival of the Chesapeake and Ohio Canal in the early part of the nineteenth century and the Baltimore and Ohio Railroad in the 1830s assured Harpers Ferry of the economic success it was to enjoy well past mid-century.

Then came disaster. In October 1859 John Brown's Raid jarred the peaceful town, and the Civil War that followed 18 months later wrecked Harpers Ferry's economy. Union forces burned the armory and the arsenal in 1861 to keep them from falling into Confederate hands. Less than one hundred townspeople were left in the community when the 12th Illinois arrived. The desolation seemed complete. Crumbling brick walls haunted the once-splendid armory, churches had become hospitals, gardens and pastures were graveyards, and private residences were barracks and stables. One soldier commented that "the entire place is not actually worth $10."[36]

Union strategists, however, deemed Harpers Ferry very worthy as a base of supplies. For Shenandoah Valley operations, the post had no equal. Union officials reasoned that a permanent garrison at Harpers Ferry would intimidate the Confederates and thus preclude incursions across the Potomac. The Federal presence there would also help to protect the Chesapeake and Ohio Canal and the Baltimore and Ohio Railroad. The Baltimore and Ohio was so important that the federal government had organized a special force to protect it—the Illinois Railroad Brigade, which McClellan appointed Colonel Miles to lead. From Washington to Baltimore and from Harpers Ferry to Winchester, Virginia, Miles had some 380 miles to protect, more than half of them in the Confederacy. He did the best he could with the 2,500 infantry, cavalry, and artillery troops in the railroad brigade. He parceled out his men so that most of the major bridgeheads were guarded against guerrilla attacks and marauding forays. His force existed for that purpose alone; he had no intention of fighting an army.[37]

Colonel Miles made defensive preparations in the fall of 1862, but he must have wondered how long his men could hold out. Harpers Ferry is between two mountains and is difficult to defend. To the north is Maryland Heights, a mountain that rises almost fourteen hundred feet above the town. To the south, in Virginia's Blue Ridge Mountains, is Loudoun Heights, a slightly smaller mountain whose highest elevation is eleven hundred feet. Both mountains are elongated, stretching westward far beyond Harpers Ferry, whose highest elevation is about five hundred feet. Both Colonel Miles and General White hoped that the two mountains were too rocky and rough to be successfully attained by a large Confederate army with artillery. As a precaution, though, they placed troops on both mountains, and the soldiers dug earthworks. If Confederate artillery took the mountains, they could fire into the town on a downward trajectory at a distance of a little less than a mile. At that range even smoothbore pieces could inflict terrible damage on Harpers Ferry and the thousands of soldiers in it. If that happened, Harpers Ferry was doomed.

Bolivar Heights, a small community almost five hundred feet above Harpers Ferry, presented another problem. If an enemy force succeeded in placing artillery on Bolivar Heights, the firing line of the guns would be on a downward trajectory at a distance of a little more than a mile. Colonel Miles had defensive positions and trenches set up at the west edge of Bolivar Heights, but his guns would be firing uphill. The Confederates would have the advantage.[38]

Before the war and during its early days, both Stonewall Jackson and his chief subordinate, A. P. Hill, whom he had assigned to capture the town, had spent a large amount of time in and around Harpers Ferry. Both men knew that Loudoun Heights on the Virginia side of the Potomac and Maryland Heights across the river dominated the region. They had been artillery officers in the old United States service and were well aware of what could be done with the guns if they were properly sighted and aligned. At eleven o'clock in the morning on 13 September, Jackson's column arrived at Harpers Ferry.[39]

The 12th Illinois Cavalry and the other mounted Federal units had been in town for less than ten hours. They were assigned immediately to scout the surrounding area and report to Colonel Miles on the positions of the incoming Rebels. A. P. Hill moved his batteries into place near Bolivar Heights and began to shell the Union Line. This diversion allowed Major General Lafayette McLaws time to establish his batteries on Maryland Heights. While McLaws was ascending Maryland Heights, General John G. Walker, Jackson's 2nd Division commander, was occupying Loudoun Heights. Each of them had a tough time finding roads and trails that could accommodate both men and artillery. And each man had serious fighting to do when he reached the top of the mountain because Miles's troops were well fortified. But the Union troops were inexperienced. Once the Confederates had reached the top, the Federal troops fought well for a while, then broke. The Confederates spent most of the morning following their victory sighting their guns and signaling to each other with flags while they prepared for the assault on the town.[40]

A. P. Hill had all of his famous light division artillery on Bolivar Heights: nine rifled guns (excellent weapons for long-range fire), eight Napoleons, and thirteen short-range pieces. All of the weapons were within one thousand yards of the Federal lines. When the crews finally aligned their pieces, more than fifty guns were arranged so that the Confederates could enfilade all Federal positions. One of Hill's gunners wrote poetically, "The great circle of artillery opened, all firing to a common center, while the clouds of smoke, rolling up from the tops of the various mountains, and the thunder of the guns reverberating among them, give the sound of so many volcanoes." For a good part of the day, Miles's battery commanders returned Rebel fire until they ran short of long-range ammunition and had to replace it with solid shot. And even most of the solid shot was exhausted by midmorning of the following day.[41]

The men of the 12th Illinois Cavalry were garrisoned across the river from Loudoun Heights on the west end of Shenandoah Street near the industrial area of Virginius Island. They had been active since their arrival by train the day before, scouting and reporting to Colonel Miles on the disposition of the various Confederate commands while Jackson's corps advanced on Harpers Ferry. On the morning of 14 September the men of the 12th were standing beside their mounts awaiting orders when the Confederate batteries opened fire from Loudoun Heights. The Confederate gunners were concentrated their attention on the cavalry camps because those were the most easily recognizable.

> The 12th Illinois had been in the saddle since daylight and were now resting. Horses were unsaddled and officers and men were sitting about watching the enemy and discussing the situation, when suddenly a puff of smoke appeared on Loudoun Heights, and the next instant a shell came screaming into camp. It was followed by another in quick succession, and they soon came thick and fast. There was no time to ask for orders, and calling to the men to saddle up.

The men of the 12th moved to the comparative shelter of the trees on Virginius Island, where they were able to find some protection.[42]

Amazingly, there were few casualties from the shelling. Although the accuracy of the Rebel gunners was very good, comparatively few of the shells exploded. The Confederates were using impact, or percussion, ammunition, and apparently the plunger device that activated the charge often failed to function in the island's sand. But the constant shelling was beginning to take its toll. Lieutenant William M. Luff of the 12th Illinois recalled the chaos of that morning, the constant screeching and occasional bursting of shells in close proximity to the men and horses. There was almost no shelter. The men would be shelled out of one position and would be in another for less than five minutes before the Confederates would have their range and the shells would begin to come again. "Surrounded on all sides by the enemy," Luff wrote, "with no hope of succor or opportunity to make an adequate defense, and with the prospect of early capture or surrender, the minds of officers and men naturally turned towards escape."[43]

Escaping Harpers Ferry had become the only option. The town was under siege. A garrison of twelve thousand men, seventy pieces of artillery (some of which, according to Trooper Ashley Alexander, had been spiked, or disabled, "by that damned fool Miles" because the men were out of long-range ammunition), and some thirteen thousand small arms were in the balance. Mounted troops could do little in such a situation. If the cavalry surrendered, the Rebels would get about fifteen hundred good horses that they desperately needed. The Confederate cavalry had been mounted on thoroughbred and saddlebred horses at the beginning of the conflict, but both of these demanded more care than army troops constantly on the march could give. Many of the Confederate cavalry animals were starting to show the effects of the war, and remounts, never in great supply in the Confederacy, were desperately needed. No one in a Union command wanted the arms and horses to fall into Confederate hands. No one wanted to be incarcerated in a Confederate prison camp.[44]

Twelfth Illinois executive officer Lieutenant Colonel Hasbrouck Davis and ranking Federal cavalry officer Colonel Benjamin "Grimes" Davis, a West Point–educated Mississippian who had cast his lot with the North, consulted one another about a plan of escape. They then approached General Julius White, under whom they both had served for most of the summer in Martinsburg. White received them cordially and arranged for them to meet with Colonel Miles, who initially disapproved of the plan, believing it to be highly risky. After consulting with White and other officers, however, Miles granted conditional approval pending the identification of a suitable escape route.[45]

Grimes Davis suggested moving along the west side of the Potomac as far as Kearneysville and then crossing the river at Shepherdstown, but Colonel Miles had received reports that Rebel cavalry patrols were operating in that direction, and he feared that the Federals would be discovered. Luff recalled that there was also a proposal "to cross the Shenandoah near the point of confluence with the Potomac and march down the Potomac toward Washington, but upon exploring the ford it was found to be full of holes and dangerous to cross." Finally, the officers agreed on a plan "to cross the Potomac on the pontoon bridge to Maryland Heights and to endeavor to reach McClellan's army in that direction." The pontoon bridge, located in a breach in the seawall that surrounds Harpers Ferry, had been built in the early days of the war after the Confederates destroyed a railroad bridge between Maryland Heights and Harpers Ferry.[46]

The escape would have to take place at night, something that was never popular during the Civil War. A large number of mounted men would have to cross the Potomac River single-file on an improvised bridge in the darkness, then turn left and follow a climbing road over the north end of Maryland Heights to Sharpsburg. If a company got lost, certain capture and a Rebel prison camp would be the result. Special Order Number 120 was issued at the Harpers Ferry headquarters on 14 September 1862 by the aide-de-camp, H. C. Reynolds. It stated:

> The cavalry force at this post, except detached orderlies, will make immediate preparations to leave here at 8 o'clock tonight, without baggage wagons, ambulances or led horses, crossing the Potomac over the pontoon bridge, and taking the Sharpsburg Road. The senior officer, Col. Voss, will assume command of the whole, which will form the right at the quartermaster's office, the left up Shenandoah street, without noise or loud command, in the following order: Coles Cavalry, 12th Illinois Cavalry, 8th New York Cavalry, 7th Squadron Rhode Island Cavalry, and the 1st Maryland Cavalry. No other instructions can be given to the Commander than to force his way through the enemy's lines and join our own army.

The tents and baggage of the 12th Illinois, as well as the instruments of its brass band, were to be left to the Confederates. The Illinois troops were less than three months out of the training camps at Camp Butler, so most were probably leaving cherished personal possessions behind. The thought of escape, though, was a good motivator to part with material things.[47]

The column was to depart at eight o'clock. Silence was the order of the march because a word or a command could give away the position of the passing column. "Hemmed in on all sides, as they had been, harried by shot and shell, without being able to strike back and with the gloomiest forebodings of the future, the spirits of officers and men had been depressed to the point of despondency." The troops were quite anxious for a chance to escape to freedom.[48]

It was a tenuous chance at best. To get out of Harpers Ferry, the officers knew, required discipline, strict obedience to orders, and total control of the mounts. The men were forming their ranks under the very muzzles of the Confederate guns on Maryland Heights. If the men were discovered once they were on the other side of the river, the Rebel gunners could lower the muzzles of the twelve pounders and use canister rounds, which in the form of large sawed-off–shotgun shells would be devastating against men on horseback. Once the troops were out of range of the artillery on Maryland Heights, they would face the unknown. The men preparing the escape were not aware that the Confederate force was growing. The third wing of Lee's army, returning from the Battle of South Mountain, "was moving from Turner's Gap towards Sharpsburg and Longstreet was at Hagerstown, with part of his command near Williamsport on the Potomac, so that the enemy was in heavy force between Harpers Ferry and McClellan as well as along the entire route taken by the cavalry as far as Williamsport."[49]

Shortly after dark the column crossed Potomac Street and began the descent to the seawall. It entered the approach to the bridge regiment by regiment, single-file, and proceeded at a walk. The slow movement had a dual purpose: to put less strain on the bridge and to make less noise because no one believed that the column could survive if it was discovered. As soon as each regimental company reached the Maryland side, it turned to the left, spurred its horses to a gallop, and took the road over the heights leading to Sharpsburg. The night was very dark, and with each company breaking into a run upon reaching the comparative safety of the other side of the river, a soldier could determine his location only by stopping and listening to the clatter of hooves and the rattle of sabers. In that part of the country the origin of sounds was not easy to determine.

There was one mishap that could have resulted in disaster. When Company D of the 12th Illinois crossed the pontoon bridge, it missed the rear of the preceding company and turned to the right instead of to the left. It advanced down the road toward the small village of Sandy Hook and "soon struck the enemy's pickets. The Captain [George H. Shears] was convinced he had made a mistake, and turning hastily to the right about, he returned to the bridge in time to take [his] place in the column."[50]

After the regiments crossed the bridge, they proceeded along the Harpers Ferry–Sharpsburg road at a very fast pace. Because the roads were curving and narrow, the troopers stayed in rows of two for about one mile as they passed between the Chesapeake and Ohio Canal and the bluffs of Maryland

Heights. Then the road suddenly veered to the north straight up the side of a mountain. Corporal Isaac Heysinger of the 7th Rhode Island Cavalry wrote that it was "so steep that I had to grasp my horse's mane" to be safe from sliding back or shifting in his saddle. As the column began to descend the north side of Maryland Heights away from the Rebels, Heysinger could look back and see the Confederates' signal rockets, which were being sent up at fairly close intervals, but the Rebels either did not see the Union troops or saw them and ignored them.[51]

After descending Maryland Heights the column proceeded at what Lieutenant Luff described as a "killing pace and very hard work." The command pushed on toward Sharpsburg and didn't slow down until it neared the town. On the outskirts of Sharpsburg the Federals ran into Rebel pickets, who retreated at first. The advanced pickets of the 12th Illinois were to avoid contact, but if contact was made, they were to ensure the column's safe passage.[52]

The 12th Illinois Cavalry, now in the lead of the entire command, "proceeded at a gallop, driving the pickets into their reserve and through the principal street of Sharpsburg on the road towards Hagerstown." Here the command slowed to a walk, moving slowly in the darkness, which was suddenly illuminated by a sheet of flame, the "stillness broken by a rattling volley of musketry." Corporal Heysinger and the 7th Rhode Island were at the rear. Heysinger vividly recalled the volley and the way the rifles "sent their leaden messengers about our ears." The fleeing Federals could distinctly hear the sounds of Rebel commands and the movement of Rebel artillery wheels, and they searched for a way out. A local scout named Tom Noakes took the advance and guided the column through the town so that it emerged on the Sharpsburg-Hagerstown Turnpike. The Confederates sent a few shells after the mounted column as Noakes maneuvered it between the camps of the Rebels, who slept through the din of the night. The column continued north through Tilghmanton and stopped at the home of a Dr. Maddox, a Union sympathizer, who told them that the Confederates they had encountered were the advance guard of Lee's main army retreating from South Mountain.[53]

After leaving the doctor's house, the Federal column crossed a number of farmers' fields until it reached a local mill, then it turned onto the Boonsboro-Williamsport Turnpike. The column advanced at a slow walk, and the troopers, now some twenty miles from Harpers Ferry, began to show the strain of the harrowing march. Men began to fall asleep in the saddle, and Lieutenant Luff relates that "one would awake, and, finding he had lost his place in the column, rejoin it only to go to sleep again and repeat the process."[54]

In the gray of first light at about five o'clock in the morning on 15 September, the column came upon a large Rebel camp just north of Williamsport, Maryland. The 8th New York was leading the column, and as

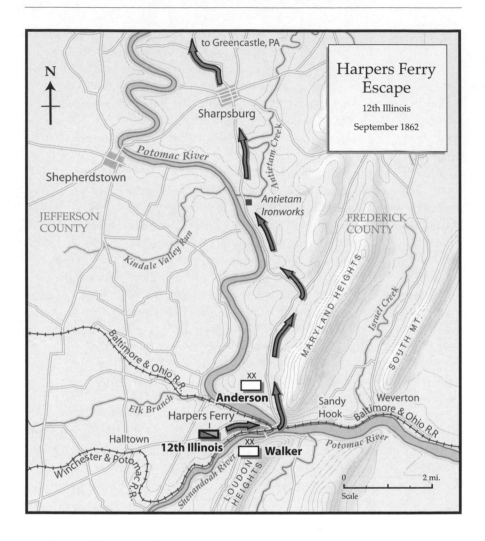

N

to Greencastle, PA

Harpers Ferry
Escape

12th Illinois

September 1862

Sharpsburg

Potomac River

Shepherdstown

Antietam Creek

Antietam
Ironworks

JEFFERSON
COUNTY

FREDERICK
COUNTY

Kindale Valley Run

MARYLAND HEIGHTS

Israel Creek

SOUTH MT.

Baltimore & Ohio R.R.

Elk Branch

XX
Anderson

Sandy
Hook

Weverton

Harpers Ferry

Baltimore & Ohio R.R.

Halltown

12th Illinois

XX
Walker

Potomac River

Winchester & Potomac R.R.

Shenandoah River

LOUDON HEIGHTS

0   2 mi.

Scale

the unit approached the turnpike, its men heard the rumbling of wheels, a sound that indicated the approach of either artillery or wagons. It was an anxious moment, and Grimes Davis and Hasbrouck Davis decided to attempt to capture the guns or the wagons, whichever they happened to be.

The 8th New York immediately formed in line facing the road on the north side, and the 12th Illinois did the same south of the road. The Maryland and Rhode Island cavalries were held in reserve.

All was done in silence and it was still too dark for our troops, concealed in the timber which skirted the road, to be seen. The approaching column proved to be a train of army wagons (97 in number) loaded principally with ammunition and escorted by infantry; four or five men accompanied each wagon, with a detachment of cavalry in the rear. When the head of the train came up it was halted and the guard ordered to surrender, which it did without a shot being fired on either side.

The road curved and turned to the left at that point, so the teamsters in the rear had no idea that the lead wagon had been captured. When each wagon reached the point where Colonel Grimes Davis was posted, it shared the fate of its predecessor. The Rebel escort was easily captured with scarcely a halt or check of the column, and the whole train was taken north to Greencastle, Pennsylvania, arriving there at ten that morning. The capture of the immense wagon train was a stunning success for the weary men who had been fleeing for their lives just hours earlier, and it had occurred within earshot of a sizable camp of Rebel infantry. If the Confederates had been roused, they would have had enough men to prevent the capture of the train.[55]

The citizens of southern Pennsylvania welcomed the Union troops as heroes. They had been apprehensive at the approach of the Confederate army, they hoped that the Federal cavalry would deliver them from the threatened danger. At one large house Lieutenant Luff and his platoon "breakfasted sumptuously," and his host informed him that he had given breakfast to a hundred men. All of them were grateful. The men of the 12th Cavalry had not eaten in twenty-four hours, and they had been without rations since leaving Harpers Ferry. The command had marched close to sixty miles from Harpers Ferry, and the men and horses were nearly exhausted.[56]

After a brief restoration period, they were sent south to aid General McClellan at Antietam, but they arrived after the battle had ended. The 12th Illinois was stationed at Jones Crossroads near Tilghmanton on the extreme right flank of McClellan's army. The captured wagon train, which contained reserve ammunition intended for Confederate Major General James Longstreet's corps, was escorted by Union troops to the Federal ammunition depot at Chambersburg.

When the Federal attacks at Antietam sputtered out in the afternoon of 17 September, Lee considered a counterattack by Longstreet's corps, but Longstreet told him that he could not launch a counterattack because he was low on ammunition. Longstreet's exhausted corps did not initiate any further action that day. Even though the South was the strategic invader in the 1862 campaign, it was on the defensive at Antietam, and many units of the Army of Northern Virginia had been fighting all day. It is hard to estimate what numbers would have been added to the 24,000 already wounded and dead on the field at Antietem if the 12th had not captured Longstreet's ammunition train.

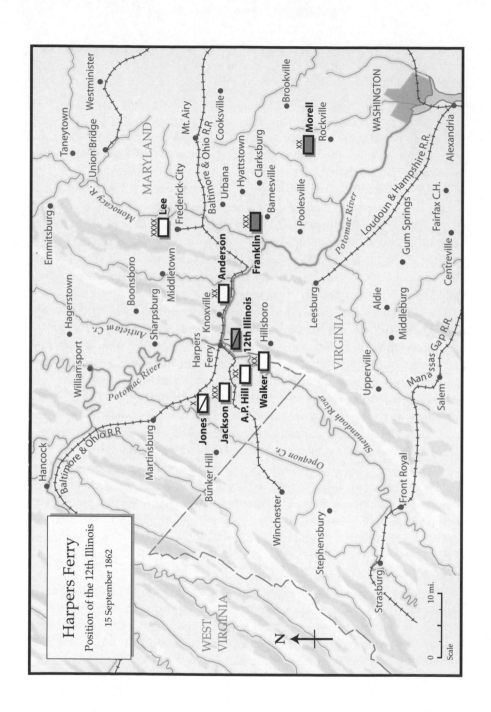

Harpers Ferry
Position of the 12th Illinois
15 September 1862

From a foreign-relations viewpoint the South needed a victory at Antietam, and Robert E. Lee was pugnacious, a gambler who was aggressive to the extreme. It is hard to imagine that Lee could have resisted the urge to counterattack and humiliate McClellan, even with exhausted troops, if he had had enough ammunition to ensure success. Isaac Heysinger of the 7th Rhode Island believed that the capture of the wagon train influenced the outcome of the battle. If Longstreet had been in possession of that extra ammunition, the attack would have been launched, and the Confederacy just might have been victorious that late afternoon in mid-September. A Confederate victory at Antietam would have altered the course of American history.[57]

Today one can follow the route of the 12th Illinois Cavalry's escape from Harpers Ferry. The pontoon bridge is gone, but the opening in the seawall is still there, and the iron ringbolts that were used to anchor the bridge are embedded in the wall. There is a place where the Harpers Ferry–Sharpsburg road rises almost straight up to the top of Maryland Heights. One can understand why 120 years ago men had to grab onto their horses' manes to keep from falling. It no longer is possible to cross the farmers' fields near Tilghmanton, but by weaving north through Williamsport and turning onto the Williamsburg-Hagerstown road one can find the exact location where the 12th Illinois captured Longstreet's wagon train. The state of Maryland has erected a marker to commemorate the daring exploit. The men of the 12th Illinois, exhausted from battle and an all-night ride to safety, made its mark on history.

CHAPTER THREE

"Picket and Reconnaissance Duty"

Thehe end of the Maryland campaign brought relief to both armies. Seventeen September was the bloodiest day in all of American history. Nearly six thousand men died; three times that many were wounded. Historian James McPherson notes that "the casualties at Antietam numbered four times the total suffered at the Normandy beaches on 6 June 1944. More than twice as many Americans lost their lives in one day at Sharpsburg, as fell in combat in the War of 1812, the Mexican War, and the Spanish-American War combined."[1]

Two days after the last gun was fired at Antietam, the Confederate Army of Northern Virginia, unable to continue the fight, began its withdrawal from Maryland. Lee's plan was to cross the Potomac near Shepherdstown, proceed southward, and move his weary, hungry army to Opecquan Creek in what is now West Virginia in search of provisions. The plan for the retreat was drawn up by Jeb Stuart's engineer officer, Captain William Willis Blackford, who stated in his memoirs that Stuart remained near Williamsport, north of Sharpsburg, and therefore on the extreme right flank of McClellan's army, to create an impression that the Confederate leadership was contemplating a serious attack on Williamsport and the enemy flank. Stuart, the highly competent commander of the Army of Northern Virginia's cavalry, rode to war on a thoroughbred wearing little gold spurs and a gray horseman's cape lined with red satin, and carrying a French Le-Mat revolver and a short French cavalry saber. Despite his wearing of such finery,

Stuart was a superb leader of light cavalry. Any Federal unit pitted against Stuart's superbly led horsemen found itself up against one of the best cavalries the world has ever known.[2]

The Federal high command appears to have been completely fooled by Stuart's maneuvering. McClellan slowed his pursuit of Lee and ordered his flank secured. Brigadier General John Kenly, whose large cavalry force was dispatched by McClellan, reported on 20 September that Williamsport was occupied by Confederate troops. Kenly appeared to realize that the occupying force was only Stuart's cavalry, but it would take more than Kenly's detachment of six hundred to drive out Stuart's one thousand men.

Kenly's force included seven out of the twelve companies of the 12th Illinois Cavalry, which amounted to about 350 sabers, two independent companies of Maryland cavalry numbering about 100 men, and about 120 additional troops to operate the eight artillery pieces that Kenly had in his command. The Federal generals bolstered Kenly's force with an additional infantry regiment and a six-gun battery of artillery, bringing his total troop contingent to about 1,200 men and fourteen guns.[3]

The Union's high command seemed to be far more concerned about guarding the Potomac waterway than about an attempt by Lee to initiate a flanking movement. Kenly was ordered to advance toward the Potomac and to protect the maze of locks and dams that made the river such an important military asset. His force moved quickly toward Williamsport with the 12th Illinois Cavalry in the lead. They arrived near the river and the town of Williamsport with such stealth and rapidity that Company I found itself surrounded by retreating Confederates for two days. A sharp little fight occurred, and one member of the 12th Illinois, Private H. Thomas from Sterling, Illinois, was killed by a bullet that entered through his nose and exited through the back of his head. Private William Henry Redman left the area of the skirmish on the dead man's horse. Redman and his small detachment evaded capture for the next two days and eventually returned to Sharpsburg to camp on the Antietam battlefield only three days after the fighting had ended there and Lee had withdrawn from Sharpsburg. Army and civilian grave-digging parties worked almost around the clock, but it still took the better part of September to bury all of the bodies. The weather was warm, and by the time the 12th Illinois camped on the battlefield, "the stench was sickening."[4]

The men of 12th Illinois Cavalry returned to their camp at the sleepy little hamlet of Jones Crossroads on 23 September and settled down to what they thought would be boring and tedious picket duty. They were posted from their camp southward about eight miles to Clear Spring, Maryland, over gently rolling countryside ideal for cavalry patrolling operations. Their assignment was to keep an eye on the various fords, or shallow crossing areas, of the Potomac. If Lee and the Army of Northern Virginia were to attempt another invasion of the North, these areas would be of prime importance. The main crossing was McCoy's Ford, located just south of Jones Crossroads and Clear Spring.

This assignment offered relative rest and relaxation. Redman wrote that it was a beautiful time. The 12th Illinois enjoyed the calm and the fall weather while they watched the Rebel pickets gallop across the countryside to trade coffee for tobacco during nighttime off-duty hours. Rest gave the men time to reflect on the war, themselves, and their unit. They had been in the eastern combat theater for a little more than five months. There had been a handful of desertions: out of 760 men, about thirty, or 4 percent, had fled. They had been involved in a number of skirmishes and had taken few casualties but, they believed, had inflicted many. They had avoided capture at Harpers Ferry, escaping after dark at the head of the whole Union cavalry contingent there. Their escape had spared almost all of them from potentially lethal incarceration at one of the horrible Confederate prisons and had deprived the Confederate army of many hundreds of valuable horses, saddles, carbines, boots, spurs, and revolvers. Stonewall Jackson himself had asked after the surrender of the Union forces at Harpers Ferry, "Where were the horses?" When he was told of the cavalry escape that the officers and men of the 12th Illinois had engineered, Jackson said that he would rather have had all those horses than the many Federal prisoners who had fallen into his hands.[5]

Most of the valuable horse country in the South was in Union hands by that time, and horses—particularly large, fast, riding horses—were in great demand in the Confederate army. The Confederates made a brief attempt to regain Kentucky in October, but most of Maryland and northwest Virginia and major portions of Tennessee were in Federal hands. Of the states that were good sources for horses, only South Carolina with its large quarter-horse farms was still exclusively in the possession of the South. The 12th Illinois Cavalry's escape with the horses and its capture of Longstreet's wagon train, which may have made a difference in the Sharpsburg fight, gave the regiment reason to look back on its accomplishments with a great deal of satisfaction.[6]

That fall the men were interested in the talking about the draft. The Lincoln administration had just instituted a conscription act that would take effect in July 1863. The need for conscription rankled the men already in the army almost as much as it riled the civilians at home. The civilians were angered because the draft would force all able-bodied men between the ages of eighteen and forty-five to be listed for possible military service. Although at first the number drafted would be quite small, if a man was called, the only way out was to hire a substitute or to pay the government three hundred dollars. Many men who wanted no part of the war would have to serve. The soldiers, on the other hand, were even more upset that more men were not already involved. Redman expressed his resentment in a letter to his sisters: "I emphatically denounce all able bodied young men who are not in the Army now unless they have been prevented by their parents." He added that a father who would not let his son enlist should not be allowed to live in the North. He was proud, he said, to have enlisted to "fight for my Country"; he had enlisted neither to avoid the draft nor to win a cash bonus.[7]

If the Federal Conscription Act was on the minds of the men of the 12th Illinois, the Emancipation Proclamation apparently was not. Lincoln had issued the preliminary proclamation after the Battle of Antietam. The executive order was to act as a carrot and a stick toward the South. The Lincoln government would liberate slaves only if the states that were still in rebellion refused to lay down their arms and rejoin the Union by 1 January 1863. The proclamation was issued also quite possibly to thwart British intervention on the side of the Confederacy. The British people were firmly against slavery and probably would have ousted their government if it intervened in a civil war on the side that declared slavery to be an integral part of its social and economic structure. This meant that at last, after over a year of war, the issue of slavery was forced onto center stage as the main reason for the war. The reaction of the states still in the Union was mixed. In the counties of northern Illinois, home of the 12th Cavalry, there was hardly any reaction at all. Soldiers did not refer to the proclamation in their extant correspondence, and local newspapers, such as the *Rock River Democrat,* mentioned it in passing and were more middle-of-the-road than proemancipation.[8]

In the second week of October 1862 the Lincoln administration began to urge McClellan to move southward and do battle with Robert E. Lee. In autumn Virginia roads were usually firm enough to support large armies and their cumbersome wagon trains and artillery. The rains that so often accompanied the early snows in the upper South were still more than a month away. "You must move now while the roads are good," warned Lincoln, but McClellan, despite the beautiful fall weather, refused. He always had an excuse: not enough horses, not enough wagons, not enough ammunition, not enough men. His unwillingness to move had frustrated Lincoln since the peninsula campaign of that spring, and it angered Lincoln now in October. And Lincoln was not the only one in the Union military machine who was tiring of McClellan's inaction. Major General Henry Halleck, who once had been a supporter of McClellan, wrote that the general's immobility "exceeds all that any man can conceive of. It requires the lever of Archimedes to move this inert mass."[9]

On the other side of the Potomac Jeb Stuart was planning the Chambersburg Raid, an escapade that would further embarrass McClellan and would rank as one of the greatest cavalry raids in the annals of the Civil War. For glory and suspense the Chambersburg Raid has few if any equals, but for what it actually accomplished in interrupting Union communications and destroying Union property its merits are debatable. The 12th Illinois did its best to foil the grandiose expedition. If its warnings had been heeded, Stuart might have been forced to turn back, and McClellan's dismissal might therefore have been postponed. But the actions the 12th was allowed to take were too little too late.

Lee had contacted Stuart in early October while the cavalry chieftain was enjoying the fall social season at a mansion called the Bower, near Charlestown in northwest Virginia. The mansion was the home of Adam Dandridge, who was related to Martha Washington, and it still stands high on a hill overlooking Opecquan Creek in a serene and secluded area. At the Bower, with many young ladies in attendance, Stuart and his dashing staff enjoyed light duty and lightheartedness. They would recall these as some of the finest days and weeks of the war. Young men talked of daring deeds, and their commanders planned to make use of these eager youths to further their mission.[10]

Lee reasoned that Stuart should cross the Potomac to see what McClellan was up to. It undoubtedly was the time for McClellan to strike, and Lee had to be prepared. Stuart was to take note of the position of the various units of the Army of the Potomac in relation to the road networks in southern Pennsylvania and northwestern Maryland. This cavalry reconnaissance plan was all highly secret, eyes-only information, and it was kept that way during most of the first week of October.

The reconnaissance plan was risky. Long cavalry raids were hard on horses, and the horses of both the Confederate and Union armies in the East were in poor shape. There had been an epidemic of "greased heel" in both armies, horses were scarce, and a raid that would cover more than one hundred miles was of questionable value unless it produced much-needed information. Lee felt that he had no alternative. His need for accurate information was critical. The Federals had the advantage of the hot-air observation balloon and had used that advantage successfully at the First Battle of Bull Run and even more successfully during the peninsula campaign.[11]

Stuart had always come through with information for Lee. He had ridden around McClellan during the Seven Days campaign earlier that summer and had done the same sort of thing in August during the second Manassas campaign. The latter sojourn, which was undertaken at night during a rainstorm, had netted the Army of Northern Virginia valuable intelligence about the position and comparative strength of various Federal forces. It had enabled Lee to institute his daring flanking movement under the command of Stonewall Jackson that had led to the Confederate victory.

General Lee's orders dated 8 October 1862 tell Stuart cross the Potomac at Williamsport with between twelve and fifteen hundred men. (Stuart took closer to eighteen hundred men and four pieces of artillery.) Stuart then was to proceed north, bearing west of Hagerstown and Greencastle and heading to Chambersburg, Pennsylvania, where he was to destroy the railroad and get all available information on Union position, force, and intent. Then Stuart was to add a modern twist to this first of modern wars by taking some hostages who could be exchanged for Rebel prisoners.

Stuart was to determine on his own how he would return to Charlestown and the Confederate lines. He decided that Wade Hampton, one of his most capable brigadiers, would lead the first six-hundred-man detachment, W. H. F. "Rooney" Lee would lead the second, and Colonel William E. Jones would lead the third. In case of trouble in either the front or rear of the column, a four-gun artillery detachment commanded by Major John Pelham would be between Lee and Jones. On 9 October Stuart and his staff attended a dance at the Bower, which had served as the headquarters for the Cavalry Corps of Northern Virginia since the Battle of Antietam. At eleven o'clock the music stopped, and Stuart and his inner circle prepared to leave for Darkesville and then to continue on to the small town of Hedgeville, where they would spend the rest of the night before crossing the Potomac early in the morning of 10 October.[12]

On the other side of the Potomac the Federals were expecting something from Stuart because he had been idle too long. After the Antietam campaign, they had put together a force that they hoped could contest river crossings. The force, with twelve guns and more than eight hundred men under Brigadier General John Kenly, seemed impressive enough. Company A of the 12th Illinois, under the command of Captain Thomas Logan, was assigned to northwestern Maryland near McCoy's Ford. The force of about fifty men had seen some action, and by October they were alert and ready for more.[13]

The 12th Illinois was responsible for patrolling the tortuous and narrow roads around McCoy's Ford in the rolling low hills of the countryside that borders the Potomac River. The McCoy's Ferry Road twists and turns for almost a quarter of a mile until it runs into the narrow and winding Big Spring Road. Even today it is very difficult to see the road ahead, and motorists often sound their horns when they drive over the hills and around the curves. In the 1860s most of the roads in the area were even smaller and narrower than they are now, particularly on the turns, and each crossroads was an excellent site for an ambush. The McCoy's Ferry Road went under the Chesapeake and Ohio Canal, which runs from Georgetown to Cumberland, Maryland, then met with Big Spring Road, which runs eastward until it forks. One side of the fork goes northward to Clear Spring; the other runs east to Williamsport. In 1862 the fork was called Green Spring Furnace.[14]

Captain Thomas Logan and Company A of the 12th Illinois had been in Clear Spring since 7 October. Logan was accompanied by Captain William Treichel, who was commanding two companies of the 6th Pennsylvania Cavalry, and Captain Charles Russell, who led an independent company of Maryland cavalry. Logan established a headquarters near Clear Spring and posted a picket reserve of sixteen men in a rotating shift near McCoy's Ferry. He placed four men at Green Spring Furnace "where the Cherry Run road crosses the road from the [Fairview] mountain to McCoy's ford," only about a half mile from the ferry. Four more men were placed at a schoolhouse two miles from Cherry Run, and another four men patrolled the road connecting Cherry Run to Clear Spring.[15]

The men were not allowed to have fires; a move by Stuart was anticipated. Logan's men were armed and their horses were saddled and bridled on the morning of 10 October. The men probably sat on their horses facing the Virginia shore with their Burnside carbines resting on their thighs. This was dangerous duty. There was always the possibility of attack by a bushwhacker or guerrilla: an attacker would shoot a cavalryman, take his horse if he could, and leave his body behind as a warning to others who stopped to enjoy a pipe and admire the fall scenery.[16]

As dawn broke on 10 October, a heavy fog shrouded the Potomac valley. On the Virginia side one of Stuart's most trusted scouts, Lieutenant James Phillips, and twenty-five men dismounted and crept across the river. They did not make a sound. The 2nd South Carolina Cavalry regiment awaited the signal to rush across the river and secure McCoy's Ford. The silence was broken by pistol shots, and the South Carolina men splashed across the river and secured the area. A trooper of the 12th Illinois and some horses were captured by Stuart's command, but the Rebels had been seen by Federal cavalry.[17]

At 5:30 on that foggy morning, a Mr. Jaque, who lived near the ford, rode to Logan's reserve, which had been moved to Green Spring Furnace, and informed the headquarters section that the Confederate cavalry was crossing the Potomac in strength. Logan quickly ordered his baggage wagon toward Clear Spring and sent couriers ahead toward Williamsport to warn Kenly and the rest of the brigade. Within five minutes the rest of Logan's command of about forty men was drawn up in line of battle across the Clear Spring Road. Logan knew that the McCoy's Ford crossing was likely to cut his pickets off from the rest of his command. He ordered Sergeant E. N. Pratt to proceed with three men and attempt to pass the crossroads at Green Spring Furnace and to gather up all the soldiers on picket duty before the enemy occupied the area. They were then to head to Fairview, north and west of Clear Spring, then to rejoin the command, which by that time would be on its way to battle the Confederates or would be falling back to Williamsport to protect the locks and the railroad. Pratt rounded up most of the pickets, but not all of them. At one time he was surrounded by Stuart's troops for hours. The sixteen men in Pratt's command maintained self-control and control of their mounts. They evaded capture and returned to the Federal lines.[18]

Stuart's advance elements neared Logan's pickets at Green Spring Furnace at about 5:40 A.M. The Confederates fired on the pickets, and the Federals fell back so that the Rebels would commit themselves to their objective, which at that stage was unclear to the Federals. As soon as the gray horsemen occupied the crossroads and Green Spring Furnace, they brought up artillery (only one gun according to official records) and trained it on the Clear Spring road. Logan, alarmed, quickly sent dispatch riders to inform Kenly that the Rebels were pulling artillery. The Federals in Kenly's brigade were well stocked with artillery; Logan undoubtedly hoped to even the odds at Clear Spring.

Upon receiving the message that the Confederates had field artillery, Kenly's brigade headquarters sent a courier dashing off to Logan and directed him to fall back to Dam Number 5 on the canal. Logan had already retreated via four locks to evacuate everything of value to the Rebels. He stayed on the Clear Spring road, prepared to contest every inch of it. A Rebel column of Stuart's advance guard approached and fired on Logan's rear guard. The men of the 12th Illinois returned the fire and killed one man and wounded one horse. Because the firefight was small and largely ineffectual, Logan believed that the Rebels had orders not to engage.[19]

Logan remained in visual contact with Stuart's column until nine o'clock in the morning, and he estimated that it included twenty-five hundred men and eight pieces of artillery. His estimate was about six hundred men too high, and he reported twice as many guns as Stuart actually had. Nevertheless, Logan was the first to report that Stuart was north of the Potomac. The signal stations that the Yankees had so carefully set up from South Mountain to Catoctin Mountain had not picked up Stuart's movements at all. Stuart's column took National Road up to the Pennsylvania line, and by 10:30 on the morning of 10 October he was in Chambersburg. The 12th Illinois had left Stuart before he crossed into Pennsylvania, and for the rest of the raid they became, like the rest of the Federal cavalry, observers of one of the most famous cavalry raids of the Civil War.[20]

But Company A had done its part. As a picket force it had spread the alarm numerous times. The Federal high command of Kenly, Pleasonton, and McClellan had plenty of notice of Stuart's presence within the Union lines.

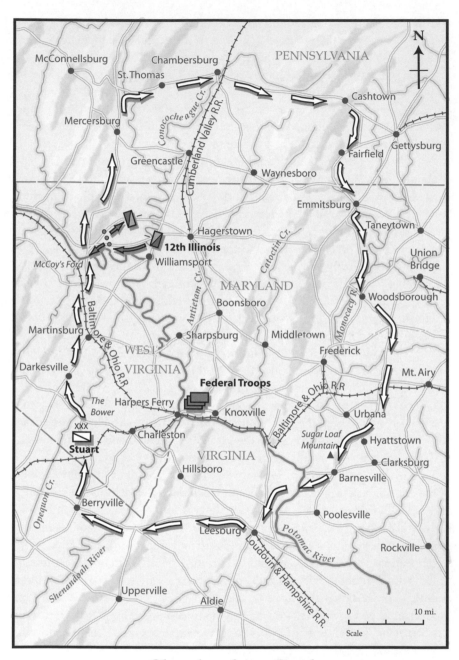

Chambersburg Raid
Position of the 12th Illinois
October 1862

They failed, however, to intercept him. Stuart entered Chambersburg and went through the farce of installing one of his subordinates, Wade Hampton of South Carolina, as military governor. Stuart tried to rob the bank in Chambersburg, but a quick-thinking bank employee had left town with the money before Stuart arrived; he hid out in the countryside until the Rebels left and rode east. Stuart's subordinates also tried to burn the bridge over Conococheague Creek, but they could not because it was constructed of iron.[21]

The next morning Stuart's raiders discovered the Union army depot, which contained army overcoats, clothing, underwear, and socks—vital supplies for the winter—and five thousand new rifles and numerous pistols and sabers. Stuart's men wrecked several trains, cut telegraph wires (then tied them together to make it difficult for Federal repair crews to find the locations of the cuts), and destroyed several machine shops. Mostly, however, they stole horses from the wealthy Pennsylvania farmers, who were the most successful agriculturalists in the country, according to engineer William Blackford. The horses the Rebel raiders took were not riding horses but were large draft horses of Norman, Percheron, or Belgian stock. The horses were well suited for use in the artillery or quartermaster service but wholly unfit for cavalry purposes. Most of the horses had been used in the fall harvest, and they were usually taken in harness because the Confederate army quartermaster had no collars that "would have fitted these huge, bull-necked animals."[22]

The Federal cavalry officers studied the Chambersburg Raid and learned from it. There were many elements in Stuart's "impossible" accomplishment. Men had been carefully selected to ride the fine Virginia bloods that had carried the Confederate cavalry through the first year of the war. The selection process produced a far more dedicated command than a random ordering of average regiments would have. As Stuart's raiding column traveled almost fifty miles behind enemy lines, spare horses were also invaluable. The column used more than twelve hundred horses, including captured mounts. No party of raiders, no matter how elite or well mounted, could have maintained Stuart's pace without additional horses.[23]

Excellent guides were also necessary to the successful raid. Stuart had made it his business to learn from which state and county each of his regiments had been organized. Therefore, when he needed reliable guides for a specific area, he knew in which regiment to start his search. For example, Captain Elijah White of White's Comanches, the Maryland independent battalion, knew the area very well, having grown up in Jones Crossroads, one of the areas patrolled by the 12th Illinois Volunteer Cavalry. Two of Stuart's men had even lived some of their early years in the Chambersburg, Pennsylvania, area, so that when the Confederate raiding column approached, at least two troopers were aware of most of the important roads. The raiders also benefited from the intangibles of teamwork and plain luck. Stuart's men were confident and dedicated, but it was the fog and good fortune that allowed his men to evade detection for so long. The raiders were well into Pennsylvania before they were discovered by anyone other than the pickets of the 12th Illinois Cavalry.[24]

These lessons that the Federal cavalry learned were not based on a central source of military information or on the work of staff officers who were assigned to study Stuart and other successful Confederate raiders. Rather, the lessons were based on knowledge gleaned by regional and local commanders. The model of a modern army with a general staff whose officers study and evaluate real or potential threats belongs to the American military experience of the twentieth century.[25]

During the final weeks of October Stuart's men, posted along the Potomac fords, began to suspect that McClellan and the Union host were at last on the move. On 19 October the men of the 12th Illinois traveled from their base camp in Clear Spring, Maryland, to raid a town in Berkeley County (now in West Virginia) called Bath. They rode all that night and returned to base camp the next, completing a round trip of forty-four miles as the crow flies. It is difficult to ascertain from Private Redman's letters, the report of the adjutant general, and the official records just what they were supposed to find, but it was clear to Redman that the great Union behemoth was about to move. This would be his unit's first expedition, and he did not know what was about to happen, but he believed that before long the 12th Illinois would do something besides "picket and recon duty," and he was certain that they would be successful.[26]

On 26 October, further indications emerged that the Army of the Potomac was finally coming to life. The brigadier general commanding the cavalry on the Potomac, Alfred Pleasonton, led a large reconnaissance force that crossed the Potomac at Berlin, Virginia, and began to scout the countryside near Leesburg and the northern Virginia communities of Aldie, Middleburg, and Philomont, towns that were deep in Loudoun and Fauquier counties in Confederate territory. On 3 November Pleasonton was joined by an additional brigade under the command of Brigadier General William Woods Averell. "The ranks were thin; nevertheless, here was cavalry obviously operating in brigade strength, and here were two brigades engaged in a joint operation." Pleasonton hoped to find out where the main Confederate army was, but more important was his assigned task of deceiving the Confederate cavalry into thinking that McClellan was preparing for a major move toward the Shenandoah Valley.[27]

Lee hoped that McClellan would attempt to move toward the Shenandoah

Valley, but he realized that McClellan probably would not and might suddenly shift southward toward Richmond, so he stationed his forces accordingly. To cover the Shenandoah Valley, Lee stationed Stonewall Jackson to the north in the city of Winchester. To cover a move to the south, Lee stationed his second corps under the command of Major General James Longstreet at the ancient town of Culpeper. Culpeper was within a day's move by rail to the valley, so Longstreet could support Jackson if needed, but he was also in position to move southeast toward Richmond if the Yankees chose that route. Between Jackson and Longstreet were the passes through the Bull Run and Blue Ridge Mountains. The Confederate cavalry's function was to keep those passes secure so that prying Federal eyes could not see who was being moved to support whom. It was the Federal cavalry's mission to find out which wing of Lee's army was moving on the other side of those passes. Hence, there were bound to be clashes as Averell and Pleasonton tried to find out what the Rebels were up to and Stuart and his superb brigades did their best to foil them.[28]

By the end of the first week in November the Army of the Potomac had a new commander, Ambrose Burnside. Lincoln was frustrated with McClellan's inaction. Repeated attempts to get him to move after Lee's army had been rewarded by a foray into Virginia during the final days of October. A small Union force of cavalry and infantry under the command of Major General Andrew A. Humphreys had brushed aside Stuart's pickets, had advanced almost to Martinsburg, and had found that Lee was still in the Shenandoah Valley. The force had then retraced its steps, going back across the Potomac with the encouragement of Stuart's cavalry and a brigade of Stonewall Jackson's infantry. Nothing could entice McClellan to move aggressively after Lee. Lincoln decided to replace McClellan just after the first Tuesday in November, an election day in most states. Lincoln, the wise politician, did not want to make McClellan's dismissal an election issue.[29]

Democrats swept to victory in Illinois that election day, reflecting the hard economic times the men of the 12th had left at home. There had been a general economic depression in Illinois throughout the 1850s, and many banks had not survived. Bonds issued by Southern states backed two-thirds of Illinois bank notes. When the state auditor demanded more securities, most banks were unable to afford them. For farmers things were just as bad or worse. Commodities piled up in warehouses. Some were delivered to the South during the opening months of the war, but the majority of them spoiled. The farmers also suffered when hog quotations in Chicago were halved and corn sold for as low as six cents a bushel. Military buying in the North and three years of crop failures in Europe helped to trigger a some economic recovery, but bitter memories remained.[30]

After the election Lincoln completed his transfer of power in the Army of the Potomac with nary a whimper from the general public. His order was brief: "By direction of the President it is ordered that Major General McClellan be relieved from the command of the Army of the Potomac and, that Major General Burnside take the command of that Army." The rank and file of the Army of the Potomac was disappointed and angry. After all, McClellan had organized, trained, and equipped the army, and the troops knew he would not send them into battle unless he was almost positive that victory was assured. The men in the Army of the Potomac would have three more commanders before the end of the war, and they would serve them with grudging respect, but they would never serve another commander with the devotion that they gave George B. McClellan. To show their regard for him, the men "gave McClellan immense demonstrations of affection in telling him good-bye, and he devoted a day to receiving them." In the two Illinois regiments that served in the Army of the Potomac's cavalry, the re-action to the change was mixed. Private William Henry Redman evidently felt much as the rest. He wrote home that he felt that the bad fortune of the Army of the Potomac was attributable of McClellan's inner circle of advisors and not to the "young Napoleon" himself. "We only ask for good leaders and we will give the North good news to read in a very short time."[31]

One of Burnside's first acts was to reorganize the Army of the Potomac into three grand divisions and a reserve division. Each grand division was made up of two corps of infantry and a cavalry component. There were about thirty-one thousand infantry troops in each division. The cavalry regi-ments, though, numbered only around six thousand men, and they were split among the three grand divisions. The reserve division had even fewer cavalry; Stephen Starr does not even mention the reserve-division cavalry in his study of the Federal cavalry in the Civil War. Two companies of the 12th Illinois formed a part of the reserve cavalry detachment. Company A pro-vided personal bodyguard protection to reserve corps commander Major General Franz Sigel during the early days of the Fredericksburg campaign. Two other companies of the 12th were detached to form the provost guard, or military police, for the entire Army of the Potomac.[32]

Logistically the reorganization into grand divisions was a wise move. In-fantry and artillery soldiers attached to the grand divisions received much-needed clothing, and there was plenty of good food. The morale of the Army of the Potomac greatly improved. For the mounted soldiers, however, the reorganization was an incomplete evolution. It was an improvement over the situation under McClellan, but the men believed that their com-manders had yet find a proper role for the cavalry.

Logistics and supply, though, were not the reasons Lincoln chose Burnside. The reason—and Burnside knew this—was that Lincoln wanted action: he wanted another battle before the winter snows stopped military operations in Virginia. Lincoln had observed that the Army of the Potomac was closer to the Confederate capitol in Richmond than was Lee's fragmented army. If Burnside would move quickly, he could threaten the Rebel capitol before Lee could react. Burnside agreed. He came up with a plan, and the president gave it qualified approval because of his concerns about weather and conditions of the roads.[33]

The plan held that Burnside would concentrate his men near Warrenton as if he were planning an attack on Longstreet, who was based at Culpeper with his corps. While Longstreet was reacting to this feint by moving back toward Gordonsville, Burnside would accumulate three or four days worth of supplies and then shift to Fredericksburg with the intention of moving upon Richmond.

In order to accomplish this goal Burnside had many things to take into consideration. He believed that his line of communication along the Orange and Alexandria Railroad was exposed to the risk of a sudden strike by Stonewall Jackson, who was operating out of Winchester in the Shenandoah Valley far to Burnside's rear. The risk of such an attack would steadily increase as he moved directly south from Warrenton. The single-track railroad was rickety, it was doubtful whether it had the capacity to supply Burnside's large army without interruption. An advance southeast through Fredericksburg would be easier to support logistically, but it would mean crossing wider rivers. Burnside could use Aquia Creek as a supply base, and because the creek is a tributary of the Potomac River, he would have a secure line of transport from Washington. Burnside having such could force Lee to react more quickly than the latter might like, and Burnside would perhaps have a chance to destroy the Confederate commander. The most critical aspect of the proposed operation was the Rappahannock River—crossing at Fredericksburg. The Rebels had burned the bridge there, and crossing the river would be a problem. Therefore, Burnside would order a pontoon train from Alexandria to Falmouth, Virginia, and the assembly of supplies would be stockpiled at Falmouth, Aquia Creek, and Belle Plain, all within the immediate vicinity of Fredericksburg.[34]

Lincoln approved the plan on 14 November 1862 but warned that "it will succeed if you move very rapidly, otherwise not." Burnside's Right Grand Division, under the command of Major General Edwin Sumner, began to leave Warrenton on 15 November. The Confederates did not detect the move right away. Three days later Lee found out about it and ordered Longstreet to intercept the Federals.[35]

Confederate horses were worn down from all the marching and fighting.

Like the Federals, Stuart's command was affected by the epidemic of greased heel. There had been seven major skirmishes with the slowly improving Union cavalry between the last week in October and 10 November alone, and many animals had been destroyed or abandoned in battle. Horses that lacked proper forage carried soldiers in constant raids and in reconnaissance over many miles of poorly maintained roads and rolling Virginia hills. The supply of horses diminished, and many of Stuart's horsemen were horsemen in name only.[36]

As Burnside's reserve corps moved south, Company A of the 12th Illinois, the corps commander's bodyguard, was ordered to take part in a rather unusual assignment. Major General Franz Sigel was camped in the Warrenton area with his reserve corps when the order came to move south to the Rappahannock. Apparently Sigel thought that if he moved quickly he would be the first to get to the town of Fredericksburg. Once he was there he could get a look at the river and see how much damage the Rebels had done to the bridge. Then he could send some soldiers into the community to assess the Confederate strength near Fredericksburg and report everything back to Burnside. Sigel hurriedly put together a mounted force to accomplish his purpose.

From his staff Sigel chose bright, energetic Captain Ulrich Dahlgren to lead the expedition. Dahlgren was a "born adventurer," the sort of man who loved danger. He held many hazardous positions in the Union army; he lost part of a leg on one mission and lost his life on another later in the War. Dahlgren selected sixty men (almost all of the officers and men in Company A) and "attacked the town, . . . routed the rebels and drove them three miles. He found five companies of the 15th Virginia Cavalry and three companies of the Ninth Virginia Cavalry," which Stuart had left to garrison the town. Sigel reported that Dahlgren and his bodyguard "also captured thirty-nine prisoners and two wagon-loads of clothing, destined for the Southern army."[37]

Dahlgren's primary mission, however, was the gathering of intelligence about the bridges, and in this too he succeeded, reporting that the bridges on "the Potomac Creek and Accokeek Creek (of the Aquia Creek and Fredericksburg Railroad) were destroyed." So Burnside knew on 10 November that he needed to get his pontoons to Fredericksburg before Lee realized what was happening and moved to block the Federal advance toward Richmond. Burnside, though, failed to get the pontoons in time, and Lee beat him to Fredericksburg. What resulted was, for the Union, a disastrous battle.[38]

It was, in reality, an artillery battle, at least on the Confederate side, with the infantry acting in support. Burnside finally got his troops across the Rappahannock after a costly battle with a brigade of Mississippians under the command of General William Barksdale. Once they were over the river the

Major S. Bronson, Wheaton, Ill. Photo by Brand's Art Gallery,
Chicago. (From Papers of William Henry Redman (MSS 7415), Special
Collections Department, University of Virginia Library)

Lt. Henry Richardson. Photo by Mansfield's City Gallery, St. Louis, Mo.
(From Papers of William Henry Redman (MSS 7415), Special Collections
Department, University of Virginia Library)

Lt. Col. Hasbrouck Davis
commanding the 12th Illinois
Cavalry, 1863–1865. (From
Massachusetts Commandery,
Military Order of the Loyal
Legion of the United States
(MOLLUS) Collection at the
U.S. Army Military History
Institute, Carlisle Barracks, Pa.)

Brig. Gen. John Buford commanding 1st Cavalry Division
at Gettysburg, 1 July 1863.
(From Massachusetts Commandery, MOLLUS Collection at
the U.S. Army Military History
Institute, Carlisle Barracks, Pa.)

Maj. Gen. George Stoneman
commanding the cavalry
column during the Chancellorsville Raid, May 1863.
(From Massachusetts Commandery, MOLLUS Collection at
the U.S. Army Military History
Institute, Carlisle Barracks, Pa.)

William Henry Redman.
(From State Historical Society
of Iowa–Des Moines)

Federals looted the town, which they had already ruined with an artillery barrage. Burnside's staff thought that a large cannonade would deal with Barksdale's sniping infantrymen. It did not, and Federal infantry had to brave the rifle fire and then again deal with the Mississippians house by house and street by street.

Once Burnside secured Fredericksburg, he realized that the Confederates were deeply entrenched at a plantation called Maryes Heights, about three miles from the Union lines. The position at Maryes Heights was at the extreme left of an immense Confederate trench network that stretched nearly nine miles to Hamilton's Crossing. Burnside should have either fortified the town or withdrawn across the Rappahannock, slipping further north and attempting to turn Lee's flank. But Burnside was Burnside; the plan had been made, so he attacked on the afternoon of 13 December, and his grand divisions put on quite a show. They advanced in perfect order, and they were shot down in perfect order. Lee's artillery was so accurate, and he had so much time to position his guns (Barksdale made sure of that), that when his artillery opened up, a "chicken couldn't live on that hill." Burnside stopped his assaults as the sun set. He lost more than twelve thousand men in that one afternoon.[39]

In a battle such as the one at Fredericksburg, cavalry was of little use. In the days just before the general action, some of the cavalry of the Army of the Potomac had delivered dispatches and served as orderlies, but most were just watching. They were on the north bank of the Rappahannock near the artillery, and they stayed there until the general retreat on 15 December, two days after the battle.[40]

With the exception of Company A, which made the opening raid, the majority of the 12th Illinois had stayed north in Maryland. But that did not hinder some of them from making their feelings known about the needless slaughter at Fredericksburg. Sergeant Ashley Alexander wrote home that he felt that the war would be lost. Alexander was willing to go even further: he would bet a hundred dollars on the ultimate decision. "Eastern generals were so poor," he wrote, "that our men have been slaughtered like hogs."

After the battle Burnside ordered the rest of the men of the 12th Illinois down from the Potomac and away from the Maryland Brigade and their base camp at Clear Spring near McCoy's Ford. They had spent a wonderful autumn there. Stuart's Chambersburg Raid and the Bath expedition had been their only challenges. But shortly that would change.[41]

Fredericksburg had been a terrible day for the Union; for Lee and his Army of Northern Virginia it had been an easy victory. After Fredericksburg Lee said to his senior corps commander, James Longstreet, "It is well that war is so terrible, we would grow too fond of it." Lee now wanted to keep the Yankees guessing, wondering what he would do next, and he had the perfect instrument to accomplish that task: Jeb Stuart. Lee turned him loose on Burnside's communications and supplies again, tired horses and all, not once but numerous times. Stuart struck the Union rear near Aquia Creek, its supply base. The 12th Illinois was based near there at a little town called Dumfries, and there they met Stuart's troops again.[42]

The bulk of the regiment was ordered to the Fredericksburg area on 9 December 1862. They had been ordered to leave their base at Clear Spring, Maryland, and ride to Harpers Ferry, the site of their harrowing escape back in September. The weather was bitter. They began to move out of Clear Spring at sunset on the sixth, the coldest night of the year by the account of one witness. The mountain roads were icy, and the horses were "smooth shod." "Many of the horses fell, and only superior horsemanship saved the boys from being seriously hurt." The men had to walk their mounts along the narrow paths so they would not lose them over the precipices. Once the men were at Harpers Ferry, a large fire warmed them, and they remained there in what was almost a ghost town for the better part of three days. While they were there, two companies of the 12th—A and C, numbering about 120 men— became involved in some picket duty, which some of their members described as "fun" in the mountain cold. The rest of the companies moved on toward Williamsport, then south, escorting the 12th Army Corps.[43]

Companies A and C finally left Harpers Ferry on 12 December. According to Sergeant William Henry Redman, they had some "fun with the rebs" on the way. They moved toward Williamsport via Hillsboro, Wheatland, and Leesburg. Near Leesburg on the night of the thirteenth, the two companies, moving slowly while guarding the regimental supply wagons, were attacked by about three hundred guerrillas. A *Rock River Democrat* correspondent identified these partisans as "White's Guerrillas" (Major Elijah White and his 35th Maryland Battalion, known to both sides as the Comanches). Sergeant Redman did not identify which Rebel unit Companies A and C were facing. Instead he described what the Confederate unit did and how badly the 12th Illinois mauled them. We "killed several of their men and lost four of our boys. One of ours was killed and three taken prisoners." Companies A and C retired from the field in a hurry, abandoning two of their three wagons to the Rebels. Redman himself captured a revolver that was worth thirty dollars. Redman added that his unit, Company C, usually was the rear guard and had some action if there was any to be had.[44]

Redman wrote to his mother that she would be "hearing things, big, big things before too long." One of the things she undoubtedly heard about was the need for warm clothing because the wagons that Redman had abandoned to White had carried the winter supplies for the entire regiment. This meant the troops were without necessities such as woolen overcoats, tents, extra woolen underwear, spare boots, and gloves. The weather remained cold through most of December in central Virginia, and the 12th Illinois, without warm clothing, had to sleep rolled up on the cold ground for many nights in the extra blankets they carried on their horses. Redman wrote of this in an almost cavalier fashion, stating that they all were kept warm by roaring fires and that he was all right. He "could stand such fare as long as anybody." If Redman was being truthful about the warm fires and the bravado of his fellow cavalrymen in the face of the cold, in the end some of the soldiers saw things differently. When they requested pensions long after the war had ended, they insisted that the effects of the continual exposure to the cold would be with them for the rest of their lives.[45]

These were times of frustration for the men of the 12th Illinois. After Burnside was defeated at Fredericksburg, the 12th Illinois, now a part of Daniel Slocum's 12th Corps, had to fall back from Fredericksburg twelve miles. The forty-thousand-man 12th Corps started out from Williamsport with the 12th Illinois regiment as escort, then found out late at night that no one had thought to supply them with food. Company A reported in the *Rock River Democrat* that on one of those chilly nights deep in "Sesech country," the men did "double-picket" duty, which combined the standard guard with the taking of forty-nine chickens, turkeys, and ducks from surrounding farms so they would have at least one meal for everyone in the regiment. After completing their double-picket duty and rejoining the entire corps, the 12th Illinois had to help pull General Slocum's wagons along the rutted Virginia roads, which by mid-December were quagmires of mud.[46]

Almost all the troops were months behind in pay. The *Rock River Democrat* reported that President Lincoln had been introduced to an army paymaster who was wearing the dress blue uniform of a major. When the paymaster remarked that he thought he would pay his respects to the president while he was in Washington, Lincoln replied that from what he heard from the soldiers, respects were about all any of the paymasters did pay. The men of the 12th Illinois did receive their pay in January, which for Redman amounted to about sixty dollars. As he saw it, as a sergeant he was paid seventeen dollars a month for dodging Rebel bullets and sleeping on the cold ground.[47]

The 12th Illinois was sent to camp at Dumfries, Virginia, on 20 December. As one of Burnside's largest supply depots, Dumfries was vital to the army. It was located on the Potomac about twenty miles southwest of Washington, D.C., near Aquia Creek, and served as important cogs in both the Army of the Potomac's communications via the telegraph and the overland supply route from Washington. The forces on the other side of the Rappahannock knew of this supply base and decided to see if they could destroy it—or at least enough of it to make Burnside withdraw from the Fredericksburg area.[48]

The Confederates had good success at raiding far into the Yankee rear that winter. On 27 November, just before the Battle of Fredericksburg, one of Stuart's brigade commanders, Wade Hampton, made a raid and returned with ninety-two prisoners and a hundred horses. On 10 December, with about eight hundred troops, Hampton hit the town of Dumfries. He suffered no losses and met little resistance, and he returned with fifty prisoners and twenty wagons with stores, which he brought to the Rappahannock. Hampton cut some telegraph wires and would have destroyed more communication lines if he had not run into General Sigel's corps on the telegraph road to Occoquan Creek. Stuart endorsed the Dumfries Raid as one of the most successful of the war. Hampton, with "a command thinly clad and scantily fed, displayed, amid the rigors of winter and on the desert track of an invading host, an activity, gallantry, and cheerful endurance worthy of the highest praise and the nation's gratitude."[49]

Hampton struck again on 17 and 18 December, capturing 150 prisoners and twenty wagons. But now Lee needed information on what Burnside was doing, and he turned to Stuart. Stuart decided on a raid that would center on the Federal supply base north of Fredericksburg at Dumfries where the 12th Illinois was encamped. It was quite an ambitious undertaking with broken-down horses, the winter weather, poorly dressed troops, and a hundred thousand Federal troops in his front. Stuart did not hope to capture the supply depot. His immediate objective was to capture some of the heavily laden supply wagons passing the Dumfries area.

Stuart started out on the day after Christmas in 1862, crossed the Rappahannock at Kelly's Ford, and made camp the following night near Morrisville. The Federals had been expecting something of this kind and had stationed a large force of cavalry and infantry, including the 12th Illinois, in the Dumfries area for just such a contingency. Lieutenant Colonel Hasbrouck Davis was in command of the 12th Illinois and had standing orders to patrol all roads to and from Dumfries. He had his forces disposed in the following manner:

A detail selected from Company G, consisting of 1 sergeant and 6 enlisted men, was sent, on the morning of the 27th, to patrol the Telegraph Road for about 4 miles southward, to meet patrols from Aquia Creek, and another detail of 1 commissioned officer and 23 men, from the same company and Company B, was sent to patrol and picket the road at Lindsays [Lindsley's] farm, about 5 miles out and beyond, toward Dyer's Mill and Independence Hill.[50]

This was standard patrolling procedure in the Civil War. Whenever there was a town that was central to the road network that surrounded it, a good cavalry commander would keep his main body in the center of the town so as to move at any time in any direction. He would then send small detachments out on all the roads with orders to rendezvous at a predetermined position. The relief commanders would stay near the city boundaries with a sizable contingent of mounted troops ready to respond on the roads assigned to them. When met with superior numbers, the relief force could act as a delaying force if the patrolling elements were overwhelmed in an attack or waylaid in an ambush. This procedure had been gradually developed during almost two years of war and was the result of many methods that worked and a few that did not. The problem was that by December 1862 the Confederates were well aware that the procedure was becoming standard among Federal cavalry units. And Stuart knew the system better than most.

Stuart had obtained Federal uniforms; after the debacle at Fredericksburg there were many of them to be had. In actions that raise some questions about the rules of war, he clothed some of his advance detachment that rode along Telegraph Road in Union blue, and they attacked a detail of the 12th Illinois commanded by Sergeant Crowe. Crowe, it appears, was waiting for the relief detail from Aquia Creek to advance and give the call sign when Stuart's troops, whom he thought to be Federals, drew carbines and charged.[51]

As soon as he was attacked, Crowe dispatched a courier to Davis, who was with the main body in the center of the town of Dumfries, but the messenger ran right into Stuart's Confederates. Davis's men were overwhelmed so quickly that they did not even know whether they had inflicted any harm on the enemy. Sergeant Redman and his squad had just left their picket patrol and returned to camp twenty minutes before the Rebels struck. Redman counted thirty men lost in the opening minutes of Stuart's attack.[52]

The other picket detachment was commanded by First Lieutenant John H. Clybourne. "Their vedettes were driven in about noon by another body of the rebel cavalry [probably Rooney Lee] and at the same time another body of rebel cavalry advanced on them from their rear [probably Hampton] and charged upon them." The men dismounted, plunged into the bushes, fought from tree to tree, and disappeared into the woods. By the time he was writing the after-action report, Colonel Davis stated that only one detachment had returned to camp. When Sergeant Redman and his detachment returned to Dumfries to the sound of the guns, they found the 12th Illinois and its supporting infantry regiments, the 66th Ohio, 7th Ohio, and 5th Ohio, drawn up in line of battle. The main event was at hand.[53]

A brisk cannonade opened up. Captain M. W. Henry's battery, assigned to Stuart's horse artillery, unlimbered and began to shell the town of Dumfries. Henry's guns were firing shell and canister at a range of eight hundred to one thousand yards. The artillery fire was bothersome but not overly dangerous.

It did, however, cause some anxious moments for Colonel Davis and the 12th Illinois. When the firing had started Davis had moved them into the center of the town where the Rebel guns were dropping most of their shells. "One shell struck the saddle of Captain R. N. Hayden and glancing upon his hip inflicted a severe injury," reported Davis. The colonel withdrew his men out of range. Then he received word to advance through the town. The 12th Illinois advanced through the artillery barrage, the shells falling close around them. "One spherical case shot struck just in front of our column of twos, and, ricocheting over the heads of the first files, passed the whole length of a company between the files, inflicting no further injury than the disabling of one horse." The men of the 12th Illinois then proceeded to an area near their camp ground, dismounted, and remained in a defensive position until the Confederates attempted a flanking movement.[54]

If it were not for the distance, many may have perished under the Rebel cannonade. The extreme range for a canister, which is a tin can filled with about sixty musket balls, is about eight hundred yards. A canister did not have an explosive charge once it left the barrel of a gun, so while it was deadly to massed columns of infantry or cavalry at ranges of four hundred yards or less, it had little or no pattern left and little velocity at a range of half a mile. A spherical case round was a little better for medium-range shooting because it had a timed powder charge that exploded at a predetermined time after it left the barrel. Distance, however, was the savior, and in the battle at Dumfries the 12th Illinois was left relatively unharmed.

Davis now moved the 12th Illinois forward to a hill that commanded the road approach to Dumfries. After they had occupied the hill, the men of the 12th discovered a Rebel column that was advancing up the road. The 12th charged them and drove them back into some woods, where the Rebels dismounted. This area was not cavalry country; it was well covered with scrub timber that concealed the enemy. Davis decided that he would have to fight dismounted. To protect against an attack from the rear, Davis sent Lieutenant Thomas Drennan and his company to hold the road to Occoquan north of the town. Then he concealed his men at the crest of the hill that they had occupied for most of the afternoon. The Rebels charged and recharged down the declivity of the Federals' front, yelling "run there—you damned Yankees—sons of Bitches." The men of the 12th Illinois rose to their feet and delivered devastating volleys from their Burnside carbines, ending each of the five charges attempted by the Confederates that afternoon.[55]

Davis believed that when the Rebels first charged they had thought the hill was unoccupied by any Federal troops, or at most occupied by a very small force. Therefore, they were surprised by the continuous volleys from the 12th Illinois. Evidently the Rebel lines were close to the Federal camp, for Davis recalled that the Rebel campfires burned brightly all night. The men of the 12th Illinois could hear the Rebel pickets converse until 9 or 10 P.M. That night, two days after Christmas in 1862, the men from northern Illinois slept on their arms "with the bridle reins in our hands," and the Rebels left in the darkness. With the exception of Captain Hayden, whose wound was caused by the glancing artillery round, none of the members of the 12th Illinois had been hurt. Thomas Logan, who had opposed Stuart in the first hours of the Chambersburg Raid and had just been promoted to lieutenant colonel and mustered out of the regiment to take a command of his own, had volunteered his assistance to Davis and was of great help. But the 12th Illinois did not escape unscathed. Twenty-eight men from Company G and three from Company B were captured by Stuart's men.[56]

On 28 December, Company C of the 12th Illinois was selected to go on picket six miles from Dumfries "at the same place where the thirty men from Company G were captured" during the Stuart raid. Once they were in the vicinity, Redman was ordered to take a squad of men to patrol the road to Fairfax Station for a length of six miles. Redman wrote proudly to his mother that he had captured a straggler, one of Stuart's cavalrymen, and was entitled to keep the man's horse and his weapons. He brought the man back to headquarters at Dumfries and found the regiment once again sleeping on their arms, anticipating an attack from Stuart who by then was many miles away. The men had been sleeping on the ground, but the weather was mild and the men had plenty of blankets. In January the weather would worsen, and the men of the 12th Illinois would suffer exposure from which some would never recover.[57]

CHAPTER FOUR

Raids

In January 1863 the entire Army of the Potomac saw the famous mud march. The 12th Illinois Volunteer Cavalry participated in the unnecessary operation, which began on 21 January and lasted two grueling days. Burnside was so upset with his useless assaults against Maryes Heights that he had contemplated ordering another attack with himself in the lead of his troops—an interesting method of ensuring his own death. His staff talked him out of the foolish move, and Burnside came up with the idea of trying to flank Lee out of his position on the south side of the Rappahannock. In order to accomplish this plan, Burnside ordered his entire army to move north along the river and to cross at the many fords above Falmouth, but the weather caught up with him in mid-January, and the ground turned to mud. Burnside's march was a failure almost from the first, and afterward he had to retrace his steps into his old positions. The soldiers were miserable, the animals were miserable, and the entire operation, which involved more than one hundred thousand Federal troops, went down in history as a catastrophe.[1]

For the first twelve days of 1863, the 12th Illinois was also involved in standard patrolling and picket operations around the Dumfries area. The weather was cold, the men were exhausted, and not surprisingly many mistakes were made. In the case of Sergeant William Henry Redman of Company C, mistakes meant capture.

Redman was in charge of a detail of three men on 8 January when he was ambushed and captured by fifteen

Confederates about five miles west of Dumfries. Redman's three charges made their escape by running into the bushes at the side of the road. Redman wrote that he should not have been captured but that his horse had become entangled in the thickets. The Rebels took him thirty miles to the rear and kept him at a citizen's house. Redman escaped when the guard took off his boots and went to sleep. That day he traveled ten miles in three hours. He lay in the woods all the next day and traveled all the next night, and he made his way back to Sigel's corps safely. Weary and sore after making his escape, Redman was soon "alright and ready to try to thrash the Rebs again." He had lost everything, "his horse, saddle, four blankets, one carbine, one revolver, one overcoat, and one pair of buckskin gloves," but he would get replacements in a couple of days. He wrote his mother that the Rebels had treated him very well. He was with them only one night, and had traveled for two days with nothing to eat except for a piece of cornbread and some boiled pork.

Redman would have gone to Richmond "like the other boys did" if he had remained captured, and if the Confederates took him to Richmond it almost certainly would have meant a stint in Belle Isle Prison until he was exchanged–and in 1863 prisoner exchanges were becoming less common. There must have been many captures during the months of January and February of 1863. Orders came down from higher headquarters that an officer would be relieved and placed under arrest awaiting a general court martial if his command was surprised by an ambush and his men were captured.[2]

In the middle of January the men of the 12th Illinois returned to their old organization, the Railroad Division, under the command of Brigadier General Benjamin F. Kelley. Most of the members of this Railroad Division were organized into four brigades and were posted along the Orange and Alexandria Railroad, which came down to Fredericksburg and was a major supplier of Burnside's Army of the Potomac. By and large, the brigades were made up of infantry with some artillery support and a company or two of cavalry to act as a roving picket.

The 12th Illinois was supposedly stationed to the north on the Baltimore and Ohio Railroad at New Creek, Clarksburg, North Mountain, Romney, and Springfield and on the line of road between New Creek and the Ohio River. The cavalry brigade assigned to this area was made up of the 12th Illinois, the 1st New York, the 54th Pennsylvania, the Maryland Potomac Home Brigade, and one company each of the 12th and 14th Pennsylvania, with a battery of Pennsylvania artillery. In reality, the men of the 12th Illinois never left the Dumfries area the entire spring. They remained there until the Chancellorsville campaign, when for the first time they thought they would have a major role in one of the largest cavalry raids of the war. Before they could assume that role, though, a command change occurred, and for the cavalry service the change was for the better.[3]

General Order Number 9 from the War Department adjutant's office, dated 25 January 1863, stated that the president of the United States had directed that Major General A. E. Burnside, at his own request, be relieved from the command of the Army of the Potomac. After the president accepted the resignations of Generals E. V. Sumner and W. B. Franklin, Major General Joseph Hooker was to be assigned to the command of the Army of the Potomac. Lincoln formally transferred the command to Hooker on 26 January.[4]

This was Lincoln's fourth command change in the Army of the Potomac since the First Battle of Bull Run in July 1861. He was searching for a commander who would be able to defeat Robert E. Lee. With the exception of McClellan's tactical victory at Antietam in September 1862, the Federals had lost every major battle fought in the Virginia theater of the war. Almost from the first days of his command it appeared that Hooker was the man to defeat Lee. He meant to change things in a positive way to achieve a certain victory in the spring.

One historian wrote that Hooker "ironed ineptitude and indolence out of the medical services, flogged quartermaster and commissary functions into a fine piece of efficiency, . . . and inaugurated an intelligence-gathering system far ahead of its time in that staff-poor era." The soldiers had experienced sometimes more than their share of ineptitude, harassment, and frustration and therefore the army had a high desertion rate. But suddenly the men were being issued hearty rations, with fresh produce and soft bread. Unsanitary camps were cleaned up, liberal furloughs were given, and paymasters came up with six months of back pay.[5] Morale, which had been flagging, began to soar, and health conditions improved. Hooker expanded the use of shoulder patches to create unit pride and a sense of identity. Most importantly, though, Hooker reorganized the cavalry. His General Order Number 6 of 5 February 1863 said in part, "The cavalry of the army will be consolidated into one corps under the command of Major General George Stoneman, who will make the necessary assignments for detached duty." The Army of Northern Virginia had done this with Stuart's brigades much earlier.[6]

On 12 February Stoneman announced that he would organize the corps into three divisions made up entirely of volunteer regiments: the 1st and 2nd Divisions, under Brigadier Generals Alfred Pleasonton and William Woods Averell, respectively, would each contain seven regiments and an independent squadron. The 3rd Division under Brigadier General David M. Gregg would have six regiments and an independent company. In addition, there would be a reserve brigade under the command of Brigadier General

John Buford composed of five badly understrength regiments of regulars. With the exception of the Railroad Division, which included the 12th Illinois Cavalry, and a few other nondivisional formations, the entire cavalry of the Army of the Potomac had been reorganized by the middle of February 1863. Now Hooker would test his commanders in a series of probing actions against Jeb Stuart's Confederate brigades.[7]

The 12th Illinois stayed in the Dumfries area, or "Camp Dumfries" as William Redman called it in his letters. During those drab days in February and March, when the roads in Virginia were almost impassable, the 12th Illinois, like most other Federal cavalry units not attached to Averell or Pleasonton, spent the time fighting the weather, the roads, and the spring illnesses that plagued almost all Civil War regiments. Private Abner Frank, who joined the 12th Illinois in February and kept a detailed diary, fell ill during this time. His first patrol action was postponed because of a sore throat that sidelined him for the better part of a week.[8]

The men of the 12th Illinois now had time to discuss politics, and there were many controversial issues to ponder. Lincoln had issued the preliminary Emancipation Proclamation in September 1862 and the final Emancipation Proclamation on 1 January 1863. Twelve days later the government formally authorized the raising of African-American troops for the South Carolina Infantry, to be commanded by Colonel Thomas Wentworth Higginson. Later that spring the famed 54th Massachusetts Colored Infantry began training outside of Boston. There is little mention of any of this in the surviving diaries and letters of the 12th Illinois. William Redman wrote to one of his sisters that spring saying that he hoped that blacks would never be given commissions as officers. He would also never accept a commission as an officer in an African-American regiment.

The feelings on the 12th Illinois's home front about black regiments show an evolution that indicates a maturation of thought. Editorials from both the *Rock River Democrat* and the *Mount Carroll Mirror* had first conveyed skepticism about the use of black troops, but by the end of spring the tone of the editorials changed to cautious optimism. After the 54th Massachusetts sacrificed more than 40 percent of its men at Fort Wagner on the South Carolina coast and black troops performed commendably in the Vicksburg campaign, the editorials became entirely positive. Still, although whites in the Federal army may have accepted the presence of black troops fighting for the Union, they never accepted them on an equal basis.[9]

Despite all the problems of weather, illness, boredom, and incursions by Rebel cavalry, the Federals felt that change was in the air. As spring progressed and the weather became milder, inspections became more frequent and more severe and discipline was tightened. Something seemed to be astir.

Trooper Winthrop S. G. Allen of the 12th Illinois wrote to his sisters about the change in the cavalry organization and the rigid, almost daily inspections. He realized that the inspections were not just for the purpose of keeping the troops occupied, and "if a soldier lacks in anything, clothing, equipment, he is supplied immediately." Private Abner Frank noted in his diary that in April there seemed to be continual drill, mounted if weather permitted, and dismounted, often with the saber, if the bottom was out of the roads.[10]

William Henry Redman and Company C of the 12th Illinois were detailed to obtain some extra horses for their regiment. They were probably sent to Giesboro, Maryland, a 625-acre site where there was provision for fifteen thousand animals. The men undoubtedly were extremely careful during this mission because horse contractors for the Union army were an unscrupulous lot. They often sold horses that were unfit for service, "doctoring" their injuries and abnormalities so that nothing would go wrong until the replacement mounts were at their far-away destination and it was too late to return them.[11]

There was the hint of a raid in all of the activity, and this time the Union troops would be on the offensive. Almost everyone agreed that Lee would not be the attacker that spring. Winthrop Allen indicated that the men openly talked about this in camp, and letters and memoirs reflect restlessness among the mounted troops.

Food and forage were scarce. Longstreet had taken two divisions to confront Union troops in southeast Virginia, and Lee had only sixty-four thousand men along the south side of the Rappahannock facing twice that many troops on the north bank. Confederate cavalry had dispersed to find grass for the horses, further weakening Southern forces. Hooker, on the other hand, had consolidated his cavalry into a single corps that was well armed and ready for action.[12]

Hooker had a plan, and it was a good one. There would be no more direct frontal assaults like Burnside's debacle in December. Instead, by extending lines northward along the fords of the Rappahannock and Rapidan Rivers, Hooker would flank Lee, or "turn him." Hooker carefully selected the fords he would use. He kept track of the depth and speed of the current and the accessibility of the riverbanks on the south side. That way he would be able to cross both rivers and be in Lee's rear before the Confederate general became aware of his presence. Presumably Lee would not fight against such odds but would retreat into the interior of Virginia via his rail lines. To prevent Lee from getting away, Hooker planned to send the majority of his cavalry corps, under the command of General George Stoneman, to raid far into Lee's rear. Stoneman's forces would tear up railroad tracks and sever telegraph wires, moving in to cut off Lee's retreat and setting the stage for his destruction. Hooker became so infatuated with the plan that he supposedly stated, "My plans are perfect. . . . may God have mercy on Bobby Lee, for I shall have none."[13]

Hooker divided his army into three parts: seventy thousand infantry and supporting artillery were instructed to proceed to the fords several miles beyond Lee's left flank while the second half of Hooker's army feigned an attack at Fredericksburg. If both of those maneuvers were completed on schedule, Lee would be in a trap. The third part of the army, consisting of almost ten thousand horsemen under the command of General George Stoneman, was supposed to cross the fords ahead of the advancing infantry corps and head for the Confederate railroads at Lee's rear. Hooker kept only three regiments of cavalry, which were formed into one brigade to be his eyes and ears once he got across the Rappahannock and Rapidan Rivers.

Keeping only that single brigade of mounted troops did much to hamper Hooker's movements against Lee, particularly when the Federals entered the wilderness. During most of the Battle of Chancellorsville Hooker was unaware of Lee's countermoves; he was militarily blind. Hooker's one brigade of cavalry was never used as a moving screen and scouting force as it should have been; rather, it was broken down and used as a courier force to run messages back and forth between the various corps commanders.

Hooker's plan was supposed to be undertaken in mid-April, but logistics and weather got in the way. For the 9,200 cavalry troopers who were to lead the way, the first fifteen days of April were a time to be endured. Supplying the largest assembly of cavalry on the North American continent posed a problem. During his rebuilding effort Hooker had decided to replace the wagon trains that customarily followed cavalry units with pack mules, which could travel much faster. Following the massive reorganization the men of the 12th Illinois and their new colleagues in the brigade and division had many questions, most of which remained unanswered because of the necessity of military secrecy.

The 12th Illinois had become part of the 3rd Cavalry Division under the command of Brigadier General David M. Gregg, a West Pointer of the class of 1855 and a native Pennsylvanian. Gregg's impressive record on the peninsula the preceding summer had earned him the rank of brigadier, and he was considered one of the rising stars in the Union cavalry. The 12th Illinois was assigned to the second of the two brigades that made up the 3rd Division, and they would be commanded by a young soldier of fortune, Colonel Percy Wyndham, the son of a British army cavalry officer.[14]

As if getting used to their new and dashing commander was not enough of a challenge, the men of the 12th Illinois also had to prepare their equipment for the upcoming expedition. Preparing the ammunition was a particular concern. Each man was to carry forty rounds of carbine ammunition and twenty rounds for his .44-caliber Colt revolver. The ammunition for the Burnside was no problem because it would be carried in a bandolier slung over each trooper's shoulder. Spare rounds for the Colt were a different proposition. The Colt 1860-model army revolver, standard issue for almost all Federal cavalry, was not the easy-loading six-shooter that became standard in the late nineteenth century. It was a cap-and-ball percussion weapon that took a long time to reload because powder and a ball had to be placed individually into each cylinder. After the soldier loaded the cylinders, he had to seal them, usually with animal fat, to prevent the chain fire, or flashover, so common in early firearms. He then had to load a percussion cap individually onto each percussion cone so the weapon would fire. Quickly reloading the Colt during the pressure of a firefight could be a life-or-death matter.

The best thing to do was to procure a Remington. The Remington loaded the same way as the Colt, but it had a key advantage. A soldier could, after lowering the rammer, detach the entire cylinder and replace it with a freshly loaded one in a matter of seconds and be ready to fire another six rounds. Officially only one .44-caliber Remington revolver was ever issued to a member of the 12th Illinois. Many of the officers and enlisted men probably purchased their own.[15]

There was also the problem of personal gear. In late spring the short, woolen shell jacket should have been enough, but freak snowstorms were not unknown, so a trooper had to decide whether to carry his greatcoat. Boots and socks were particularly important, especially if a man's horse gave out or if he was captured. A captured soldier would almost surely be relieved of his boots at gunpoint if they were new or even looked new. He would be left with his army-issue socks of double-footed wool, which were warm and had enough padding so that they were at least a good substitute for walking barefoot.

Each soldier also carried a saber and saber belt, a canteen, a haversack, spurs, gauntlets, a rubber poncho, a forage cap, a carbine sling, and possibly a pair of field glasses. He also needed horse tack, a McClellan saddle, a picket rope, saddle bags, a saddle blanket, a farrier's pocket knife for potential problems with a horse's feet, a metal curry comb for horse grooming, a girth belt, a regulation grub kit, and three days' forage and grain. The forage and grain alone weighed twenty-four pounds.[16]

Soon the men were equipped, brigaded, armed, and ready. William Redman, anticipating what was about to happen, wrote home asking his mother to send him various personal articles, especially a good pair of boots with the instep built up. Redman seemed ready to accept whatever the army had for him in the way of duty. He saw Lincoln when the president came to review the troops, and he said he was a fine-looking man who inspired utter confidence. This was a far cry from the impression Lincoln made on a member of the 8th Illinois Cavalry, who wrote of Lincoln in the fall of 1862, "Poor man, . . . he is as homely as a mud fence."[17]

Everything was ready to go, but the weather did not cooperate. Melting ice and snow coupled with the spring rains saturated the soil, leaving it soft, and the rivers were rising very quickly, the currents increasing to dangerous levels. The 12th Illinois Cavalry camped at Belle Plain on the Potomac River with the rest of the 2nd Brigade of the 3rd Cavalry Division. The aggregate strength of that division on the day they broke camp was 2,905 officers and men. From Belle Plain, the entire brigade moved to Morrisville in preparation for crossing the Rappahannock at Kelly's Ford. Detachments of scouts found that a substantial Confederate force was guarding the bridge over Kelly's Ford. Rebels were also dug in at another crossing, Beverly Ford, two miles above the railroad bridge. Stoneman decided that he would force the crossing on the morning of 15 April.

The division camped for the night at Bealton, which lies astride the Orange and Alexandria Railroad tracks north of the Rappahannock River, about three miles north of Rappahannock Station. At this point the 12th Illinois, in the lead of the 2nd Brigade, was occupying ground fifteen miles from the extreme right of the Union lines at Fredericksburg. During the night a heavy, pelting rain began to fall, "and at the hour designated for the crossing of my division at Beverly Ford . . . it was evident that a crossing was impossible for the artillery and pack trains." Then the rain turned to hail, hailstones as large as hen's eggs made the horses "kick and rear like fun." Even when the rain subsided, the currents remained too swift and the rivers remained too deep to cross. "The first Maryland cav crossed," Abner Frank wrote in his diary, "and lost three men."[18]

While the cavalry waited for the rivers to return to normal, Lincoln began to urge Hooker to take the offensive. Hooker deferred to Stoneman's judgment regarding the rivers, and the various Union cavalry commanders fumed privately and publicly about weather and other situations they could not overcome. On 28 April, Stoneman, who had steadily outflanked the Confederates, put his forces in motion. Because his cavalry corps was so large, he chose to cross the Rappahannock at both Beverly and Kelly's Ford. Gregg's division, of which the 12th Illinois was a part, was put on the march at five o'clock in the evening and reached Kelly's Ford at eight o'clock the next morning. The entire 5th Corps used the bridge across the slough near the ford, preventing Gregg from crossing until about noon. At sunset the division marched in the rear of Buford's reserve brigade and halted at the crossroads beyond Mountain Run. It was cloudy and rainy all that day, and the column had marched about twenty miles. All of the rations and forage were transferred to the serviceable horses during the night.[19]

The pack trains, all wheeled vehicles except those of the artillery, all wounded and sick men, and unserviceable horses were taken off the rolls and sent to Germanna Mills. The men were allowed to get a little rest by lying down in front of their animals, reins in hand, in the middle of the road. The division crossed the Rapidan at Raccoon Ford at about six o'clock on the evening of 30 April and encamped for the night. No fires could be started because they would be in full view of the Confederate signal station on Clark Mountain. The column was drawn up in close order. The night was cold. The mud froze so solid that it was able to support the horses, and the wet, exhausted men were miserable. Still, they slept.[20]

The men did not rest for long. At one o'clock in the morning, the order came to stand to horse and prepare to march. The fog, however, continued to be a problem. It covered the valley of the Rapidan, severely restricting vision. The column got under way at around four o'clock in the morning for what would be a fifty-mile march. Right before the column departed, Stoneman had spread his maps, called in his division and brigade commanders, and briefed them on "what we were to do and where we were each to go." Hooker detailed Stoneman and his horse soldiers to "ricochet with deadly effect through Confederate rear areas, freeing Federal prisoners, tearing up the railroads, breaking an aqueduct on the James River and forcing a frightened Lee to fall back from Fredericksburg." To accomplish all he had been assigned, Stoneman decided to divide his command. Averell's division was supposed to be detached from the main body and to proceed to the Orange and Alexandria Railroad depot at Brandy Station by nightfall. There it would communicate with Gregg's column—which Stoneman would accompany—via nearby Stevensburg.[21]

As Stuart had anticipated, one Confederate unit awaited Stoneman's force, the brigade commanded by Brigadier General Rooney Lee, son of commanding general of the Army of Northern Virginia Robert E. Lee. Rooney Lee had but two regiments under his direct command, the 9th Virginia and the 13th Virginia. These two regiments had about fifteen hundred troopers a couple of pieces of artillery. They opposed a Federal force of almost seven thousand troops and twenty-seven pieces of artillery. Rooney Lee's mission was, first, to contain Stoneman, limiting his damage to Confederate government property, and, second, to follow and harass the large Federal column wherever it went. The Confederate cavalry also was to confine the Federals to the main roads and to make sure they did not penetrate the rural areas near the horse farms. Stoneman was pleased that his column would be able to replenish lost or wounded horses by getting replacements from the many horse farms that he found along his route. Robert E. Lee, needing every available horse, sent orders to his cavalry commanders that Stoneman must be restricted in his operations "or we shall be ruined." Rooney Lee positioned his forces near Louisa Court House and Trevilians Station and back up the Orange and Alexandria Railroad to the town of Gordonsville. There he could protect not only the southwest run of the Orange and Alexandria, but also the spur of the Virginia Central Railroad that led east-southeast toward Richmond.[22]

Stoneman's main force, which included the 12th Illinois, left Orange Spring at six o'clock in the evening on 1 May and arrived "within three-fourths of a mile of the Court House at three A.M. on the following day." Once the men were at the Louisa Court House, the work of destruction began. Stoneman took heed from Stuart at Dumphries five months before, when the Confederates had intercepted Union messages, and stationed a Union army telegrapher on the line to intercept Confederate dispatches to Robert E. Lee's army at Chancellorsville. Then Stoneman's raiders destroyed the telegraph. They demolished the water tank, and by midday they had laid waste to eighteen miles of railroad.[23]

In the afternoon Stoneman ordered his command south, deep into Confederate territory. They crossed the South Anna River and reached Thompson's Crossroads late in the night on 2 May. There the column captured a supply train with sixty-four wagons. The captured wagon train was a blessing to the tired and anxious cavalrymen of Stoneman's command. It was packed with surveying equipment and a section of recent topographical maps of central Virginia. The maps Stoneman had brought with him were based on topographical surveys done before the outbreak of the Civil War. Now that he had accurate maps to guide him, he could move with more assurance.

Stoneman was one of the first Federal commanders to appreciate a most important intelligence-gathering "apparatus" of the conflict, the slave. As early as 1 May, when Gregg's division was preparing to pounce on Louisa Court House, a major of Gregg's staff rode up with a male slave on the horse behind him. The slave knew the road network south of Louisa and could enlist the help of several other knowledgeable people when the command separated. He could then either seek safety by his own navigation or return to the column.[24]

Stoneman decided to divide his forces into four parts. He was undoubtedly thinking of Hooker's original orders to him that he cause the maximum damage possible, and he was unnerved by the sound of artillery some thirty-five miles distant. Historian John Bigelow writes:

Colonel Percy Wyndham with the 1st New Jersey and 1st Maryland, about 400 men, were to strike the junction of the James and Rivanna Rivers at Columbia, destroy, if possible, the canal aqueduct over the Rivanna, and proceed along the canal in the direction doing all damage possible. Colonel Judson Kilpatrick, with the 2nd New York, took about 400 men to push the Chickahominy railroad bridges over. Lieutenant Colonel Hasbrouck Davis took about 300 men from the 12th Illinois to penetrate to the Richmond and Potomac Railroad, and if possible to the Virginia Central, and destroy communications. Brigadier General David Gregg, with the 1st Maine and 10th New York and two pieces of artillery, was to destroy the bridges including, if possible, the two railroad bridges on the South Anna. The bulk of Buford's Reserve Brigade and the 6th Pennsylvania Lancers remained in camp as a reserve and provost guard.

The raiders were on their way by three o'clock in the morning on 3 May. They had orders to strike their targets simultaneously twelve hours later so that the Confederates would not have time to communicate with each other and prepare for the raiders. To ensure their own security, Colonel Wyndham and General Gregg were to return to the main column, while Colonel Hasbrouck Davis, at the head of the 12th Illinois, and Colonel Kilpatrick were to push on down the Virginia Peninsula to either Yorktown or Gloucester Point.[25]

The 12th Illinois was ordered to penetrate the Virginia Central Railroad and destroy communications, then head for Williamsburg, which Davis thought was in possession of the Federals. Davis reported that his men passed down the bank of the South Anna through a region never before occupied by Union forces. They burned one bridge, which Davis did not name, pushed aside a poorly mounted guerrilla force, then struck Ashland Station at about one o'clock in the afternoon.

Lieutenant Frederick Mitchell and about a dozen men were the first to charge into town, and they caught the civilian population by surprise. "Words cannot describe the astonishment of the inhabitants at our appearance," wrote Davis. Ashland was the sleepy little college town of Randolph Macon College for Men, most of whose students were in Confederate service and away from campus that spring, so it had mostly a female population. Sergeant Redman wrote that the women of Ashland were like "baboons and monkeys peeping out of the windows and over the fences." The soldiers quickly went to work cutting the telegraph wires and "tore up half a dozen rails, and, piling a quantity of boards in some trestle-work south of town, made an immense fire which soon consumed the entire structure."[26]

While the 12th Illinois was destroying all property within sight that belonged to the Confederate government, a train came into the station from

Fredericksburg with a cargo of more than five hundred wounded Confederate soldiers from the Battle of Chancellorsville. Davis released the prisoners after he heard their version of what was going on to the north. He left the railroad cars for the benefit of the wounded, disabling only the engine and tender with the aid of a mechanic from the ranks. The men of the 12th Illinois then destroyed twenty wagons, took the horses and mules that they could use, and left Ashland by six that evening. A few miles from the town the Federal column received word that another convoy of eighteen wagons was encamped in the nearby woods. Captain Charles Roden, with Companies B and C, was sent to destroy the train and take its animals. That capture made a total of thirty-eight wagons destroyed by the 12th Illinois alone during that part of the raid.[27]

The men of the 12th Illinois then struck the Virginia Central Railroad at Hanover Station at eight o'clock in the evening, but found no one but rear eschelon support troops. They "captured and paroled about 30 men" and destroyed "the trestle-work, which reached about ten rods to the south of the depot. The work was effectively done by the same process as at Ashland, and by its blaze we could clearly discern the Confederate guards passively standing at the other end." They also set fire to a culvert, cut the telegraph wires, and destroyed all buildings and train cars belonging to the Confederate government. They burned about one hundred wagons and destroyed one thousand sacks of flour and corn and a large quantity of clothing and horse tack. They left Hanover Station by the light of the burning buildings and proceeded southeast to Hanover Court House. A detachment of the 12th Illinois under Captain James Fisher had already taken possession of this little hamlet, which had been a courthouse since colonial times, and when the main body arrived, they set fire to almost the entire village.[28]

The scene at Hanover Court House at this stage of the raid is not hard to imagine. Colonel Davis had about three hundred men, almost all of whom had been without sleep for days and were riding exhausted horses. There was only one well from which to water as many horses and men as possible in a very short time. Word had spread of the force's presence in central Virginia, and measures were almost certainly being taken to capture or eliminate the entire command. Davis had to decide at this point among several courses of action. Should he move out of Hanover Court House and, if so, which way should he go? How far should he push his tired men and their horses? It was nearing midnight, and from what Davis was able to learn from Confederate prisoners there had been no brilliant Yankee victory near Fredericksburg–rather the opposite, Fredericksburg (Chancellorsville) had been a Yankee catastrophe. Therefore, there would be no assistance from the main Union force. Kilpatrick's was the nearest friendly column, and his men were fewer in number and just as exhausted. General Gregg, originally Davis's superior officer, was leading his own column, the only formation remaining that had any artillery, but Davis did not know Gregg's location. Furthermore, Gregg had standing orders to return to Stoneman, who was sitting out the night of "the exploding shell" at Thompson's Crossroads far to the west. The 12th Illinois was on its own.[29]

Davis knew he could not stay at Hanover Station. It was on a direct train line, and if trains can move wounded men, they can move combat troops. It was doubtful that the men of the 12th Illinois had cut the telegraph lines before the Richmond garrison was notified, so an intercepting force was probably on the way. Davis had to proceed southeast as quickly as possible. The new maps procured from the Confederate surveying team captured at Thompson Crossroads, as well as reports from slaves, would surely have been helpful in determining which road to take. But Davis took his cue from history.

What little American history was taught in public schools in the 1840s, when Davis and his staff would have been students, tended to concentrate on American wars, particularly the American Revolution. One of the most dramatic maneuvers of that struggle was Washington's trek from the Northeast to Virginia in the early fall of 1781. Accompanied by Count Rochambeau and the French contingent, the American commander had marched his troops to entrap Lord Cornwallis in Yorktown in October 1781. The road used to move the troops down the Virginia Peninsula (now Hanover County Route 301) would have been well known to every school boy who had read about those stirring times. The road had been improved since then, and Jeb Stuart had used it during the famous Chickahominy Raid in the summer of 1862. At the time of that raid two companies of Illinois cavalry known as McClellan's Dragoons, now part of the 12th Illinois, had been the personal bodyguard of George McClellan, who was then the commander of the Army of the Potomac. They undoubtedly had a good knowledge of the area and would have counseled the use of that road. It was the most direct route to Yorktown, the nearest friendly base in Virginia.

Davis set out for Yorktown, but he could not push the column all the way there that night; the effort would have cost too much in men and animals. At about two o'clock in the morning on 4 May, he ordered the men of the 12th Illinois into camp on the road, less than seven miles from the Confederate capital of Richmond. It was a beautiful night to get some rest—the first for the 12th in a couple of days. Davis's report states that the regiment remained in bivouac until eight in the morning, but that probably is an error, for remaining inactive deep in enemy territory for several hours after the sun is up is would have invited trouble. The diary of Abner Frank indicates they left

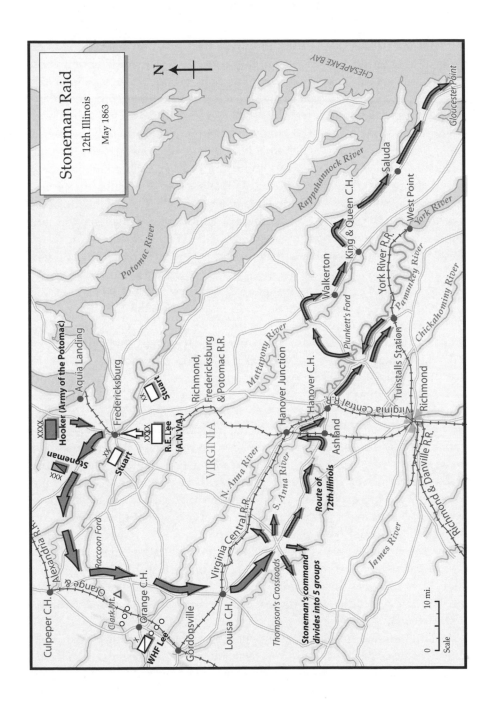

Stoneman Raid
12th Illinois
May 1863

Hooker (Army of the Potomac)

Stuart

R.E. Lee (A.N.VA.)

Stuart

Stoneman

Aquia Landing

Fredericksburg

Richmond, Fredericksburg & Potomac R.R.

VIRGINIA

Potomac River

Rappahannock River

CHESAPEAKE BAY

Gloucester Point

Saluda

West Point

York River

King & Queen C.H.

Walkerton

Plunkett's Ford

York River R.R.

Pamunkey River

Chickahominy River

Tunstalls Station

Richmond

Hanover Junction

Hanover C.H.

Ashland

Virginia Central R.R.

Mattapony River

N. Anna River

S. Anna River

Route of 12th Illinois

Thompson's Crossroads

Stoneman's command divides into 5 groups

Louisa C.H.

Gordonsville

WHF Lee

Orange C.H.

Clark Mt.

Culpeper C.H.

Orange & Alexandria R.R.

Raccoon Ford

Virginia Central R.R.

James River

Richmond & Danville R.R.

N

10 mi.

0   Scale

much earlier, at daylight. The 12th moved on without incident until about eight o'clock in the evening, when they came to a little town on the Richmond and York River Railroad called Tunstalls Station. There "a train of cars filled with infantry and a battery of three guns, was run out to oppose us."[30]

Davis decided to attack with his leading element made up of Companies D and F. He would attempt to break through the crossing before the Rebels could position the battery. He hoped his Confederate counterpart would not have time to place his infantry behind the railroad embankment, which would be an ideal defensive position. The charge was "gallantly made," Davis noted, but it was not made quickly enough. The Confederate infantry was able to fill the railroad embankment and fire a quick volley into the 12th Illinois. Davis reported that two men were killed and "several wounded" in the desperate charge at Tunstall Station. Among the wounded was Lieutenant Frederick Marsh, "who was one of the foremost in the charge." Sergeant William A. Arter of Company D was captured, but he was paroled the next day at City Point, Virginia, and remained with the 12th Illinois until he was mustered out in New Orleans on 28 February 1866. Wallace Ball, a private with Company D, was slightly wounded, captured, and admitted to a military hospital in Richmond. He was released on 15 May 1863 and sent to City Point, Virginia, where he was exchanged.[31]

The 12th Illinois's losses could have been much worse. At Tunstall Station the ground was low and flat from the scrub timber east via the Washington-Rochambeau road to the railroad. The trees were about a quarter of a mile west of the tracks. Davis must have set his two lead companies to a maneuvering gallop so that they could swing into line about a hundred yards after emerging from the scrub timber. That way, each trooper would have been able to make maximum use of his carbine as soon as he closed with the Confederates in the embankment at a range of fifty or so yards. The line also would have made the troopers less of a target for the hurriedly aiming Rebel infantry, especially in the half-light of dusk. A marching column would have offered a denser target. At first the Confederate artillery probably was not loaded, and once it was loaded, the ammunition was probably solid or case shot, which was not as effective as canister against charging cavalrymen.

In all likelihood the Rebels were able to fire only one volley, and rifled muskets sighted for five hundred yards would have fired well over the heads of the horsemen. So the Confederates must have fired only one shot before Davis's troopers were on top of them. At that point the cavalry troops must have been among the Rebel infantry, and shooting must have been at extremely close quarters. The quick-loading Burnside carbines and Colt revolvers would have prevailed over the bulky, awkward muzzle-loading

Confederate weapons. The quick cavalry charge, then, kept Union losses to a minimum.[32]

The Federals were greatly outnumbered. Davis broke off the action quickly. They had been ordered to avoid contact, destroy as much property as possible, and get back to the safety of their own lines. Moreover, Davis had discovered that there were rifle pits to the left of the road, which meant that his flank would soon be turned. He retreated back up the road to the nearest fork, set his men to a gallop, and proceeded to Plunket's Ferry on the Pamunkey River.[33]

The men of the 12th Illinois crossed the Pamunkey River late at night on 4 May. About sixteen men at a time crossed on the available boats, apparently without incident. The regiment then proceeded to the Mattapony River near the little village of Walkerton. At this point Major Samuel Bronson was detached from the column. He joined what appears to have been selected troops who stayed at Walkerton to set up courier stations along the way from there to Gloucester Point.

The column was at last near the Union lines at Gloucester Point, and Davis wanted to allow no opportunity for Rebel cavalry or infantry to get between the 12th Illinois and friendly lines. It had been a long ride, and the troops were near exhaustion. The Southerners who saw them could tell that they had been in the saddle for about five days. But still there was the very real possibility that the column would be captured or attacked, for the alarm in the Confederate capital had sounded all day on 4 May. Special troop trains had been readied on the Richmond tracks, and almost every able-bodied man in Richmond had been rounded up, organized into battalions, and sent to the guns on the city perimeter.[34]

On the morning of 5 May the 12th Illinois crossed the Mattapony River near Walkerton. As soon as the regiment was over the river, all of the ferry boats, which belonged to a local noncombatant, were burned, and all of the horses that were available at local plantations, most of them of fine-blooded stock, were taken. The troopers left their government-issue mounts in exchange and proceeded southeast. Two men in the advance column were captured, an officer and a private. First Lieutenant Frederick Mitchell soon escaped; the private did not.

From Walkerton the men of the 12th Illinois went to Stevensville, home of a local academy, then turned south toward Farmers Rest and King and Queen Court House, when the alarm was sounded from the rear of the column warning that they were being attacked. The order was given: "Fours [columns of fours] right about," and the 12th Illinois prepared to receive the Confederate attack. But the sighted troops were not Rebels. They were Kilpatrick's 2nd New York Cavalry. Once positive identification was made, the 2nd New York fell in to the rear in columns of fours, and the march continued.[35]

The 12th Illinois moved on without incident through a rainy night on 6 May and captured another supply train near the town of Saluda that was made up of eighteen wagons "loaded with corn and provisions." The men arrived at the Federal lines near Gloucester Point late in the afternoon of 7 May. They were very wet and very tired. For the next three days they ate, slept, tended to the horses, and sent out patrols for stragglers. Finally, on 12 May they received four months back pay, and for a very short time they thoroughly enjoyed themselves.[36]

The 12th Illinois had brought with them to Gloucester Point some one hundred mules and seventy-five horses. They had destroyed a number of bridges and railroad yards, as well as property that their commander valued at more than one million dollars. During the raid the 12th Illinois lost two commissioned officers and thirty-three enlisted men. In his 8 May report from Yorktown to Major General Henry Halleck, division commander of the V Corps, Brigadier General Rufus King hailed the Stoneman Raid as one of the finest feats of the war. King also lauded the performance of particular units. The 12th Illinois and the 2nd New York Dragoons under the command of Judson Kilpatrick received high praise.

As a cavalry raid, however, the Stoneman operation does not go on historical record as a particularly remarkable exploit. To some of the participants the raid seemed to be poorly planned and executed. Major General Hooker saw nothing worthwhile in the expedition. In search of a scapegoat for the loss at Chancellorsville, he soon replaced cavalry commander George Stoneman with Alfred Pleasonton, and he said that he "would give fifty dollars to see a dead cavalryman." Years later, at the 12th Illinois Cavalry reunion in October 1918, Homer Calkins of Company I remarked that when Hooker was replaced, the cavalrymen of the 12th Illinois "saw a defunct Hooker without paying fifty cents."[37]

Sergeant Redman wrote to his mother that from his perspective the expedition had been one of the great raids of the war. He claimed that he personally had put millions of dollars worth of property to flame, but that the rain had made things very difficult for both the men and the animals. Thirty-five men had been lost, and their horses had become worn out and unfit for service.

The men hoped that they would be able to rest at Gloucester Point for at least a short time. The raid had given the troopers a tremendous amount of self-confidence. The 12th Illinois had camped within seven miles of the Confederate capital during a major campaign without being caught. The other units attached to Stoneman had made it back to the Union lines at various times. Some, like Gregg's detachment, which had been reinforced by some of Colonel Wesley Merritt's troopers, had attempted to strike the important South Anna bridge near Hanover Court House and had found themselves nearly cut off by large numbers of regular Confederate troops and home guards that had been called out to pursue Hasbrouck Davis's men. Kilpatrick's troopers had burned bridges over the Chickahominy, had destroyed three large trains of provisions in the rear of Lee's army, and had burned all of the stores at Aylett's Station and a large commissary depot above the Rappahannock River.[38]

The two railroads that Kilpatrick and Davis had torn up were repaired within a week, but still the injury to the Confederate war effort was severe. In the Civil War the railroads were critical, and because the Confederacy had much less iron and steel with which to build rails than the North did, the Rebels were far more injured by their destruction. In the week before Stoneman started on his raid, the presidents of the major rail lines that traversed the Confederacy had met in Richmond. They said that to maintain the tracks for military purposes would require the manufacture of 49,500 tons of rails per annum. The rail works in Atlanta and the Tredegar Ironworks in Richmond, the largest foundry in the South, could not produce more than 20,000 tons a year. Resources and production were stretched thin, and Kilpatrick and Davis's exploits had exacerbated the crisis.[39]

After the Stoneman Raid "a portion of the Twelfth remained at Gloucester Point, while one Battalion was sent to General John A. Dix, commanding at Fortress Monroe, and the remainder [four companies, or about 240 men] reported at Alexandria." Before the end of May the men at Alexandria would report to Brigadier General John Buford, one of Stoneman's former subordinates, to form the 1st Cavalry Division, which would play a prominent role in the Gettysburg campaign. A detachment of about one hundred men remained at Gloucester Point as part of the overall command of Fort Monroe at Hampton Roads. The detachment that remained at Fort Monroe was assigned to crack down on smuggling along the southeast coast of Virginia, which required "frequent excursions into the interior counties."[40]

The part of the 12th Illinois that were under the command of Fort Monroe were also involved in various authorized missions to procure badly needed horses for the Federal army. They became so successful that the regiment adopted the sobriquet "The Horse Thieves." On 13 May 1863 they received orders to proceed into the interior of the Tidewater around Yorktown-Gloucester Point, where they would be under the command of Colonel Judson Kilpatrick of the 2nd New York. The operations were clandestine. Special Order Number 130 in the official records indicates only that two short regiments were assigned to the Yorktown area under "special instructions." Abner Frank stated that on 20 May "one hundred men of our regiment started out on an expedition with a detachment of the 2nd New York and three pieces of artillery and infantry."[41]

The 12th Illinois and 2nd New York marched to Matthews Court House and encamped on a plantation owned by a man named Miller. The next morning the two cavalry regiments started out to find horses, leaving the infantry at a place called Brichey Store to keep Confederate forces in the vicinity from flanking the Union detachment. The men brought back more than two hundred good horses. As Redman informed his family, they also helped themselves to two hundred head of cattle and a great many sheep.[42]

The 12th Illinois saw few Confederates this time. There were not many to see; most were with Lee's army at Chancellorsville. The men captured most of the few Rebel bushwhackers they encountered. In response to being harassed by these bandits, the 12th Illinois burned several gristmills full of wheat and flour. The men continued northeast for a few miles, raiding from Gloucester Point to Gloucester Court House, then they turned northwest toward Urbana. As they left Gloucester County, they crossed the Rappahannock and proceeded east to Heathsville in Northumberland County. Once at Heathsville they were able to procure the horses they needed. Like many Federal raiding parties, the men of the 12th Illinois were not particularly judicious in their acquisition of animals. Samuel B. Rice of the 9th Virginia Cavalry, which opposed the 12th Illinois, indicated that the Virginia civilian population suffered such deprivation following the Yankee raids that almost all of the servants ran off. The Union troops helped themselves to whatever they wanted—horses, carriages, bacon, flour, wheat, money, valuables, anything that the raiders could carry with them. They went into smokehouses and took "hams, flour and so forth which we find in abundance." If Rice's letters to his wife are representative of the conditions in tidewater Virginia, particularly regarding the lack of horses, then the damage wrought by the 12th Illinois and the 2nd New York was formidable.[43]

In a letter to his family from Potomac Creek, Virginia, William Redman stated that it was usually standard operating procedure to take all the horses that were fit for cavalry service. He explained that slaves would ride the horses away from their plantations. If the horses were broken to harness as well as to the saddle, they were hitched to carriages, buggies, or carts that African-American women would drive. If there were more women and children than were needed to drive the carts or ride horses, they would be loaded into the various vehicles and taken to the Union lines.[44]

In spite of all of this pillaging, sometimes the Illinois troopers were treated with kindness. Near Urbana toward the end of May, as one battalion of the 12th Illinois was en route back to the Army of the Potomac, Redman and his companions became acquainted with two young women who "lived in a large mansion made of imported brick which had been built a hundred and fifty years before. Oh, you ought to have seen their garden and door yard." The two women, Mattie Christian and Henrietta Robinson, seem to have been members of the Tidewater aristocracy. Miss Robinson's brother, John A. Robinson, formerly a captain in the 25th Virginia Infantry, had just been elected to the Virginia legislature. Redman struck up an immediate friendship with Christian and Robinson while his regiment was taking their horses, mules, and slaves, and he was concerned that he would appear to be captivated by the women.[45]

Because the raids were occurring after emancipation and Virginia was still in rebellion, the only property for which owners were compensated in Federal money was horses and mules. During the Civil War the three major modes of transport—rail, boat, and horse—were invaluable, and the loss of any of them could jeopardize the existence of a plantation or a community. In its exploits in the Virginia countryside the 12th Illinois had made it presence felt.[46]

Forcing the Rebels to Deploy

The division of the 12th Illinois regiment into two battalions began after the Stoneman Raid in May of 1863 and did not end until after the Gettysburg campaign. The division was probably based on which troopers had horses that were serviceable enough to get them to Alexandria, Virginia, or to Loudoun County, where the Army of the Potomac sat, ready to make its next move. About 250 men of the 12th Illinois remained at Gloucester Point to continue raiding in the Tidewater area. These men could replace their mounts by requisitioning from the planters in the area. The rest of the men, about four companies comprising a little more than two hundred soldiers, were sent northwest back to the Army of the Potomac. The commanding officer, Lieutenant Colonel Hasbrouck Davis, stayed in the Tidewater until after the Battle of Gettysburg. The four companies sent north were under the command of the senior captain, George W. Shears. They reported to Colonel George H. Chapman of the 3rd Indiana, who commanded those four companies as well as his own 3rd Indiana during the Gettysburg campaign.[1]

Hasbrouck Davis became involved in another small raid into the Tidewater in late June. Along with a detachment of Pennsylvania cavalry and some Massachusetts horsemen, the 12th Illinois was able to penetrate Confederate lines near the Pamunkey River and approach a small plantation called the White House. It was the home of Brigadier General Rooney Lee, who was recuperating from a thigh wound received in the action at Brandy Station in June 1863. He was unaware that enemy units were approaching even though a twelve-man Confederate guard was stationed around his home. Davis and his men captured Rooney Lee and at least eight other Confederate army and naval officers, ninety-four unsuspecting enlisted men, thirty-five wagons, five hundred mules, two hundred horses, small wagons, carts, harnesses, and a large quantity of grain and hay, burning all but the men and livestock.

Zora B. Custer of Company I had been searching the manor house and "stumbled onto a gentleman who he thought too fine haired for a soldier. He investigated and, sure enough, he proved to be General Lee, home with his wife's people on sick furlough. But he [Rooney Lee] proved to be able to take up the line of march to Fortress Munroe." When he could no longer keep up, Lee was carried the remainder of the journey on a blanket between two cavalry troopers. While on the way to capture Rooney Lee, Colonel Samuel P. Spears of the 11th Pennsylvania Cavalry, who commanded the expedition, captured a Confederate agent and "took from him about $15,000, Confederate bonds. He was making payment for purchased stores."

Following this remarkably successful mission, Spears said his "warmest thanks are due to Lieutenant Colonel Davis, his officers and men, for his hearty cooperation." Rooney Lee's capture must have been sweet success to Davis and the men of the 12th Illinois. It had been the men under Lee's command who had pushed and harassed them near Gordonsville only a month before during the opening days of the Stoneman Raid.[2]

While recovering from his wound at Fort Monroe, Rooney Lee was told that his wife was dying and that she wanted to see him before she succumbed. The Lincoln administration refused to release him and publicized the capture of the son of the commander of the Army of Northern Virginia. When the Confederate government tried to exchange several Union brigadiers for Rooney, the offer was turned down. Custis Lee, Robert E. Lee's oldest son and an aide to the Confederate president, even offered to take Rooney's place. But the Yankees held their prisoner while his wife died calling for him. When Rooney Lee was finally released, he returned to Richmond a hero, and he stated without hesitation that General Benjamin Butler of New Orleans had treated him with every courtesy and consideration.[3]

While Hasbrouck Davis and half of the 12th Illinois were making plans to capture as many men and goods as they could on the Pamunkey River in Southeast Virginia, four companies of the 12th, including William Redman's and Abner Frank's, were sent to the Washington, D.C., area to once again become part of the cavalry corps of the Army of the Potomac, which was under the command of Major General Alfred Pleasonton. Pleasonton assigned the men of the 12th Illinois to the newly formed 1st Cavalry Division commanded by Brigadier General John Buford. Buford was a Southerner, born in Woodford County, Kentucky, in 1826. He emigrated to Illinois with his family, and followed his older half-brother, Napoleon Bonaparte Buford, and his cousin, Abraham Buford, to West Point. He graduated from West Point with the class of 1848. John Buford served on the frontier and in the Utah expedition, then brought his regiment to Washington, D.C., at the outbreak of the Civil War. He held the position of inspector general of the army until it was finally recognized that an officer of his talents should not be confined to a desk; then he was promoted to brigadier general and given a field assignment.[4]

Buford soon understood that in this war of the rifled musket, the repeating rifle, and rifled artillery, cavalry should be used as mounted infantry. The cavalrymen should use their horses to get to a particular place on the battlefield and then to dismount them and fight as foot soldiers. He was unaware that he shared this perception with a little-known Indiana colonel named John T. Wilder and a famous Confederate cavalry general of the Tennessee theater named Nathan Bedford Forrest, under whom Buford's Confederate cousin Abraham would command a division of mounted troops. Buford also saw the value of using cavalry as a scouting element. According to one historian, "After skirmishing . . . at Thoroughfare Gap, Buford sent [Union General John] Pope information about Confederate strength and positions that might have prevented the disaster of Second Bull Run had it been acted on properly."[5]

In early June 1863, the 1st Cavalry Division had been part of a large cavalry force dispatched by General Hooker to learn of Robert E. Lee's whereabouts and intentions. Lee had started to move his army toward the Shenandoah Valley. Historian Shelby Foote notes: "Hooker's balloons were up and apparently spotted the movement, for the bluecoats promptly effected a crossing below the town [Fredericksburg]. It was rumored that Lee had expressed a willingness to 'swap queens,' Richmond for Washington, in case Hooker plunged south while his back was turned." These aggressive movements exploded in the First Battle of Brandy Station on 9 June 1863, a battle the 12th Illinois Cavalry did not participate in. On that date they were just leaving Alexandria, Virginia, where they had been refitted after the Stoneman Raid.[6]

It was vitally important for the Federals to track Robert E. Lee's army. They sent up hot-air balloons, but their visibility was limited in the Blue Ridge Mountains, which were often covered with haze. A more practical way to get information was to send the Union cavalry into the gaps, the critical mountain passes in the Blue Ridge and Bull Run Mountains. The Bull Run Mountains are east of and parallel to the Blue Ridge Mountains, and the two ranges are separated by a fifteen-mile-wide valley of rolling hills.

The passes through the Blue Ridge Mountains are Manassas, Ashby's, Snickers, and Thoroughfare Gaps. Once these gaps were secure from Confederate forces, the Federals could travel through them to establish stations on the highest peaks from which they could watch Confederate-army movements on the floor of the Shenandoah Valley. Securing the gaps was dangerous work because the people of that part of the country were sympathetic to the Confederate cause. The passes were guarded by Stuart and his subordinate John Singleton Mosby, a frail major who commanded a guerrilla band called the 43rd Virginia Battalion of Partisan Rangers. It was the job of John Buford and the 12th Illinois Cavalry to penetrate their screen.[7]

The 1st Brigade was commanded by Colonel William Gamble and comprised four companies of the 12th Illinois, A, E, F, and H; the 8th Illinois, which had been handled roughly the previous week at Brandy Station; six companies of the 3rd Indiana; and the 8th New York. The 2nd Brigade was composed of the 6th New York, the 9th New York, the 17th Pennsylvania, and two companies of the 3rd West Virginia. In addition, there was a reserve brigade made up almost entirely of regular troops that was commanded by Brigadier General Wesley Merritt. It included four United States regiments and one volunteer regiment, the 6th Pennsylvania.[8]

Major General Alfred Pleasonton was in command of the Army of the Potomac's cavalry corps, which was in reasonably good condition. Most regiments had been reduced to three or four hundred officers and men, but the cavalry corps had begun to replace the horses and weapons lost at Brandy Station. The draft was one possible way of replacing casualties, but a bounty was more likely to draw the needed enlisted men. A week before the Brandy Station action, an advertisement had appeared in the *Mount Carroll Weekly Mirror* asking for cavalry volunteers and authorizing the local mustering officer to pay the bounty prescribed by law for all qualified men who enlisted.[9]

Abner Frank noted that when Pleasonton reviewed the 12th Illinois, he seemed to be satisfied with what he observed. Redman thought a move was in the air but wrote that the division would not leave until the horses were shod, which would take two to three days for a three-thousand-man division. The 12th Illinois had lost many men, and the promotion of three very junior officers, Elon Farnsworth, George A. Custer, and Wesley Merritt, to the rank of brigadier general had created a morale problem in the officer ranks. The regiments that were down to fewer than four hundred men had lost a number of key noncommissioned officers, the sergeants who command small squads of men in ambushes and fire fights. In the 12th Illinois and other regiments, many sergeants had been wounded at Brandy Station or had been left in the Tidewater area assigned to the battalion that was under the command of Fort Monroe. Other sergeants had been commissioned and were now in the officer ranks even though they had no experience commanding a force of over a dozen men. The promoted sergeants had often left their squads to former privates, now corporals and sergeants who had no experience at all at command. The 1st Brigade of the 1st Cavalry Division, to which a portion of the 12th Illinois was assigned as replacement troops, reported 96 wounded at Brandy Station with an aggregate remaining of 368 enlisted men and 71 officers.[10]

The objective for the Union cavalry that June was to penetrate the Confederate cavalry screen that protected the advance of Lee's army into Pennsylvania. On 17 June Stuart placed three of his best brigades at the little town of Aldie on the Little River Turnpike (now U.S. 50). Using Aldie as a base, Stuart could move his cavalry to cover any of the three critical passes—Thoroughfare Gap, Ashby's Gap, and Snickers Gap—that led through the Blue Ridge Mountains into the Shenandoah Valley and to the flank of Lee's army, which was advancing into Pennsylvania. Hooker, sensing Lee's advance, ordered General Pleasonton to "put the main body of your command in the vicinity of Aldie, and push out reconnaissance toward Middleburg, Winchester, Berryville, and Harpers Ferry. . . . Obtain information of where the enemy is, his force, and his movements. . . . Leave nothing undone to give him the fullest information."[11]

Pleasonton gave it a good try, but perhaps Hooker should have made clear that he needed information not only about Lee's cavalry screen, but also about his main force. Forming his division at Union Mills about five miles outside of Manassas, Pleasonton advanced along the Little River Turnpike toward Aldie and Stuart's men. The four companies of the 12th Illinois who played a part in the operation left Warrenton on 15 June in the vanguard of the 1st Division, which was following Brigadier General David Gregg's 2nd Cavalry Division toward the contested area. When the fighting began that day, the 12th Illinois was near the rear and played little part.[12]

The 12th Illinois, the 8th Illinois, and the 3rd Indiana advanced with Pleasonton. They pass through Aldie, saw the destruction that followed the battles and came closer to the actual fighting. It was obvious to the men when they had reached a battlefield.

> First there were a half-dozen dead horses in the road, and the wall beside the road was broken down here and there. . . . Already the horses' bodies were beginning to bloat, and their legs pointed stiffly skyward. . . . Local farmers had gathered weapons and accouterments as souvenirs, but had left scattered in the grass the family letters, pictures, and small pocket items that are abandoned where the dead have been removed.[13]

Buford's 1st Division passed through Gregg's troops and undoubtedly witnessed the grim attitude of the seasoned veterans. As soon as the firing died away after Gregg's action, Federal soldiers started burying the dead.

> General Gregg, riding around to inspect the field, came upon a soldier, Private David Davis of the Tenth New York. Davis had dug a grave beside a fallen Confederate and was just sitting there, doing nothing.
>
> "What is the matter?" he asked. "What is stopping you from burying that man?"
>
> "I jus waiting fer 'im to die," answered the Welshman, impassively. Such macabre remarks were not uncommon when fighting men became accustomed to the sight of mangled humans.

Buford and his brigade did not stay long in Middleburg; they were ordered northwest to secure the Union cavalry's right flank. They occupied a little hamlet some three miles northwest of Middleburg called Leithtown, which was sometimes referred to as Pot House in reference to one of several buildings that had been used for decades to make pottery. Situated on high ground at a crossroads, Leithtown was now the logical point of contact between opposing outposts. The 12th Illinois and the rest of the 1st Brigade under Gamble's command occupied a stone fence in front of a ridge. Beyond a second stone fence a few yards back Gamble had an artillery battery drawn up in enfilade. The 8th New York was drawn up in formation in mounted squadrons.[14]

Confederate Colonel Thomas T. Munford, Gamble's counterpart, decided to feel out his opponent's strength for a possible turning movement that would place his Rebel forces squarely in Gregg's rear. Munford ordered Colonel Thomas Rosser forward to drive in Gamble's pickets. Then Rosser hit the main Federal defense line but recoiled under fire from Gamble's brigade. Lieutenant Colonel Thomas Marshall, grandson of the former chief justice of the United States and commander of the 7th Virginia Cavalry, was sent in to support Rosser. Marshall's troopers moved up at a trot. He sent forward his own sharpshooters and then ordered the rest of his regiment to charge. When they reached the first stone fence they had to tear a hole in it to get the troops through. They then saw Gamble's mounted columns and his artillery crews with their lanyards taut. Marshall told his bugler to sound retreat, and his squadrons wheeled about-face and galloped into the woods. The Confederates then attempted a flanking movement but were repulsed by the Federal artillery, which "loosed some canister but only a few men were wounded." The entire Federal brigade skirmished on 19 June and pushed the Rebel cavalry along the Snickersville Road, getting almost to

Snickers Gap before being ordered back to camp at Pot House Crossroads, where they supported a section of artillery. The men prepared for the next day's action and tried to sleep. It rained all night.[15]

The men of the 12th Illinois played only a supporting role in the Middleburg fight, just as they had done at Aldie, but their confidence was never higher. William Redman reported to the *Mount Carroll Weekly Mirror* that he was glad that the four companies of the 12th Illinois were brigaded with the 8th Illinois and the 3rd Indiana. They had, after all, been together a long time. They had shared the privations of war and had become a "band of brothers." The officers of the three regiments even petitioned their superiors to form a separate "Western Brigade." Their request was turned down, but the esprit de corps of the three western regiments was soaring. The high morale was needed because in the next fight, at Upperville, the men in the four companies of the 12th Illinois would play a central role, and they knew it. Buford and the other senior division and brigade commanders in the Union cavalry tended to rotate their various commands so that a different element was exposed to the initial onslaught of each action. There was no doubt that wherever contact was made next, it was the 12th Illinois's and 1st Division's turn to be in the forefront.[16]

The plan was for all three cavalry divisions to move at daylight and push Stuart into the Blue Ridge Mountains. They had the necessary numbers and equipment, but, as in many military plans, the human condition delayed the advance. Unlike other general officers of Pleasonton's command, General Buford took good care of his men. He delayed his advance more than two hours while waiting for rations and remounts. His men and horses had not eaten for two days, and some eight hundred horses were to be brought through Aldie Gap. The majority of these horses would go to Gregg's division, which had done most of the fighting, but Buford had also lost some horses. He wished to keep his command together, so he delayed his advance until he could remount his column.

The horses that were sent to Union cavalry regiments were in some cases rehabilitated animals, and the troopers often found that the rehabilitation had been incomplete. Those whose mounts were not already adapted to military service received fresh horses. As historian Stephen Starr noted:

> The depots [such as the one at Giesboro near Washington, D.C.] fulfilled fairly well, even if not to everyone's satisfaction, their primary duty of supplying horses for the cavalry, . . . but they did not "train" horses in the sense that horses for European cavalry were trained by expert horsemen before being issued to the troops. Indeed, Stoneman's depots did not train the horses at all,

and the bolting of untrained horses ridden by unskilled riders the first time they were exposed to gunfire, remained a serious hazard in the Union cavalry to the very end of the war.

A commander as careful as Buford would want at least twenty-four hours to allow the men to become accustomed to their new mounts, however challenging the horses might have been.[17]

Buford's advance finally got underway. The majority of his command passed through Middleburg at about seven o'clock in the morning and proceeded north along Pot House Road (now Virginia 626) to link up with Gamble's 1st Brigade, which had been at Pot House since the minor action the day before. After crossing Goose Creek and failing to turn the enemy's flank, Buford and Gamble began to move north along the creek. Buford became separated from Gregg's division, whose flank he was supposed to be protecting, so he detached his rear regiment, a regiment of U.S. regulars under the command of Major Samuel Starr, so it could go to Gregg's aid by doubling back and crossing the creek at the town of Millville. Shortly afterward Buford followed the detached regiment, proceeding northwest on the Millville Road. He was now roughly parallel to Gregg's forces and was protecting their flanks.[18]

The Confederates had anticipated Buford's move and had taken action to ensure that the Yankee cavalryman would not fall on their flanks. As the Union forces approached, the Confederates were deployed in line of battle on the right side of the road. Gamble moved one section of his artillery—three guns—to the front of the column. He "deployed the column in line of battle, and a few well-directed shells into the enemy's [the Confederates'] column dispersed him rapidly in retreat through the woods southward. One mile further, found the enemy behind stone walls, near a house; a few more shells drove them again toward Upperville." Each time the Confederates retreated to another prepared position, the 1st Brigade had to stop, unlimber its guns, load and sight in, fire, and reload. While all of this was happening, on the Ashby's Gap pike Stuart was very effectively delaying Gregg; Buford could not yet help Gregg except with Starr's brigade of regulars.[19]

Two miles farther along the Rebels once again sent out skirmishers, this time supported by artillery. Gamble deployed his column in line, advanced, and drove the dismounted Confederates from the safety of one of the many stone walls that characterize the northern part of Fauquier County and the southern part of Loudoun County. The 1st Brigade again advanced up the Millville Road and this time came to a crossroads and the little town of Willisville. They turned south on what is now Virginia Route 623 and continued at a trot until Buford reached a high point in the road. A half mile south on the Ashby's pike, Buford and Gamble saw Gregg heavily engaged with Stuart and decided to go to Gregg's aid. Once again, Buford placed his command in a trot and struck out across the fields. This time, though, he found the going difficult. Ditches caused by the overflow from Panther Skin Creek prevented the men from making fast progress. The column quickly became disorganized.[20]

While attempting to close up his command, Buford observed a train of Confederate wagons and a few troops marching toward Ashby's Gap. This was Stuart's supply train. It was being removed through the mountain pass because Stuart was fighting a retrograde movement and was ensuring the safety of his supplies. Buford apparently thought he could cut the supply train off by taking a little-used sunken road from Kinchloes Mill across what is now known as the Ayrshire Cattle Farm, but his command came under fire from Robert Preston Chew's battery of the Stuart horse artillery. Gamble charged with the 3rd Indiana and the 8th and 12th Illinois, and he and Lieutenant Colonel David Clendennin of the 8th Illinois were knocked down when their horses were struck in the first artillery barrage. William H. Medill of the 8th Illinois took command, and he led his men toward the Confederate artillery, which stood behind a wall that ran southeast to northwest across the Ayrshire Cattle Farm. Medill ordered his men to fire, and the wave of pistol shot forced the Confederate gunners to flee, abandoning their weapons.[21]

Buford reported that the Confederate gunners, equipped with four twelve-pound guns, had some excellent practice with the lead regiments in his command, one of which was the 12th Illinois. Each of the guns fired spherical case shot with a timed fuse set to explode at a certain point in the flight of the shell. The gunners would have been able to get off about three shots in the minute or so they had before the men of the 12th Illinois were on top of them. The twelve-pound iron spheres would have detonated above the ranks of the charging cavalrymen, and the bursting charges were not sufficient to kill or wound dozens of closely packed men riding at an extended gallop. There were some casualties, and the men of the 12th Illinois became aware that there was no way out of the situation except to make a saber charge, or "run the gauntlet," and to neutralize the Confederate artillery. They charged into two Confederate units—the Laurel Brigade, led by W. E. "Grumble" Jones, and the old nemesis of the 12th Illinois, Rooney Lee's brigade, now led by Colonel John R. Chambliss.[22]

Gamble later reported that the men of the 12th Illinois had performed well in driving the gunners from their guns. They would have captured all of the gunners had it not been for the stone walls, which were about six feet high, too high for heavily laden troop horses to clear. If the men had attempted the initial jump, they would have encountered what Gamble could

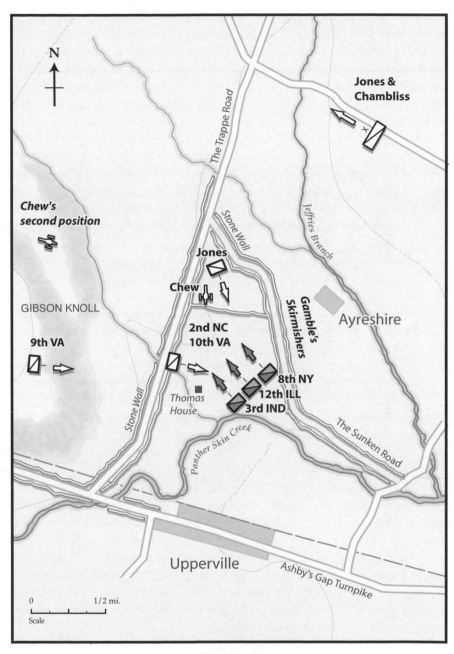

The Action at Trapp Road

21 June 1863

not see until near the end of the charge: a second stone wall that probably would have wreaked havoc with the mounts.

The Confederates, attempting to stop the Union advance, charged the men of the 1st Brigade as they hastily dismounted, turned the cannon around, and secured firing positions along the stone wall. On came the Confederates, seven regiments strong, in full, repeated countercharges. The men of the 12th Illinois, 3rd Indiana, and 8th Illinois replied with effective carbine and pistol fire and used what was left of the captured Confederate artillery ammunition for the captured gun. When things became desperate, they mounted their horses and repelled the last charge with the saber. Redman reported that in the charges and countercharges at Upperville the 12th Illinois was "hand to hand [in] the prettiest fight" he had ever seen. The Confederates then attempted to turn the Federals' flank and were repulsed by two squadrons, one each from the 8th Illinois and the 3rd Indiana, along with a section of captured artillery ably served by members of the 8th New York who had remained mounted and ready for just such an occurrence.[23]

The defeated Confederates retired through the western part of Upperville toward Ashby's Gap, a distance of about two miles, pursued by the 1st and 2nd Brigades. The brigades then returned to the battlefield at dusk to bury the dead and care for the wounded. Gamble reported that eighteen dead and more than thirty wounded Confederates were found on the field. The 1st Brigade suffered a total loss of forty-four: four killed, thirty-five wounded, and five missing. The five missing were from the 12th Illinois. They had been directly under one of the exploding twelve-pound case shells during the mounted charge. Of the four who were killed, two were from the 12th Illinois; from its two squadrons there were also thirteen wounded, including an officer, Captain Thomas Brown.

Gamble reported that the brigade had lost only thirty-six horses, which is remarkable for a charge into entrenched Confederate positions supported by four pieces of artillery. "The horses were as excited as the men, and instantly as wild. A score of animals had dropped from the artillery fire but others did not feel their wounds until the affray had ended, when dozens sank to their knees in the grass, and toppled over," the stress just too great. None of the thirty-six horses that were killed belonged to troopers of the 12th Illinois. By luck or chance, either the men had not mounted new horses or the new horses had not panicked.[24]

As the Federals secured the town, they began to hear rumors that a high-ranking Confederate was in the vicinity, convalescing from a wound received during the Middleburg fight. The Yankees went door to door looking for him, a colorful Prussian volunteer and major on Stuart's staff named Heroes von Borcke. Von Borcke had sustained a neck wound at Middleburg and had been brought to Upperville to the home of Dr. Eliason, who was serving with Stuart as surgeon. Eliason believed at first that the wound was mortal, but von Borcke had rallied. Right before the fall of Upperville, he was moved two miles south to the plantation of Bolingbrook. The Yankees never found him. The people of Upperville told the Yankee search parties that von Borcke had been killed at Middleburg and had been buried in the graveyard at Upperville. In truth, he recovered, returned to Germany, and lived to a ripe old age.[25]

From a strategic point of view, Stuart seems to have won the battles of Aldie, Middleburg, and Upperville. He prevented the Yankees from penetrating Ashby's Gap, saved his wagon train, and kept the towns of Aldie and Upperville from being shelled by Yankee artillery. He lost far fewer men in the battles than Pleasonton did, with only 510 killed as opposed to 827 of Pleasonton's men. Stuart appears to have come out ahead from a tactical point of view as well. He fought delaying actions and only went over to the offensive when the opportunity arose, and he was back in control of Upperville on the day after the battle. And Stuart was able to inflict almost twice the number of casualties that he sustained.[26]

Part of the reason that so many more Federals than Confederates were wounded and killed is that the Federals were often attacking prepared defensive positions, which in this war of rifled weapons ensured that the attacking troops would suffer. Also, Stuart's troopers were more experienced under fire than most of the Federal cavalry. The 12th Illinois had not experienced combat at Barbees Cross Roads, Kelly's Ford, or Brandy Station. Their first experiences with desperate, bloody fighting were on Pot House Road at the end of the battle of Middleburg and at the stone fence and sunken road at Dunbar's Corner northwest of Upperville.

The Federals had exhibited much bravado. Since Kelly's Ford and Brandy Station, they had able to stand their own with Stuart's brigades, and they were proud of it. Redman wrote from camp that the 12th Illinois had been in two battles and had "whipped the Rebs" both times. On Sunday afternoon of 21 June, the 12th Illinois "drove the Rebs eight miles . . . and we charged and they charged. . . . You ought to have seen us run them and heard us yell at them." Redman described the fighting skills of men who were still not quite veterans: he "shot about twenty times and I should hate to say now that I did not hit a Reb." He went on to write that "several of the boys were hit but not seriously hurt. . . . John Bowman from Mount Carroll was in it and he came through all safe—fought like a tiger." "We can whip the Rebs any time," and the men "expect battle every day." The phlegmatic Abner Frank simply stated that the brigade "marched to Upperville skirmished all day and had a pitched fight at about three o'clock in the afternoon and drove the enemy and we encamped on the field. The[y] wounded three of our squadron and the captain of my company."27

Pleasonton's report confirms Frank's description, although the dates are different. Pleasonton wrote that Buford's division operated independently on 21 June, the day of the battle of Upperville. Buford sent "a party to the top of the Blue Ridge, that saw a rebel infantry camp about two miles long on the Shenandoah, just below Ashby's Gap. The atmosphere was so hazy they could not make out anything more beyond." As a result of this reconnaissance, Pleasonton reported "that General Lee himself, and the corps of Longstreet and A. P. Hill, were in the Shenandoah Valley, on their way north."28

Upperville looks much the same as it did in late June 1863. Most of the roads are still there and appear on state maps. The sunken road where the 12th Illinois charged the men of Colonel Lunsford L. Lomax's command is now on private property, but the stone wall and Dunbar's Corner, where they withstood the charges of the Laurel Brigade, are still visible. The house where Dr. Eliason examined Major Heroes von Borcke still stands in Upperville on Ashby's Gap Pike, which still runs right through the center of town. Also in Upperville are the graves of sixteen Confederate Soldiers, two of whom are unknown, who fell in the battles of Middleburg and Upperville.29

From 23 to 25 June the men of the 12th Illinois Cavalry and the rest of the 1st Cavalry Brigade stayed around the area of Aldie to refit, remount, and rearm. They needed only thirty-six additional horses. On the evening of 25 June the men received some much-anticipated mail. That night, while the men of the 12th Illinois and other members of the brigade were enjoying their mail, Stuart slipped by Pleasonton's entire cavalry corps and proceeded north. Acting under Lee's orders, Stuart embarked on a raid into southeastern Pennsylvania, leaving Lee and the Army of Northern Virginia without its eyes and ears as it entered enemy territory. Stuart took with him three of his best brigades and left four cavalry brigades behind under the command of Brigadier Generals Beverly Robertson and William Jones, who would soon face the 12th Illinois's 1st Cavalry Brigade as they moved on almost parallel courses into Pennsylvania.30

On 26 June, the 12th Illinois moved to Leesburg, Virginia, about 15 miles from their camp at Aldie, trailing Lee's army. There had been another reorganization of the cavalry, but Buford's 1st Division was still made up of the 1st Brigade under Colonel William Gamble, to which the 12th Illinois was attached along with the 8th Illinois, part of the 3rd Indiana, and the 8th New York; the 2nd Brigade under the command of Colonel Thomas C. Devin; and the reserve brigade comprising regulars commanded by Brigadier General Wesley Merritt. Because of Battery A's autonomy, a six-gun battery was assigned to Buford's division: Battery A of the 2nd United States Artillery under the command of First Lieutenant John A. Calef.[31]

On 27 June the 1st Division crossed the Potomac into Maryland at Edwards Ferry. They then traveled over very poor roads to the Monocacy River, crossed near its mouth, and bivouacked on the east side of the mountains three miles from Jefferson. Buford halted there because a supply train was passing that belonged to Major General Julius Stahel's Federal cavalry division, which had formerly been assigned to the defense of Washington. The assignment of Stahel's 3,500-man division to Pleasonton's corps had been Hooker's idea. The assignment was Hooker's last act as commander of the Army of the Potomac, but the appointment was not made until he was relieved. George G. Meade replaced Hooker on 28 June 1863.[32]

On 28 June Buford's division moved through Jefferson and went into camp at Middletown for the purpose of shoeing and refitting. Abner Frank wrote that on 28 June the 12th Illinois marched thirty miles. As 29 June dawned, Buford's command moved northward to Middleburg, Maryland, on that day the reserve brigade was detached and moved to Mechanicstown. At that time Buford's First Brigade, which included four companies of the 12th Illinois, was at Middletown guarding the left flank of the Union army as it marched northward as fast as its infantry could go. Near Frederick Buford's men caught a spy. In quick succession, the spy was tried, convicted, condemned to death, and hanged. "A committee of citizens called on . . . Buford and wanted to know why he was hanged. . . . Buford informed them that the man was a spy and he was afraid to send him to Washington because he knew the authorities would make him a brigadier general." No doubt Buford's comment was a sarcastic response to the controversial recent promotion of three junior officers—George Custer, Wesley Merritt, and Elon Farnsworth—to the rank of brigadier general, the result of a political scheme by Pleasonton and Radical Republican Congressman John Farnsworth, a former commander of the 8th Illinois Cavalry and an uncle of Elon Farnsworth.[33]

Buford moved through Boonsboro, Cavetown, and Monterey Spring and encamped near Fairfield, Maryland, where he discovered that he was near a contingent of Confederate infantry comprising two Mississippi regiments and two pieces of artillery. The citizens of Fairfield did not inform Buford of the presence of the Rebel soldiers because they feared Confederate retaliation against their homes. Buford "literally stumbled on" the Rebels near Fairfield on 30 June 1863 while his 1st and 2nd Brigades were headed in the direction of Gettysburg. Had he known earlier of the Confederate regiments' presence, Buford wrote, he could have attempted to surround and capture the Rebel force and might have destroyed it. But Buford quickly grasped the meaning of the presence of such a force that far north. Infantry unsupported by a cavalry screen but accompanied by artillery were probably the extreme right wing of a much larger Confederate force, and Buford was taking no chances. He considered calling up his artillery and shelling the Mississippi regiments from a distance with his six three-inch ordnance rifles, but he believed that shelling the Mississippians would simply disrupt the plans of the Rebel general commanding that detachment, and Buford's function was to see where the outfit was going.[34]

So without serious incident Buford turned his column, which included the four companies of the 12th Illinois, toward Emmitsburg, and he was soon on the road assigned to him. He was moving toward Gettysburg, where he supposed he would meet other Union cavalry formations. The 1st Brigade entered Gettysburg late in the afternoon of 30 June 1863. It was just in time to meet the advancing enemy, but the brigade was able to take control of the community before the Confederates could gain a foothold. The Confederates withdrew toward Cashtown, leaving their pickets about four and a half miles from Gettysburg.

Buford then began to move his cavalry into a position from which they could prevent the rebels from entering the town. "By daylight on 1 July, I had positive information of the enemy's position and movements," he reported, "and my arrangements were made for entertaining him until General Reynolds [who commanded the nearest corps of Federal infantry] could reach the scene." Buford observed a crossroads village flanked by defensible ridges and hills, and he knew that the place was strategically ideal. On Chambersburg Pike, there were three ridges—Herr, McPherson's, and Seminary—each about a quarter mile from the other. They would make good successive positions in case he was forced to fall back. Looking backward, Buford saw that the town of Gettysburg sat up against another ridge where the local cemetery was located. If Upperville had taught him nothing else, it was the value of sturdy stone walls. Farther behind and slightly north of Buford's position was a natural fortress, Culp's Hill, and southeast were two rocky hills called Round Top and Little Round Top by the natives. If a cavalry brigade or an army fell back to those positions, it could hold out for days. Buford knew that he had found the ideal ground for a major engagement. He much preferred Gettysburg to Cashtown, snuggled against South Mountain, where the Rebels were waiting and had all the advantage of maneuver.[35]

Buford sent out his scouts first to ascertain that the force to his front was the main body of the Army of Northern Virginia. He had his patrols fan out "north and northwest, and northeast" of the town. He reported that although he had run into no main body at that point, the road to Cashtown and Oxford "is terribly infested with prowling cavalry parties." Buford wrote General Reynolds, "A. P. Hill's corps, composed of Anderson, Heth, and Pender, is massed back of Cashtown, nine miles from this place. His pickets, composed of infantry and artillery, are in sight of mine." Buford had heard "many rumors of the enemy advancing on me from toward York," and he was beginning to overwork his already tired horses and men. One rumor held that "Ewell was coming over the mountains from Carlisle." Buford queried, "When will the reserve be relieved, and where are my wagons?" In an earlier dispatch of the same day, he wrote to Pleasonton that his men and horses were exhausted and there were no facilities for shoeing.

When Buford's scouts and patrols had returned and reported that the Rebels were indeed about ready to move on Gettysburg, he moved his division through Gettysburg and out on the Chambersburg Pike. He called in his commanders and told them to place their brigades and dig in because there would be a fight the next day. When one of his junior officers told him that their position was so strong that they would hold the Rebels off without too much trouble, Buford gently replied, "No, you won't. . . . They will attack you in the morning, and they will come a booming—skirmishers three-deep. You will have to fight like the devil until supports arrive." He was preparing his men for a desperate stand.[36]

As Buford's brigades moved through the quaint little Pennsylvania town of Gettysburg, William Redman wrote his mother on the morning the battle would begin that "young Ladies came out in the streets by the hundreds—handing us bouquets and singing to us as we passed along, 'My Lover has Gone to the War'—a very beautiful song which made us all feel good." Gettysburg was a beautiful place, and "the people are truly loyal and look upon us . . . as . . . rescuers." It took great loyalty for the young women of Gettysburg to come that close to the troopers, very tired men on very tired animals, filthy with days of dust.[37]

Once out on Chambersburg Pike and McPherson's Ridge, the two Federal commanders, William Gamble and Thomas Devin, placed their respective commands. Devin was to the right of Chambersburg Pike and Gamble was to the left, and Lieutenant Calef positioned his six guns on either side. Gamble placed his brigade, three squadrons of the 3rd Indiana, the 8th Illinois, two of the four companies of the 12th Illinois, and the 8th New York, to "the right resting off the railroad track and the left near the Middletown road." Altogether they were about sixteen hundred strong. "Half of the Eighth Illinois, Third Indiana, and Twelfth Illinois were dismounted, and ordered over McPherson's Ridge and Herr Ridge and deployed as skirmishers." Buford then began to send a series of messages through couriers to General John Reynolds, commander of the 1st Corps, located eleven miles south of Gettysburg. He was asking Reynolds for help because he knew what the next day would bring.[38]

Buford continued to place his pickets, and for most of the night he roamed his lines, making sure that all of the men had dug in their firing positions as well as possible. Making these preparations was difficult because they carried few tools and the supply train had not arrived. Buford also placed a couple of companies northwest of the town on the Mummasburg road and a detachment due north watching the road from Carlisle to Gettysburg. Then he waited for the dawn. Redman informed his mother that he was lucky enough to spend the night in Gettysburg at the William Stalsmith home and that he ate breakfast with them early in the morning on 1 July before the Confederate attack. Henry Stalsmith of Carroll County, Illinois, Redman wrote, was a direct relative of William's. Redman might have been the only trooper at Gettysburg who, after riding over one hundred miles and engaging in three pitched battles, was entering the first day of fighting with a good night's rest in a bed and a meal of something besides cold dried beef and hardtack biscuits.[39]

On the Confederate side, Major General Henry Heth, commander of the Rebel infantry division nearest to Buford's cavalry on the Chambersburg Pike, had asked his corps commander, A. P. Hill, if he could take his division into Gettysburg to get some shoes that he had heard were stored in the town. He told Hill that the only opposing force was cavalry that could be brushed away without much trouble. Asked whether he had any objections, Hill answered, "None in the world." So Heth and his men headed for Gettysburg to get the shoes. Buford knew he was out there. He wrote Pleasonton at 10:40 P.M. on the night of 30 June, giving his position and carefullly detailing some of the Confederate units that opposed him.[40]

The weather was showery on that first day of July, with almost a continuous light rain. Archer's brigade of Heth's Confederate divisions deployed in the light rain in those very early morning hours and came out of the mist near Herr Ridge. First Lieutenant Marcellus Jones of DuPage County, Illinois, a member of the 8th Illinois Cavalry, commanded a small detachment assigned him by Buford. He and his men saw the ghostly gray infantry emerge out of the mist, and they picked their targets. They unleashed a couple of shots then fled back to the rest of the company on McPherson's Ridge. Buford, who had just finished a cup of coffee at a nearby farmhouse, heard the firing and hurried to the front lines. As soon as he ascertained that an attack was in progress, he hurried back to his headquarters near the front lines for a few short minutes to ensure that additional couriers had been sent out for help. Then he sprinted his horse for McPherson's Ridge to be with his men as the battle opened.[41]

The Rebels came on, as Buford had predicted, "three-deep and booming." In this first attack were two brigades made up of troops from Alabama and Mississippi. The Confederates advanced cautiously once the skirmishers on both sides became engaged, and then Calef's artillery opened up on the advancing Rebel column and did extensive damage. Almost immediately the Confederates opened up with two batteries of eight guns, and an artillery duel ensued. The Yankee gunners had the advantage of the three-inch ordnance rifles, so they were able to dislodge several of the Confederate guns and stem the advance for a short time. But the enemy advance continued, and by seven o'clock the men of the skirmish detail and other elements of the brigade were compelled to fall about two hundred yards back from Herr Ridge to McPherson's Ridge.

In spite of the retrograde movement, the detachment of only a couple of hundred men was successfully fending off three Confederate divisions numbering some five thousand. For the next two hours the men of the 1st and 2nd Brigades withstood charge after charge. At about ten o'clock in the morning General Reynolds arrived, leading the infantry advance of the 1st Corps. When Reynolds arrived, the men of the 12th Illinois undoubtedly believed that their job was over and that they would soon be relieved. So did John Buford, who watched from below the cupola next to the Lutheran seminary. His division was low on ammunition and was almost exhausted by three solid hours of combat.[42]

Relief was not in sight, however, and there were several bad omens. While the ridge was being transferred to the infantry's control, General John Reynolds was felled by a shot through the head by a volley from Heth's men, a shot probably intended for the Federal infantrymen on McPherson's Ridge. Command was transferred first to General Abner Doubleday and then to General Oliver O. Howard, so some confusion was bound to emerge.

In the midmorning hours following Reynolds's death, Confederate skirmishers were seen attempting a reconnoiter that would probably lead to an attempt to turn Buford's flank. By ten o'clock the strongly reinforced Confederate infantry and artillery under Brigadier General James Archer extended their flanks and advanced on the Federal left in an attempt to force the Union cavalry and a division of Union infantry off of McPherson's Ridge. Once again the cavalry, exhausted and almost out of ammunition, was called on to stem the enemy tide. Buford ordered the 1st Brigade to mount, move forward at a trot, and deploy in line of battle in the woods that cover the south half of McPherson's Ridge. Buford ordered Gamble to deploy half of the 8th New York, all of the 3rd Indiana, and the four companies of the 12th Illinois. They were to dismount and position themselves behind a stone wall under cover of a grove of trees. The Lutheran seminary was visible on the brigade's right.[43]

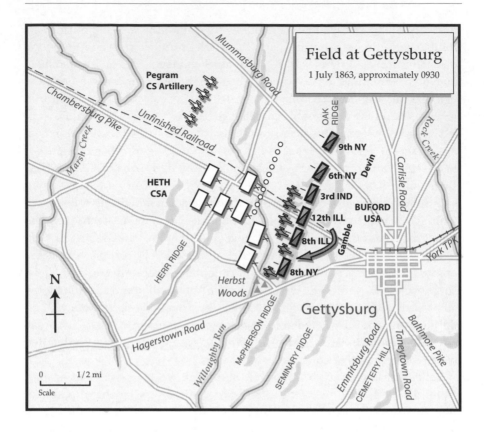

The Confederates were almost upon the horsemen before the Federals completed their alignment behind the stone wall. When the Lincoln men opened up on the Rebels, the fire was appalling. The carbine fire was so rapid that many Southerners in the first rank who were hit at relatively close range by the .52-caliber Burnside were blown back into the second and third ranks. The men of the 12th Illinois kept up the fire until the Confederates sent more and more men into the melee and finally overran the cavalrymen, who, to save themselves and their valuable horses from certain capture, rapidly fell back to Seminary Ridge where the brigade artillery had withdrawn after running out of ammunition. Buford moved the 1st Brigade to guard the left flank, posting it near the Gettysburg-Fairfield road.[44]

As the brigades of Colonel J. M. Brokenbrough and Brigadier General James H. Lane swept across McPherson's Ridge, the Army of the Potomac seemed to be, once again, in full retreat. The lead regiments of A. P. Hill's corps pushed them aside, just like the Confederates had done in most of the engagements across Virginia during the first two-and-a-half years of the war.

But all was not the same as before. The Federal infantry brigades of Brigadier Generals Roy Stone, Solomon Meredith, and Chapman Biddle had not been not routed; rather, they were falling back in good order, southeast in the direction of the Lutheran seminary. The slightly elevated, wooded ground all along the westward slope of the seminary would be easily defended by the effective Union artillery. The problem was the left flank.

The Hagerstown Pike ran at a left angle slant. As the slant ran northeast from Fairfield, Pennsylvania, to Gettysburg, the road intersected with what is now Lutheran Seminary Road. Lutheran Seminary Road also intersects with Seminary Ridge. If the Confederates of Hill's corps could cross the Hagerstown-Fairfield road, they would be able to quickly and effectively move behind Federal lines and capture all three Federal infantry brigades and their supporting artillery. For more than an hour the Confederates appeared not to grasp the connection between the Hagerstown Pike and the unprotected flank of the Federal 1st Army Corps.

The Confederate division of Major General William D. Pender began to push the attack against the Federal center. They found that the Federals had called for help and that Brigadier General John Buford had sent it. Shortly after the midmorning Confederate breakthrough on McPherson's Ridge, Buford's division had been withdrawn to the northwest part of Cemetery Hill to watch the Federal flank and await orders. There they had stayed mounted. Three Confederate brigades had moved in: J. Johnson Pettigrew and J. M. Brockenbrough of Heth's division across Seminary Ridge from the west, and the brigade of Junnius Daniel of Rode's division of Ewell's corps from the north, from Carlisle. The Federal commander on the field, Major General Oliver O. Howard, had asked his staff if they knew the location of any reinforcements. There were no reserves on the field, a courier informed him. The courier, E. P. Halsted, was sent to find Brigadier General John Buford and one of his cavalry brigades that was located on the slope of Cemetery Ridge. Halsted gave Buford the message that reserves were badly needed near the Lutheran seminary. Through his binoculars Buford observed the long gray lines of Confederate troops approaching the Union center, and he asked: "'What does he think I can do against those long lines of the enemy out there?' 'I don't know anything about that, General. Those are General Howard's orders.' 'Very well,' said he, 'I will see what I can do,' and like the true soldier that he was, he moved his command out in plain view of the enemy and formed for the charge."[45]

The enemy reacted to the movement, forming squares in echelon and allowing the Union troops that had been penned down to move to safety. Buford's men then dismounted and deployed just to the right of the Federal infantry behind and along a low stone wall that runs on the northwest side of

McPherson's Ridge. The 3rd Indiana occupied the area adjacent to the Hagerstown road; half of the 8th New York were next in line, and the other half remained mounted. Two squadrons, or about one hundred men, of the 12th Illinois were third and last in line against the stone wall. The second battalion of the 8th New York was mounted, posted southwest along the stone wall, facing southwest at a right angle to counter any flanking movement by the Confederates. With them was assigned one gun from Lieutenant John Calef's battery that had been with Gamble's brigade out on Chambersburg Pike that morning.[46]

Gamble's men had anticipated correctly. As the Confederate brigades of Pettigrew, Brokenbrough, Scales, Perrin, and Lane began to move to the attack against the Federal line on Lutheran Seminary Road, they found themselves running a gauntlet of fire from the two squadrons of the 12th Illinois Cavalry and the rest of Gamble's 1st Brigade. At a range of around one hundred yards, the 3rd Indiana, half of the 8th New York, and one squadron of the 12th Illinois had opened fire. The Rebels were completely surprised. They had not seen the Federal cavalrymen deployed behind the stone wall, and the fire was so heavy that rank after rank of Confederates in Perrin's brigade were blown back into each other by the striking power of the .54-caliber Burnside carbines.[47]

To counter the Federal cavalrymen along the stone wall, the Confederates executed two maneuvers. First, they sent the 12th and 13th South Carolina Regiments to assault the stone wall where the 3rd Indiana and 12th Illinois were keeping up the very effective carbine fire. Second, the brigade of James H. Lane moved across Hagerstown Pike to clear away the cavalry troopers with a flanking movement. At that point, just before dusk on 1 July, the Union troops began to fall back across the field toward Seminary Ridge. The 12th Illinois and the 3rd Indiana dismounted and, behind the fence and the stone wall, covered the infantry and its left flank, the 8th Illinois, before the 12th Illinois and 3rd Indiana withdrew to Cemetery Hill.

As the first day of the Battle of Gettysburg ended, the Federal infantry of the 1st Army Corps, 3rd Division, were safe. Retreating through the town of Gettysburg, they occupied the defensible heights of Cemetery Hill. The men of the 12th Illinois Cavalry and the rest of Gamble's brigade had performed a near military miracle. They had prevented the capture of an entire division by applying steady, disciplined fire at a critical moment. If the 12th Illinois or their Midwestern brothers from Indiana had broke and run, or if they had expended their ammunition less frugally, the 3rd Division might well have been captured, and the Battle of Gettysburg would have ended differently. The stand taken by the 12th Illinois, 3rd Indiana, and 8th New

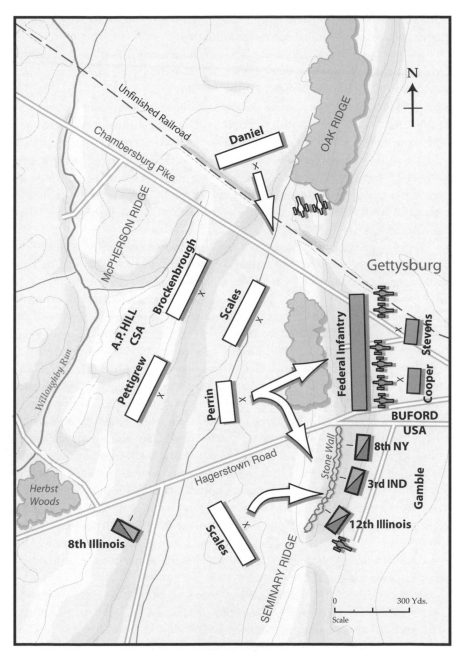

Field at Gettysburg

1 July 1863, approximately 1630

York prevented the left flank from being turned and saved a division of infantry from almost certain capture or annihilation.[48]

The casualty list from that day's action is long, and this time, unlike at Upperville, many officers were either killed or badly wounded in action. Gamble lists nine brigade officers lost. Of these nine three were from the 12th Illinois: Lieutenant Charles Conroe killed, Captain James Fisher and Lieutenant Arno Voss, wounded. Ferdinand Ushuer was the first Union soldier to be killed at Gettysburg, and other enlisted men of the 12th Illinois killed that day were Thomas G. Blanset, John Ellis, Gabriel B. Durham, Homer C. Stedman, and George Riesborough. All but Riesborough's names are inscribed on the stone monument on McPherson's Ridge in Gettysburg National Park; presumably Riesborough was wounded and died later in the day.

The case of Private Gabriel B. Durham of Company I is probably the most horrible of those of the enlisted men who were wounded. Durham suffered greatly after both of his "nates," or buttocks, were struck by a solid artillery shot. He died on 23 July. The case of Private Willet S. Haight of Company A of the 12th Illinois also stands out as a graphic example of the horrors of wounds received on the opening day of Gettysburg. Private Haight was mounted that day, acting as a courier. As he rode along the line, a shell (or perhaps more than one) exploded, killing his horse and throwing him to the ground. He was hit by a shell fragment, "which struck him in the face, breaking his left jaw badly and tearing a hole under his chin and next to his throat in such a manner that his nourishment would escape by the wound." He survived the Battle of Gettysburg and was taken to an army hospital in Harrisburg, Pennsylvania, where he was medically discharged later that year. He suffered from the wound for the remainder of his life. He could open his mouth no more than about one inch. Whenever he chewed his food, the repaired bones in his jaw would grind together, causing him great pain. The impact of the shell fragment also caused a severe injury to the back of his neck and his spine. He could "not rise himself without assistance. . . . He was unable to masticate his food and often bites his tongue."[49]

William Gamble, the commanding officer of the 1st Brigade of the 1st Cavalry Division, wrote in reply to a citizen's inquiry regarding the action at the stone wall at Gettysburg: "An hour before dusk . . . this Brigade of Cavalry was again ordered to the front, dismounted, and fought the Rebels on the Seminary Ridge and saved a whole Division of our infantry from being surrounded and captured—nothing of this is mentioned in news-papers of dispatches, yet these facts occurred with the loss of some of our best officers and men." During that terrible first day, he noted, the losses of the 1st

Brigade were "111 officers and men killed, wounded, and missing and 56 Cavalry horses killed, 13 Artillery horses killed and wounded." Gamble is less self-congratulatory in his after-action report, stating blandly: "My brigade fought well under disadvantageous circumstances against a largely superior force . . . [and] had the honor to commence the fight in the morning and close it in the evening."[50]

One historian calls Buford's stand the most valuable day's work done by the cavalry in the Civil War; another believes it was too "extravagantly praised." Such judgments are necessarily subjective and need not be accepted as incontestable truth. Historian Stephen Starr writes that reports of the gallantry of the men of the 1st Brigade and of Buford's entire division are "probably inspired more by the glamor that attaches to the most dramatic battle in American Military History, than by the facts." Yet even this most critical of American military historians states, "Buford . . . and his entire command, and Gamble's regiments in particular, are entitled to great credit for holding at bay for two hours a force of Confederate infantry outnumbering them three to one." Probably the most exact evaluation of the performance of the 12th Illinois and its colleagues came from the other side of the hill. Writing of the first day at Gettysburg almost a half century later, General Edward P. Alexander, Longstreet's chief of artillery, noted that Confederate generals Heth and Pender, who initiated the attack on Buford, got "a genteel whipping, by the . . . force they had inadvertently pitched into."[51]

The remarks and observations of the enlisted men, whose names are rarely in print because they usually do not have to write after-action reports, tell much the same story that their officers recorded. Their emphasis is on the common soldiers, who carried the burden of battle. Private Abner Frank wrote that it was cloudy and rainy all day (it was not; the weather cleared by mid-morning) and that his squadron was on picket when the fight opened. The enemy advanced on the 12th Illinois, and the men slowly fell back with the rest of the brigade until the infantry came up. The brigade was fired on all day, and the Confederates killed one lieutenant of Frank's squadron and wounded two corporals of his company, one seriously. The Union army fell back, Frank wrote, and the Confederates took possession of the town at five in the afternoon on 1 July.[52]

Redman was far more descriptive and realistic, writing to his sisters, "I thank God for His kind protection." Like Gamble, Redman wrote that the 1st Brigade opened the fight. His company "lost three men—one killed instantly with the piece of a shell—one wounded in the hip—(he is now in hospital all right)—John Burrows—(quite badly), and one wounded and taken prisoner. One Company just beside of us, of the 3rd Indiana Regt., lost 15 men and one [Company] 12, and we had a great many killed and wounded in our Regiment. We dismounted and fought on foot. I shot 10 or 12 times and if I did not hit the enemy every time, I give them close calls." The rest of the army was now up at Gettysburg, he wrote, and "I think that we will be able to annihilate all of General Lee's Army in Pa   God Grant that we may. I am willing to kill my part of the DEVILS."[53]

On the night of 1 July, Buford reported, the 12th Illinois and the rest of the division camped on the Gettysburg battlefield while protecting the Union left flank, with the "pickets extending almost to Fairfield." The first day of battle at Gettysburg was over, and the men of 12th Illinois, exhausted and bloodied, looked back with pride on the role they had played.[54]

"Fighting the Rebs for Seven Days"

The second day's fighting at the Battle of Gettysburg, on 2 July, began just after nine in the morning. Buford's "division became engaged with the enemy sharpshooters . . . and held its own until relieved by General Sickles' corps." As the battle continued, Buford was ordered to leave Gettysburg with his command and proceed to Westminster to guard an important ammunition depot, to protect wagon trains there against a raid by Stuart, and to seize any fords the Confederates might use should they retreat back into Virginia. Buford left the Gettysburg battlefield and camped at Taneytown that night. On 5 July, the day Lee's beaten army was on the road back to Virginia, the 12th Illinois Cavalry and the 1st Division "marched toward Frederick, drew supplies, and remained all night."[1]

The night before, 4 July, Lee had decided that his army, now seriously battered, must return to Virginia. The problem was how to get back home with his wounded and his trains, with as much equipment and as many men as possible. Sending for Brigadier General John D. Imboden, he detailed the disposition of his forces and his long wagon trains.[2]

Major General Alfred Pleasonton thought he had a chance to capture Lee's entire supply train. His troopers under Generals Judson Kilpatrick and George Custer caught the end of Confederate General Jubal Early's wagon train in a gap in South Mountain called Monterey Pass. Kilpatrick attacked in the middle of a thunderstorm and captured only ninety wagons and 345 prisoners, many of whom were wounded. Lee, in his report of the Gettysburg campaign, brushed the capture off as an annoyance. Pleasonton's attack was ineffectual not only because it was attempted on slippery mountain roads, but also because most of the Union cavalry were in great need of remounts after Gettysburg. During the Federal pursuit of the Army of Northern Virginia, hundreds of horses dropped from exhaustion and were left in the road where they had fallen, saddles and bridles in place, and the dismounted troopers walked along rain-soaked roads with little food. Most of the Federal cavalry was soon to be resupplied, thanks to a herculean effort by the Federal quartermaster corps and Herman Haupt's U.S. military railroad, but for the purpose of catching Lee, it was all for naught because Lee was able to escape.[3]

One of the few outfits that had cared for its horses and had refitted just before the Gettysburg campaign was Buford's 1st Cavalry Division, whose 1st Brigade, including the 12th Illinois Volunteers, was at Westminster, Maryland. They had been withdrawn after the morning of the second day of the Gettysburg battle and had therefore been spared the charges and countercharges of Federal and Confederate cavalry on the "Forgotten Field of Gettysburg." The duty of guarding a stationary depot had given their horses a day or two of rest, and Buford was ready. The men of the 1st Division, and particularly the men of the 12th Illinois, were also in familiar territory. They were in the part of Maryland where they had spent the autumn after the Antietam campaign. Federal cavalry commander Alfred Pleasonton, ordered by Meade to pursue Lee's forces, needed to make good use his 1st Division, the only one with fresh horses that had experienced some combat.[4]

It was a critical time. The armies were repositioning themselves: the Union army gearing up for the offensive and the Confederates hoping to get back to Virginia where they would prepare to fight a defensive war in the near future. In this period of armies on the move, speed had become crucial. The Federal 1st Cavalry Division and the bulk of the Army of Northern Virginia raced for the fords that cross the Potomac in northern Maryland. Lee had left a pontoon bridge in place at Falling Waters, hoping that it would survive the campaign and that his army could use it to cross the river on the way back from Pennsylvania. The Potomac was out of its banks because of the July rains, so Lee probably thought that the pontoon at Falling Waters had been washed away, but the bridge had been destroyed in a rare show of initiative by Brigadier General William H. French and a cavalry detachment from Harpers Ferry. Lee, however, had some remarkable engineers in his army, and getting across the Potomac once the rains subsided would not be impossible as long as the fords at Falling Waters remained in Confederate hands. The fords, therefore, suddenly became very important geographical positions on the maps of both armies.[5]

On 6 July 1863 the 12th Illinois and the rest of the 1st Brigade became involved in the chase for the Williamsport and Falling Waters fords. On the night before they drew supplies at Frederick had prepared to pursue the Army of Northern Virginia. Sergeant William Redman of Company C told his mother that combat would be coming soon. The unit had been moving so fast that he had fed his horse and staked it near him, eaten a supper of cold fried bacon and hard tack, and immediately fallen asleep on the ground near his tethered horse; he had not awakened until morning. No sooner had he had his breakfast than it was "boots and saddles" and on their way to find "Mr. Rebbs."[6]

Near Saint James College later that day, Buford's division discovered enemy pickets that had been driven in, and preparations were made to attack the school. About a mile and a half outside of the college, the enemy line grew progressively stronger as Rebel cavalry prepared to protect their trains. Buford placed his division in attack formation, using Merritt's Regulars with the battery to the right of the Boonsboro Road, Gamble's brigade (including the 12th Illinois) to the left of that road, and Devin's 2nd Brigade as the reserves on the extreme left. The men of the 12th Illinois knew that this would be a dismounted action like Gettysburg, so they got behind whatever cover they could find and waited. The Confederates decided to preempt a Union offensive and attacked first, and Gamble's brigade was surprised and somewhat alone. The 3rd Indiana had been detached to destroy a small train of seven vehicles and so was out of this skirmish. The only mounted units involved were the 8th New York and the 12th Illinois.[7]

John Imboden, the Confederate cavalry commander who was in charge of the train, had chosen his ground well. "The town of Williamsport is located in the lower angle formed by the Potomac with Conococheague Creek," he wrote. "These streams enclose the town on two sides, and back of it about one mile there is a low range of hills that is crossed by four roads converging at the town. The first is the Greencastle road leading down the creek valley; next the Hagerstown road; then the Boonsboro road; and lastly the River road." Imboden circled his wagons, armed his drivers with spare rifles, and placed twenty-three pieces of artillery at regular intervals between the wagons. He then sent a force made up of seasoned infantry to move on the dismounted Federal cavalry on the Boonsboro road. A sharp fight resulted, but the carbine fire, with the Federal artillery of Calef's battery, did "excellent execution" and broke up the Rebel attack in short order. The 1st Brigade did incur some losses, including Major William Medill of the 8th Illinois, brother of Joseph Medill, publisher-owner of the *Chicago Tribune*. The 12th Illinois held its position until dark and then was relieved by Colonel Devin's brigade and sent back to its old headquarters of a year earlier at Jones Crossroads, Maryland. The men arrived at midnight on 6 July, dead tired. They were late getting into camp because of a delay caused when Kilpatrick's division was driven back in confusion toward Jones Crossroads from the direction of Hagerstown. It took about six hours to move a three-thousand-man combat brigade a distance of five miles; under Buford, cavalry normally traveled at about five miles per hour. Looking back on the failed assault on the wagon train, Buford admitted in his report that he was not able to destroy it–it was "too strong" for him–but he stated that at least he had given Imboden a thorough thrashing. The Confederate losses were almost four times larger than the Federal losses.[8]

After one day of rest the men of the 12th Illinois were in another major skirmish near Boonsboro. The Rebels continued to fight delaying actions to protect valuable horses and equipment and an ambulance train as they slowly moved back through Maryland to Virginia. In the Boonsboro action of 8 July the 12th Illinois once again fought dismounted. They seem to have done quite well, driving the enemy three miles on the Williamsport-Funkstown road while under intense artillery and musket fire. One historian noted that the success of Meade's strategy of pressuring Lee's army was "thanks largely to his horsemen." These actions were not without their costs for the Union cavalrymen, although Redman wrote that he came through without a scratch.[9]

Gamble reported that three-quarters of his brigade fought dismounted at Boonsboro, which seems to have been happening more and more. The horse is an excitable, reactive creature. It must be taught everything: to turn right and left, to ford a stream, to swim a river, to tolerate gunfire and other sounds of combat. The cavalrymen were beginning to discover the dangers of replacing their mounts with half-broken horses from the remount corrals near Giesboro, Maryland. They had little more than a day to teach them what they must know to save the life of the rider and to carry out the mission assigned. In a cavalry charge worthy of Joachim Murat, more animals would be used up than could be safely replaced. But horses were not the only concern of the men of the 12th Illinois. The regiment was drawing ammunition and expected to be sent to the front at any moment. If the men had known what awaited them, they probably would have requested, and Buford probably would have granted, the double the amount of ammunition that they normally carried.[10]

Near Funkstown, Maryland, on 10 July, the men of the 12th Illinois and the rest of the 1st Brigade endured a fierce preemptive strike by the retreating Confederates. The 1st Cavalry Division was advancing under Buford's command in its usual manner, this time with the reserve brigade on the right, the 1st Brigade in the center, and the 2nd Brigade on the left, when the Confederate horse artillery of Stuart's command opened fire. The dismounted Federal troopers continued their advance until they occupied the heights of

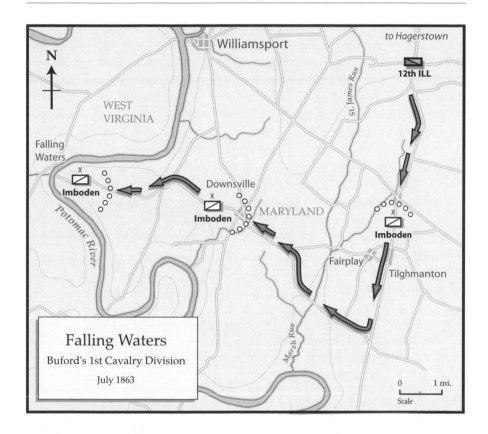

N

to Hagerstown

Williamsport

12th ILL

WEST
VIRGINIA

Falling
Waters

Imboden

Downsville

Imboden

MARYLAND

Imboden

Fairplay

Tilghmanton

Falling Waters

Buford's 1st Cavalry Division

July 1863

0   1 mi.

Scale

Funkstown. Lieutenant Calef worked his guns, returning fire and doing his best to cover the troops. The men advanced into the outskirts of the town and ran head-on into a well-prepared ambush by Stuart's cavalry with some of Jubal Early's infantry. The Rebels' purpose apparently was to contain the Federal cavalry by maintaining a screen until more Southern infantry arrived to occupy the entrenchments at Funkstown and to prevent an assault by the Army of the Potomac, which never came. Stuart maintained this screen until the bulk of the Confederate army could fall back to the ford at Falling Waters.[11]

During the Funkstown action the Federal cavalry fought until their ammunition was exhausted. By then their infantry support had come up and Gamble thought they could withdraw and resupply. But the infantry did not advance through the cavalry position or even occupy it; rather, without explanation they began to pitch tents and "commenced cooking and eating, in spite of repeated and urgent requests to the commanding officer of the infantry to occupy our excellent position and relieve us." The next day the infantry had to retake the position "with the unnecessary loss of several killed and wounded."[12]

Near Falling Waters on 14 July, another mistake in command judgment occurred. This would be the last chance to stop Lee before he crossed the Potomac and returned to Virginia. Major General Judson Kilpatrick and his cavalry brigade were assigned to capture the Confederate trench works at Falling Waters, where part of Lee's army was attempting to cross the Potomac. The 1st Brigade was in motion toward the enemy in the direction of Downsville from its camp near Bakersville. With the 12th Illinois in the lead, the 1st Cavalry Brigade marched rapidly toward Falling Waters on what is now Falling Waters–Natural Well Road in western Maryland. A division of Confederate infantry had occupied a hill that covered the ford and all approaches to it.

There was a weakness in their position, though, because the entrenchments did not cover both sides of the road and could therefore be flanked to the left, which Gamble set out to do with two brigades of the 1st Cavalry Division. His troopers were in the middle of their flanking movement when

> two small squadrons of General Kilpatrick's division gallop[ed] up the hill to the right of the rebel infantry, in line of battle behind their earthworks, and as any competent cavalry officer of experience could foretell the result, these two squadrons were instantly scattered and destroyed by the fire of a rebel brigade, and not a single dead enemy could be found when the ground there was examined a few hours afterward.[13]

Kilpatrick's foolhardy charge had alerted the Confederates, who saw that they could not hold the position and fell back to the ford before the 12th Illinois and the rest of the 1st Brigade could get around to their rear. The 1st Brigade, however, once again using dismounted tactics to the best advantage. They attacked the Confederates while they were withdrawing and captured about "511 prisoners, 61 of whom, together with 300 stand of arms, were turned over to an officer of Kilpatrick's division by mistake; also a 3-inch Parrott gun, captured from the enemy by the Eighth New York Cavalry, which was afterward sent by General Kilpatrick to the camp of this brigade, where it properly belonged." Still, the Rebels had escaped and were back in Virginia. Redman did not seem to think that the failed encircling movement was a great loss. He wrote his sister two days after the Falling Waters action and stated that the 12th Illinois "had been fighting . . . the Rebs for . . . seven days in all since he came into Pa." He thought that the Confederate army "has got enough of coming North." Redman ended his letter abruptly because "the saddle call has blown."[14]

Throughout the post-Gettysburg campaign, the men of the 12th Illinois had been rotated into the lead position time after time because of the intimate knowledge of northeastern Maryland and northern Virginia that they had gained from their service in the Railroad Brigade after their daring escape during the Antietam campaign in September 1862. Buford's division now began to move south into Virginia. On 18 July Abner Frank wrote that the 12th Illinois and the rest of the brigade had "crossed the Potomac at Berlin on pontoons and [ridden] through Lovetsville and encamp[ed] at about 10 o'clock at night."[15]

Reveille sounded at four o'clock in the morning on 19 July, and the brigade started out about four hours later, marching into Fauquier County, Virginia, and through Philomont to the village of Rectortown. There the column rested for about three hours before encamping about four miles farther on, deep in dangerous territory. The 1st Division was no longer in a part of the South where loyalties were uncertain. The people of Fauquier County were clearly "pro-sesech." Rectortown was right in the middle of "Mosby's Confederacy," and the Federals placed (and probably doubled) appropriate pickets for night security because of the guerrilla threat.[16]

Buford split his forces on 20 July in an attempt to take Manassas and Chester Gaps. Both of these mountain passes were in the possession of Stuart's cavalry, and sharp fights ensued. Gamble arrived at Chester Gap with his brigade, which included the 12th Illinois, at about 3:30 in the afternoon of 21 July. Gamble reported:

> About a mile from the Gap [on what is now the Appalachian Trail] our advance line of skirmishers encountered the enemy's pickets. I dismounted six squadrons, and drove the enemy pickets to the crest of the Gap on their reserve, which was found to consist of Picket's division of infantry, one regiment of Jones' cavalry, and a battery of six guns, occupying the Gap.

Gamble then saw, to his horror, that he had outdistanced his support—the nearest was twenty miles to the east. With only his cavalry and six guns, he easily could have been flanked and cut off from any possible line of retreat. Gamble ordered his force to fall back one-and-a-half miles and took position to cover the two available roads to Chester Gap: one leads toward Barbees Cross Roads, and the second (now Virginia Route 522) toward Little Washington and Sperryville. Gamble quickly sent off a note to Buford, stating that he had stopped Longstreet's column for a period of seven hours on 22 July. He also wrote that the next day Longstreet's corps was still passing through the gap with strong flankers, and that the Rebel army was moving on to Culpeper as fast as it could. He hoped that the Union army would move to cut them off.[17]

On the same day that Gamble sent his dispatch, Buford reported to Pleasonton that his men, the 1st Brigade, were holding their own, but that the entire 1st Division could not begin to hold Longstreet's corps coming from Front Royal through Chester Gap. There was no way that Buford's six pieces of artillery and seventeen hundred men with could hold fifteen thousand men and probably fifty pieces of artillery, especially because Longstreet, who had not been in favor of the Gettysburg campaign in the first place, was not about to be stopped at Chester Gap. Buford was realistic, and he made only a cursory delaying action in which the 1st Brigade, including all ten companies of the 12th Illinois, captured 23 prisoners, 84 horses, 12 mules, 654 beef cattle, and 602 sheep. The livestock had been on its way to the Rebel army at Chester Gap. Buford also captured the Rebel commissary agent and his son, who were in charge.[18]

Gamble's pickets reported at eight o'clock in the morning on 22 July that the enemy infantry was advancing in column on the road from Chester Gap to Sperryville. When the Confederates came within carbine and canister range—about three hundred yards—the 1st Brigade opened fire. Most of the Union men had Burnside carbines, and the artillery was firing case-shot rounds, which were hollow, cast-iron spheres containing lead balls and a small bursting charge, a good choice for between four hundred and fifteen hundred yards. As the Confederate infantry column came closer, the Federals used canister. Quickly, the Rebel infantry column fell back with its wagon train. It was George Pickett's infantry, which had been badly mauled in the grand charge on the third day at Gettysburg. With good cause, Pickett's men were very fearful of artillery that was firing case-shot and canister. Pickett left his skirmishers in place for the appearance of another attack, but decided against such a move. The men of the 1st Brigade were able to prevent Longstreet's Confederate corps from moving forward from Chester Gap until six o'clock that evening.[19]

In the late afternoon, Gamble's luck ran out. Longstreet, who was in overall command of the Confederate forces at Chester Gap and who always was one to use a flanking movement rather than a frontal assault, began to execute a turning movement against the 1st Cavalry Division. When Longstreet did this sort of thing, he always moved in force, using the topography for protection and woods for cover. Private Abner Frank wrote in his diary that a "brigade of Rebel Infantry flanked us on our left and drove us back about a mile." The attack was so sudden that Redman wrote to his sister Emeline that he had just finished a letter to their mother when the firing commenced. The letter Mrs. Redman received is about three lines long. It gives an indication of the constant danger the troops were in; Redman just wanted her to know he came through everything "alive and pretty well." He also wrote that they had "found the enemy in possession of the Gap."[20]

The men of the 1st Brigade, fighting mostly dismounted, slowly fell back in the face of the overwhelming numbers of the Confederate assaulting force. They fell back to Barbees Cross Roads and kept the vedettes on alert the rest of the night. They had to be alert. Not only were they deep in enemy country, but the 2nd United States Artillery, which was supporting the 1st Brigade, had received a shipment of faulty ammunition. In Gamble's words, only "about one shell in twelve would explode," and that one would explode prematurely over the heads of the troops it was supposed to protect. The fierce fighting ended that night. The Confederate soldiers slipped farther south, and the men of the 12th Illinois could bandage their wounds and tend to their horses.[21]

There are no official casualty reports for the 12th Illinois, and neither William Redman nor Abner Frank recorded a total. Colonel Gamble reported a total for the whole brigade in the actions at Gettysburg, Pennsylvania; Williamsport, Boonsboro, Funkstown, and Falling Waters, Maryland; and Chester Gap, Virginia, from 28 June to 31 July 1863. Twenty-five men were killed, 110 wounded, and 48 missing, for an aggregate total of 183 casualties. Many of the wounded men would soon return to action. Private William D. Clark was wounded during the fighting at Chester Gap on 21 and 22 July 1863. He received a flesh wound in the left thigh, and he was treated at the Cavalry Division Hospital, where the ball was extracted and a surgical dressing applied. He was placed on leave, then returned to the command on 8 October 1863.[22]

On the last day of July 1863, the commanding general of the Army of the Potomac, George Gordon Meade, issued orders reorganizing his army. Brigadier General John Buford remained in command of the 1st Cavalry Division; Colonel William Gamble still commanded the 1st Brigade, which included the 12th Illinois; Colonel Thomas Devin still headed the 2nd Brigade; and Brigadier General Wesley Merritt commanded the 3rd, or reserve, Brigade. Four companies of the 12th Illinois continued with the 3rd Indiana under the command of Colonel George Chapman. The rest of the 12th Illinois remained in the Tidewater under the command of Hasbrouck Davis. The 8th Illinois was under the command of Major John L. Beveridge. For the men of the 12th Illinois, then, Meade's changes were not very disruptive. The first of August saw the armies returning to familiar positions, with the Union army on the north side of the Rappahannock River and the Confederate army south of the Rapidan. Stuart's cavalry was vying with the Union cavalry under Buford and Kilpatrick for control of the land between the rivers; they probed each other's positions in an area familiar to both.[23]

The 12th Illinois Cavalry was on picket duty at Kelly's Ford, which they knew well, on 27 July. They stayed in their tents during a heavy thunderstorm on the 28th and 29th, rested and tended to their mounts on the 30th and 31st, and then "drawed 5 days rations and got orders to march" from Buford's staff. Ahead of them was a rather confused mission for the 12th Illinois and the men of the 1st Brigade. Buford's cavalry had been ordered to cross the Rappahannock and proceed to Culpeper to defend the rebuilding of the trestle on the Orange and Alexandria Railroad. Buford was unhappy to be facing a mission in the dog days of August on worn-out horses.

Buford advanced to Brandy Station and was attacked by a brigade of Jeb Stuart's cavalry on the afternoon of 4 August. Stuart's troopers were thrown back, this time having gained no usable information. Buford reported that "the First and Reserve Brigades behaved like heros." Abner Frank of the 12th Illinois agreed; he recorded in his journal that "the enemy advanced on our pickets and we were ordered out and drove them back to Brandy Station where we hauled [halted] our column and returned to our old camp." He added that "the enemy did not make their appearance" the next day, and the men stayed over in camp. Buford reported a "trifling" loss of men.[24]

The men stayed in camp from 5 August through 9 August, primarily because of the effect of the heat on the animals. The brigade rotated its pickets among the regiments everyday. When the men of the 12th Illinois were not on picket, they seem to have been used as a sort of replacement regiment, fulfilling any duties assigned to them. A couple of companies were detailed to go north to Centreville, Virginia, on the Warrenton turnpike to guard against guerrilla attacks. On 5 August, partisan forces captured a group of sutler's wagons near Fairfax and would have been gone with their booty, but "a portion of the Twelfth Illinois Cavalry lying in the vicinity, hearing the alarm, immediately gave chase, and succeeded in recapturing all, or nearly all, of the . . . stolen property."[25]

In mid-August the rest of the 12th Illinois, which had been in the Tidewater since the middle of May, came from Alexandria to the Kelly's Ford camp on the Rappahannock. Lieutenant Colonel Hasbrouck Davis, who had served at the Stoneman Raid and had been with the regiment off and on since Williamsport, again resumed command of the entire 12th Illinois Cavalry. Companies A, B, C, and D of the 12th, about 120 men, were detached from the rest of the regiment to form a bodyguard for General Buford. They left the Kelly's Ford camp and moved about a mile away to division headquarters. They were the security force for the division and followed the commander and his staff wherever they wished to go. The officers seem to have been spending a lot of time with Buford, planning for whatever was to come next. One soldier wrote that his security duties were demanding, and he hoped that the captain directly over him would return to command because he disliked having "to perform all of the duties and someone else receive remuneration" for his services. The trooper also wrote that at last the original colonel, Arno Voss, had resigned from the 12th Illinois. Voss had not been with the regiment very much since he was assigned to detached duty in Washington and elsewhere, and his men did not regret his resignation.[26]

Lieutenant Colonel Hasbrouck Davis was officially given command of the 12th Illinois in July 1863. Not everyone was happy about this. Captain George W. Shears had evidently had a disagreement with Davis as early as the Stoneman Raid, and when it became clear that Davis was going to return as temporary commander, and quite possibly permanent commander, Shears's feelings for Davis turned even more sour. On several occasions Shears made inflammatory statements about his commanding officer in the presence of other officers and enlisted personnel. He even went so far as to state that if Davis returned as commanding officer, he would not serve under him. Because of his actions, Shears was informed in August 1863 that he would face a general court-martial. He was charged with inciting a mutiny; it was one of the most serious charges of the Civil War.[27]

Because of Shears's combat record and his powerful letters of recommendation, including a letter from brigade commander Colonel William Gamble, one of Buford's most able and trusted subordinates, and because his civilian friends wrote to President Lincoln, Shears was able to obtain a court of inquiry before which he could try to clear his name. The court of inquiry was not a general court-martial, but a type of military grand jury that would ascertain whether there was enough evidence to justify a general court-martial. The inquiry was held intermittently in Washington during the months of August, September, and October 1863. Davis also asked for a court of inquiry to clear his own name. During that time, both Shears and Davis were temporarily relieved of their respective commands. From available records it appears that Shears refused to serve under Davis (and there is no evidence that Shears ever denied that charge) because of something that had happened during the Stoneman Raid in May of that year. At first glance, Shears seems to have been one of those officers who cannot get along with his superiors and cannot accept discipline. But Shears might have had a legitimate case.

In the personnel record of the regimental commander, Lieutenant Colonel Hasbrouck Davis, there is a letter written by Major Samuel Bronson from Yorktown, Virginia, on 14 May 1863. It is an appeal to the adjutant general, and later to Illinois Governor Richard Yates, to have Colonel Davis removed from command for abandoning most of the regiment in the field. The letter was written, according to Bronson, at the request of several officers of the regiment. It discusses the activities of the 12th Illinois after it was detached by Stoneman at Louisa Court House. The summary of Bronson's letter states that he

> complains of unmilitary conduct of Lt. Col. Davis, Comdg. Regt., during the Stoneman Raid;–abandoning one half his Command–going to a different ferry from where he ordered the rear to follow–leaving Walkerton Ferry, when only one half of his Command, their [sic] with him had crossed–marching so rapidly that many men were lost and abandoned on the road. Requests investigation, as early as possible.

The accuracy of these charges has never been established. The court of inquiry was dismissed in the spring of 1864, the officers in question returned to their respective units, and neither Shears nor Davis appears to have suffered sanction. Shears was allowed to resign with a clean record and was given a recommendation for reenlistment as a veteran in some other organization as soon as he settled a few minor debts with the quartermaster of the Army of the Potomac. He never reenlisted. He left the army and the state of Illinois to spend the rest of his life in the state of New York. Davis continued to command the 12th Illinois until the summer of 1864, when he was moved to brigade command. He was breveted a brigadier general on 13 March 1865 for gallant and meritorious service.[28]

Although it would be difficult to fault Davis for some of his actions (those at Tunstalls Station–not being at the front of the column–for example), he probably did use poor judgment in the countermarching orders and at both ferries. In hindsight, while he had no way of knowing he was being pursued, it might have been better for all concerned if Davis had kept his command together instead of separating the men. To scatter an already small command while deep in enemy territory has always been unforgivable for American officers. Still, nothing was done to Davis. It is possible that he was able to use the threat of a general court-martial as pressure to force Shears to resign. In order to cover himself, Davis had his second in command, Lieutenant Colonel Hamilton Dox, place a statement in his (Davis's) file indicating that Shears had resigned in early 1864 and that there was absolutely no truth in any accusation in the Bronson letter. Dox went farther, noting that almost every officer in the regiment was glad to see Captain Shears resign. The enlisted men seemed oblivious to the conflict between Davis and Shears. Redman, a member of Shears's command, does not mention the trouble in his many letters to his family. Neither does Abner Frank in his diary. The brief regimental history in the Illinois adjutant general's report also makes no mention of it.[29]

The 12th Illinois spent the rest of August 1863 near the Rappahannock

River at the camp at Kelly's Ford. For a combat cavalry unit on outpost duty in the middle of the war, the men experienced intense action, but only occasionally. There was almost no action in the closing days of August. The men of Company C of the 12th Illinois procured their food by foraging. Redman wrote his mother that the troops in his company—the commanding general's escort—went out to eat almost every day. Prices were high: chickens were fifty cents each, a quart of milk cost twenty-five cents, and everything else was accordingly expensive

> if we buy it. But we cavalrymen don't always buy. No, indeed we don't but sometimes we price what we want. Five of us boys priced a nice hog yesterday and made an old Secessionist give us all of the milk we wanted. I offered to pay in Rebel money but he would not take it. I gave him the privilege of taking his own money or none. Wasn't that fair? I think it was.

Redman knew that if the situation were reversed and the Rebel cavalry were in northern Illinois and had carried off all of his mother's hay, she would "talk pretty harsh" to them. He said he had taken a detail of men to procure hay from a Rebel citizen: "it was . . . hard to do," but he needed hay for his horses. He told "the citizens to either go south or north as their principles dictate and not stop near either army. Or I often tell them to take the Oaths of Allegiance and we will not bother them at all." He added that he thought that it would "be two or three Christmases" before he was able to "eat dinner with you at home." Redman closed with an interesting anecdote: A message had come through the lines "last night from Major General Fitzhugh Lee to our Captain Stephen Bronson complimenting our Company very much for the manner in which we have always used the people of Virginia." He did not say whether he or anyone else believed that Lee was being appreciative or sarcastic.[30]

On 27 August the men of Companies C and D were detached once again, this time from the entire division and the cavalry corps, and sent to be the personal escort of Major General Daniel Slocum, commander of the 12th Army Corps of the Army of the Potomac. Slocum was "quite an aged man and . . . a gentleman in every respect." Evidently Slocum remembered favorably that Company A of the 12th Illinois had been his escort earlier at Dumfries in the winter of 1862. The troops "all liked him well." Slocum gave each man a new suit of clothes that Redman considered to be worth twenty dollars, and the major always made sure his escort had enough food and was properly cared for. In this assignment ten men were required each day for guard duty. This meant that a soldier in this one-hundred-man detachment was only on duty one day out of ten. The men were glad for the assignment. As Redman wrote, there would be no combat, and the require-ments were to look good and be stylish. On the other hand, as August turned into September, the remainder of the troops of the 12th Illinois and their commanders complained about the excess of picketing, the long scouts, and the heat.[31]

One topic of discussion that summer was the units of black soldiers, or "Colored Troops." They had distinguished themselves in combat during the Vicksburg campaign, and in July the 54th Massachusetts, a black volunteer regiment, had engaged in the famous but suicidal storming of Fort Wagner on Morris Island in Charleston, South Carolina. A very supportive editorial appeared in the *Mount Carroll Weekly Mirror* about the enlistment and training of black troops, the editor admitting that the action at Fort Wagner had changed his mind. The opinions of the men of the 12th Illinois were less pos-itive. Old ideas and prejudices had not changed. In the fall Redman wrote that his company had employed an African-American man named George to act as a cook, and he described him as lazy, nasty, and "surely not worthy of his name." It is likely that most soldiers of the 12th Illinois Cavalry did not care whether blacks were slave or free; they had enlisted to save the Union.[32]

By the middle of September the troops were busy with something besides picketing and coping with the heat. Robert E. Lee had been weakened by the loss of Longstreet's corps, which he had sent to Georgia to help Bragg at Chattanooga. He fell back to the Rapidan, allowing Meade to occupy Culpeper. When Meade learned that Lee had sent an entire corps to Geor-gia, he detached two small infantry corps and sending them west under the command of Joseph Hooker. To see whether Lee's army was moving farther south as had been reported, Meade sent Pleasanton's cavalry to Raccoon Ford on the Rapidan. Meade also sent infantry in case Pleasonton got him-self into trouble. Pleasonton had been told not to "bring on a general en-gagement," but to make contact with enemy cavalry, to probe and harass and find out the movements of the Confederates. The action was supposed to start with a surprise attack on Stuart's cavalry at Culpeper, but that was botched because of faulty security on Meade's part. A medical doctor, a for-mer member of one of Stuart's regiments who evidently had access to north-ern lines, told Stuart of the impending movement the night before the at-tack, and Stuart was able to get his disabled horses and wagons out of the reach of Pleasonton's troopers.[33]

The Federals pitched into two Confederate cavalry brigades on 13 Sep-tember and drove them south for a few miles, then returned to their line of departure. On the following morning, the Federals once again advanced to the Rapidan, but they could not force a crossing in the face of A. P. Hill's in-fantry corps. There had been an almost continuous engagement from the

Rappahannock River to Raccoon Ford on the Rapidan, a distance of around twenty miles, and the fighting was intense at times.

On 14 September two brothers, Sergeant Napoleon B. Kemper and Private Thomas J. Kemper, were on the skirmish line of the 12th Illinois. The sergeant was hit by a miniball and fell. His brother went to his relief and was hit by a carbine round. They were both carried from the field. Surgeon Abner Hard of the 8th Illinois, the 12th's sister regiment, was the first medical officer called to see them, and he found that the ball had lodged in Sergeant Kemper's lung after fracturing a rib; it was a mortal wound. Private Kemper had been shot through the lung, so that his recovery was unlikely. Both of them were placed in an ambulance and sent to Culpeper with a number of other wounded men. The ambulance train was ordered to move slowly and to halt frequently so that stimulants could be administered. They had traveled three or four miles when at one of these stops Sergeant Kemper said to his brother, "I feel that I am dying. Surgeon Hard has said that I cannot recover, but before I go let us sing the 'Star Spangled Banner.'" Surgeon Hard wrote after the war that the two brothers rallied, raised themselves up, and sang in clear, distinct voices what is now the national anthem. After they completed the piece, the sergeant died. His brother, Thomas, was removed from Culpeper to one of the general hospitals in Washington. He lived only a few weeks more and expired there.[34]

Pleasonton moved again on 20 September, this time with a larger force of two divisions of cavalry, Buford's and Kilpatrick's. This time his mission was spelled out with precision. He was to reconnoiter from Madison Court House to Barnett's and Robertson's fords to determine the position and the numbers of the enemy, the conditions of the roads leading to the Rapidan, and "the character of the fords and of the ground on both sides where these fords cross the Rapidan, and the advantages such points afford for effecting a crossing in the face of the enemy." Buford, with the 12th Illinois, moved out at sunrise toward Gordonsville from Madison Court House, expecting to join Kilpatrick's division at the crossing of the Rapidan at Liberty Mills. At Jack's Shop, however, some distance north of the Rapidan, Buford encountered Confederate cavalry under Stuart. "The Confederates attacked at once."[35]

Buford, unable to contain his advance guard, also charged. While this skirmish was taking place, Devin's 1st Brigade, which was a part of Kilpatrick's command that had already reached Liberty Mills, was coming north to find Buford and ran into the back of Stuart's cavalry. As the rest of the 1st Brigade came up, Buford began to push forward. The Federal attack was successful, and Stuart retired from Buford's grip and crossed back over the Rapidan at Liberty Mills. From the viewpoint of the 12th Illinois Cavalry, which had been in the advance and had received Stuart's first charge and then had been rotated to the rear as fresh troops came up, the Rebels had "made no stand" in the "brisk skirmish." The 12th Illinois returned to camp on Raccoon Ford at nine o'clock that night.[36]

During the first week in October, Lee developed a risky plan to take the strain off of the Confederate Army of Tennessee. Following its stunning victory at Chickamauga Creek, the Army of Tennessee was surrounding Chattanooga and the Federal Army of the Cumberland. Outnumbered almost three to one, Lee hoped to achieve a surprising victory by marching around the right flank of the Union army. In order to make sure Robert E. Lee's movements were secret, on 9 October Stuart dispatched Fitzhugh Lee's division to hold Buford in place at Raccoon Ford. After one day, Buford realized that Fitz Lee was holding him so Robert E. Lee could slip around General Meade's flank in a move reminiscent of Lee's victory at Chancellorsville. Buford crossed the Rapidan in force below Fitz Lee's right to conduct reconnaissance. Lee attacked him immediately, and with the support of two brigades of infantry, he drove Buford from the Rapidan. Buford struggled to protect his supply trains–slow-moving wagons drawn by slow-moving draft animals–from falling into the hand of Lee's army.[37]

That area of central Virginia along the Rapidan was densely covered with scrub timber and vegetation. The riverbank slopes downward abruptly, so an offensive force on either side of the river is at a disadvantage. Buford needed to cross the river and buy time as he retreated to Stevensburg. Buford's men would have to repair Mortons Ford while the entire division and its artillery were crossing it. Buford was fearful that Fitz Lee and his Confederates were waiting and preparing to capture or annihilate Buford's entire command, so he first sent the 12th and 8th Illinois and the 3rd Indiana, now commanded by Colonel John Chapman, and two batteries of artillery across the ford to set up a blocking force along the north bank. They completed their preparations just in time. Almost immediately Fitz Lee's entire division came down on the men of the 1st Brigade, charging into the face of twelve pieces of artillery and two thousand carbines. The attackers were thrown back in confusion. Fitz Lee then advanced his infantry, but Chapman and the troops under his command simply withdrew toward Stevensburg. Their mission of covering the crossing for Colonel Devin's brigade had been accomplished.[38]

Lee pursued Buford to Stevensburg. A detachment of the 12th Illinois had been left to guard the division's forage, and as the Confederates who were following the main body came near, the men of the 12th Illinois set fire to the forage, which would have been invaluable to Stuart. When the 2nd Brigade connected with the 1st Brigade near Stevensburg, the two brigades were followed closely by Fitz Lee and his division. Buford decided to protect a number of Union supply wagons until they crossed Kelly's Ford on

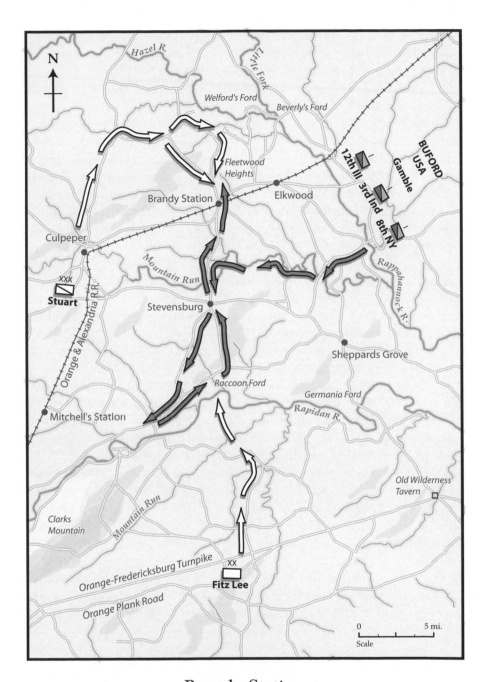

Brandy Station
Buford's 1st Cavalry Division
October 1863

the Rappahannock. The men of the 12th Illinois were forced to use long-range rifled muskets to engage infantry troops rather than the shorter-range cavalry carbines. They fought dismounted from behind very hastily prepared obstacles and were able to hold the Confederate infantry at bay until the wagons safely cleared the area.[39]

To the north of all of this, Stuart had been in combat with Judson Kilpatrick's division for most of the day. When he found Kilpatrick's men drawn up in line of battle outside of Culpeper, he knew how badly he was outnumbered, and he decided on a turning movement. He withdrew to the south, moving toward Kilpatrick's right and rear, which would place him above Fleetwood Heights on the old Brandy Station battlefield. Kilpatrick, assessing what Stuart was trying to do, headed to Fleetwood Heights. Stuart's and Kilpatrick's cavalries were in sight of each other on the converging roads, and the advance elements of their commands began to charge and countercharge. Buford's command, which included the 12th Illinois, arrived on Fleetwood Heights first, so his men had the advantage of elevation for their artillery. They were occupying the same high point Stuart had held during the First Battle of Brandy Station.[40]

But the Federals were by no means out of danger. Rebels were around them front, flank, and rear, and the Second Battle of Brandy Station ensued. While Buford's division was held in reserve, the brigade of George Custer of Kilpatrick's division led a series of attacks that gradually wore down the Confederates. Stuart attempted in the late afternoon to retake Fleetwood Heights, but he was unsuccessful. Soon after the Confederates withdrew, the Yankees moved across the Rappahannock to consolidate their lines. They returned the next day to find Fleetwood Heights unoccupied and were gratified that they could care for their wounded. Some of them had been abandoned the previous day and, as Buford wrote, they would have surely perished. Trooper Abner Frank of the 12th Illinois states simply that his division and regiment had fought all day and that one of his company was killed and four of his squadron wounded.[41]

Two enlisted men of the 12th Illinois were killed, nine were wounded, and four were captured or missing. The regiment lost twenty-one horses—its heaviest loss of men and horses on any one day in the war. The two men killed were the two Kemper brothers from Greene County, Illinois. The 12th's sister regiment, the 8th Illinois, suffered an aggregate of twenty casualties. Buford reported that in the four separate actions of the 1st Cavalry Division sixty enlisted men and three commissioned officers were captured.[42]

As planned, Lee took advantage of the distractions to move the bulk of the Army of Northern Virginia past Meade, who then hastily entrenched north of Bull Run, while the Confederates concentrated near Manassas Junction. After assessing the situation, "General Lee, mainly for logistical reasons, ordered a retreat to the Rappahannock." Lee's cavalry, under Stuart, covered his withdrawal. At the end of this Bristoe campaign, the men of the 12th Illinois were once again detached from the 1st Division and moved north. Day after day, they were stationed along the Warrenton turnpike to guard wagon trains that were supposed to supply Meade's army. Most of the Army of the Potomac moved slowly northward after Meade's army, and Lee always kept a respectful distance.[43]

On Tuesday, 26 October, a train of forty to fifty wagons was en route to Warrenton from the supply depot at Gainsville. Except for its two companies that were protecting Major General Slocum, the 12th Illinois was assigned to protect the wagons, and was aided by a sizable force of infantry and artillery. On the pike about two miles from New Baltimore, the Confederate partisan ranger John S. Mosby, commanding fifty men, attacked the train. He struck it in the middle because the escort was at the head of the wagon column and at its rear. Mosby unhitched more than twenty of the wagons and started them off. He was going to burn the rest when the men of the 12th Illinois arrived just in time to put an end to Mosby's raid. Abner Frank wrote that Mosby captured twenty-one wagons that night. Mosby's own report of the raid, written the day after it occurred, indicated that he got far more than twenty-one wagons; he also captured "145 horses and mules, and upward of 30 Negroes and Yankees (among them 1 captain)." Six officers, mostly infantry and none of them from the 12th Illinois, were sent into the Confederate lines as prisoners.[44]

From the first of November until Thanksgiving, the men of the 12th Illinois moved slowly toward Washington, camping where the night found them. For a seventy-five-dollar bonus, Abner Frank signed his name on 12 November to reenlist in what was called the veteran corps. "On the 20th of November it [the 12th Illinois] was formally relieved from duty with the Army of the Potomac, and ordered home to reorganize as Veterans. This distinguished privilege was awarded the Regiment by the Secretary of War, for 'brilliant services in the field.'" On 23 November members of the regiment turned in all their horses, and two days later they turned in their weapons. The following day they began the long trip home by train.[45]

CHAPTER SEVEN

Search and Destroy

The train that was carrying the men home for their first furlough since they had left for war stopped in Pittsburgh at about supper time, and the good citizens of the city fed the entire regiment. The 12th Illinois arrived in Chicago on 29 November. A cold front had just moved into the city, so rather than go out in bad weather, the 12th stayed overnight at the National Guard armory, and on 30 November the members took various trains for their homes in the northern and southern counties of Illinois. After about five weeks of rest at home, more than 80 percent of the regiment reenlisted. "At the conclusion of the brief season of rest the Regiment, which had been recruited up to the maximum number of 1,256 officers and men, reassembled at Camp Fry [on the south side of Chicago]." More than four hundred men were turned away from the 12th Illinois that winter, and most of them joined the 17th Illinois. By January most of the veterans had returned, and William H. Redman, acting as the orderly for his company, was busy making out muster rolls. He reported that the barracks at Camp Fry were "comfortable and pleasant." Redman went on to say that two men from Mount Carroll had left Camp Fry that morning to join a new cavalry regiment, the 17th Illinois.[1]

Shortly thereafter, Redman was granted a brief furlough home. He wrote that he had a good time in Mount Carroll and enjoyed seeing his friends at the seminary and in the community. It must have been a good week for Redman: as a sergeant he received a reenlistment bonus of $175. While in Mount Carroll he had an Ambertype—a photograph—taken, and he left it at P. Dulls at Lanark, Illinois, for his friends and family. No sooner had Redman returned to Camp Fry than he was placed on provost duty, arresting soldiers who could not control their consumption of liquor—"drunkards and City loafers" he called them—men who were drowning their troubles and fears about returning to combat.[2]

In February 1864 Redman wrote that the 12th Illinois Cavalry had marching orders to move the next day to St. Louis, Missouri. They were rumored to be Texas-bound. The barracks were in an uproar, the troops packing everything they could for the move south via rail. Once again Redman was detailed to provost duty to pick up the unwilling members of the regiment. He had to physically force one man back to camp, which resulted in a "[k]nock-down fight" in which Redman injured both hands. He reported that he was in such pain that if his condition did not improve by the next day it was time for "ambulance call."[3]

After staying in St. Louis for about three weeks during the month of March, the 12th Illinois was sent by steamboat down the Mississippi to New Orleans. During this time the regiment's horses were taken by General Grant's army, and the men were informed that they would remain dismounted for an unspecified period of time. This decision was promptly appealed to Major General Nathaniel Banks, commander of the Federal army in Louisiana. After hearing that the 12th had "been dismounted and their horses transferred to General Grant's army," Banks requested of Halleck "that the Twelfth Illinois Cavalry shall be immediately mounted and forwarded to New Orleans." When Halleck informed Grant of Banks's request, Grant responded, "mount them and forward them to Banks without delay." The 12th Illinois was to remain a cavalry unit for the duration of the war. The 12th Illinois was not returned to Virginia because the Army of the Potomac already had many veteran cavalry units, but General Banks was commanding the Red River campaign in Louisiana and was in great need of veteran mounted regiments.[4]

Redman wrote from Cairo, Illinois, to tell his mother that once again he was company orderly. The 12th Illinois was on the riverboat steamer *Edward Walsh* and was leaving from the levee of Cairo. He wrote that they had left St. Louis on 30 March and had traveled about two hundred miles. Like most of the river steamers during wartime, the *Edward Walsh* was heavily overloaded. The river was low, and quite often the boat would run onto sandbars. On the fourth day of April, the *Edward Walsh* docked at a former Confederate river fort named Fort Pillow, about fifty miles north of Memphis, Tennessee. The Federals had been in possession of Fort Pillow since the spring of 1862 and had garrisoned it with heavy artillery that manned by one regiment of black troops and two regiments of white infantrymen. The men of the 12th Illinois were in Fort Pillow only one night before they continued on down the Mississippi to New Orleans. Only eight days after they left, the most feared Confederate cavalry leader of the war, Major General Nathan Bedford Forrest, and his cavalry division captured Fort Pillow on a raid deep behind enemy lines and massacred a great number of the black troopers—after they had surrendered.[5]

The 12th Illinois arrived in New Orleans, the largest and most cosmopolitan city in the South, on 15 April 1864. The city had been a Union possession for almost two years. By the time the 12th Illinois arrived, the inept General Banks had already been humiliated at Sabine River Crossroads and Mansfield as well as at Pleasant Hill on 9 April. The 12th Illinois readied itself to go to Banks's aid as quickly as possible. Joining the 12th Illinois in New Orleans were the 2nd and 3rd Rhode Island cavalry regiments, followed later by the 2nd Maine, the 3rd Maryland, the 6th Massachusetts, and the 2nd New Hampshire, as well as the 11th, 14th, and 18th New York.[6]

The Illinois troopers had their pick of horses because upon their arrival in New Orleans the men of the 12th acted as the provost guard, and Banks told them to take whatever mounts they needed from the citizenry. The men of the 12th Illinois were fortunate in being able to acquire their mounts from the city's populace. Most cavalry regiments assigned to General Banks had to make do with whatever horses they could find. Redman acquired what he thought to be a trained mount, which he referred to as his "Gallant Steed." He wrote that it was a "splendid black horse," and he rode it to downtown New Orleans. As first sergeant Redman drilled the company during what little time was available, using foot drill in the morning and mounted drill in the afternoon. Most of the men who had horses that were less well trained than Redman's were able to get them under control by the end of the afternoon of the nineteenth. Drill was relentless, tiring, and difficult; the objective was to tire the animals so that the breaking period would be at a minimum. The veteran men of the 12th Illinois had learned the importance of well-rested and well-trained mounts.[7]

The men of the 12th Illinois didn't stay long in the Crescent City. By 19 April two companies had already departed northward on a steamer from New Orleans headed for the Red River. The remainder of the 12th Illinois, including Redman, would go on the first available packets.

On 21 April Redman began his "last steamboat ride . . . very likely for some time. We are going up Red River . . . to see what 'Johnny Rebbs' are doing with General Banks. We shall soon resume our place as a Regiment in the active field." He added that he wanted to do all he could to "clear the country West of the Mississippi River of traitors in Arms." With bravado, he wrote: "We will clean them out—yes, that we can do." The 12th Illinois encamped on the Red River just above Alexandria, Louisiana, on 25 April. Redman said he liked the camp and its warm days and cool nights, but that it was rumored that Rebels were all around them. They could hear artillery far off to the north. The men of the 12th Illinois were experienced in combat now, and they knew that before long guerrillas would fire into the regiment. Already Redman had distributed twenty rounds of ammunition per man "to be ready to use at a moment's warning. I have loaded my carbine and am ready to use it now."[8]

Word filtered to the men that Banks had been beaten yet again. His force, they believed, had never been strong enough anyway. As the Union commander for the region, Banks had an army of more than thirty thousand men to defend Alexandria. The Confederate force against him was commanded by Lieutenant General Richard Taylor, former brother-in-law of Confederate president Jefferson Davis and son of former president Zachary Taylor. Outnumbered five to one, Taylor had wrested control of almost all of northwestern Louisiana from Banks by using of turning movements and exploiting the low water level of the Red River. South and east of Alexandria there was constant fighting as Taylor tried to close off all the roads into the town and to shut down all of Banks's communications with Federal forces that might come to his aid.[9]

On 6 May 1864 Company C of the 12th Illinois was defending one of the roads (the rest of the regiment was being held in reserve). Taylor ordered skirmishers to dislodge the Yankee cavalry. The men of Company C charged, but the topography did not lend itself to a massed cavalry charge because the area, not unlike the country northeast of Upperville, Virginia, was crisscrossed with ditches that were six to eight feet wide. The troopers crossed the ditches then captured half of the Rebel skirmishers while under constant infantry fire. During the crossing Sergeant Redman survived what every cavalryman feared. His horse fell and pinned him underneath. Redman at first thought his left thigh was broken (it was badly bruised). With the assistance of one of the troopers who stayed with him, he was able to get the horse to stand, and he mounted it. In extreme pain, he rode off the field. The regiment charged onward, with Companies I and D coming onto the field to aid Company C.

> The Captain of Company "I" [William Luff] was shot through the head—the ball entering in his upper lip and coming out on the back of his neck. He is not dead and there is strong hope for his recovery. Sergeant Langley of Company "D" was shot through from breast to back and it is thought that he will live. Several of the regiment have been killed, and more wounded.

Luff was sent to an army hospital in New Orleans, where he underwent the first of eight reconstructive surgeries to restore his appearance. After the war he became a member of the Military Order of the Loyal Legion of the United States and spoke to many audiences about his experiences.[10]

According to Redman, the 12th Illinois was earning a reputation as the best regiment in the Department of the Gulf and Eastern Louisiana. Their experience in the Virginia theater was invaluable, but occupying Louisiana was a different matter altogether. The Southern citizenry in this area was far from starving. Most of the large plantations had a surplus of almost every-thing that a soldier would want: "Corn, Sugar, Pork, Beef-cattle, Potatoes and Vegetables . . . there is no end to cotton." Bale after bale of cotton fell into Union hands as a result of cavalry raids; most of it was destroyed. Red-man adds almost as an afterthought that the real injury to the Southern war effort was the flight of the slave-labor supply: the slaves would "generally pack up and follow our troops." But the soldiers were much more interested in a private from the 12th Illinois who "sent into camp three very fine silk dresses and two silk velvet capes . . . all of the best silk goods." Some of Redman's squad were so "lucky as to find money—gold and silver—others get valuable jewelry."[11]

But the enemy was always on the minds of the soldiers of the 12th Illi-nois. The Union troops, according to Redman, were experiencing just what Confederate general Richard Taylor wanted them to experience, the feeling of being surrounded and almost cut off. Nathaniel Banks's ineffective leader-ship and poor coordination between the army and the navy caused the dis-aster known as the Red River campaign.

When Banks's expedition finally reached safety after the Red River cam-paign, the war in Louisiana changed for the men of the 12th Illinois. Banks's offensive had been the last large-scale offensive in the state. From that point on the forces of both the North and the South would expend treasure and lives in small operations and would seek to win the hearts and minds of the civilian population of Louisiana. The 12th Illinois was stationed at Napoleonville, some seventeen miles west of the Mississippi River and about eighty miles above New Orleans near a large waterway known as Bayou LaFourche. Small steamboats plied the tributary and helped to keep the regiment supplied from its main base at New Orleans.[12]

From Napoleonville the 12th Illinois began to conduct wide tactical sweeps deep into enemy-held areas to root out suspected Confederate guer-rillas. Fighting guerrilla troops takes infinite patience and devotion to the cause, and it is usually better done by troops that have experience fighting insurgents. The men of the 12th Illinois had little experience with guerrillas. There had been a couple of incidents when they had to deal with Mosby in

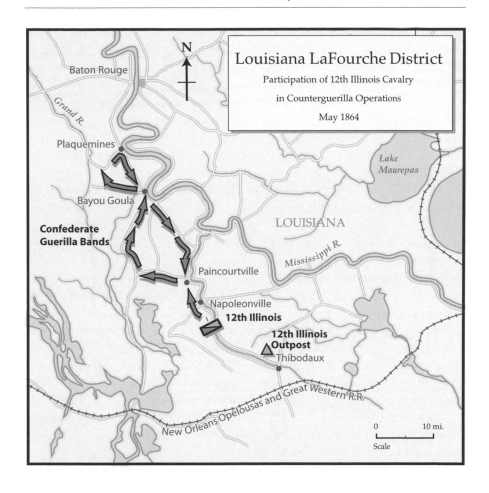

Louisiana LaFourche District

Participation of 12th Illinois Cavalry

in Counterguerilla Operations

May 1864

Fauquier and Loudoun Counties in Virginia, but they had seen little action that was not against regular Confederate forces.

The 12th Illinois slogged through the swamps of Louisiana in the summer and early fall of 1864, attempting to control a guerrilla-infested land. In this environment the men from northern Illinois operated almost as an independent unit, responsible for a certain amount of geography on a headquarters map. The outposts, base camps, and supply lines were targets of the guerrillas, and frustration levels grew. The function of the 12th Illinois and other mounted units was to appease the economically powerful elements of that part of Louisiana, the sugar planters and their buckra accomplices. The Federal troops were to try to restore order to at least part of one of the former Confederate states that was slated for readmission and reconstruction by the Lincoln administration.

It was punishing duty for cavalry. A year earlier, under John Buford, a wise and prudent general officer, the men and animals of the 12th Illinois had been carefully used and properly maintained. Buford knew the value of the horses and knew that they had to last. They had to be constantly watered in extreme heat and only pushed when life depended on it. For many days in the latter part of August 1863, the men of the 12th Illinois had lain idle because of the oppressive heat. They had survived and had performed well. But that was under Buford and in Virginia, which now seemed a different and faraway world. Compared to Louisiana, Virginia was cool and mild. Louisiana, particularly the southeastern part of the state, is warm and humid and does not cool off until November, and the men of the 12th were dressed in woolen uniforms and high leather boots, standard wartime issue. Also, they were coming off a winter furlough in frigid Illinois and were not acclimatized to the weather of the extreme South.

The men's letters home speak of the terrible climate, where putrefied fog rose from the ground, where the men were forever wet and their clothes never dried, where sleep and mosquitoes occupied much of their time. Redman wrote that the rain came every day and that as of the first of August it had rained for forty-five straight days. Sergeant Henry Richardson of Company H stated that "the Red River Campaign had been a hard expedition on man and beast." The regimental order books are filled with page after page of special orders warning of the dire consequences of riding horses in the cantonment area at any pace faster than a walk.[13]

Lieutenant Colonel Hasbrouck Davis, recently exonerated of all implications of misconduct in the court of inquiry for Captain George W. Shears, was sent to Louisiana in command of the 12th Illinois, then was given a brigade to command and was promoted to full colonel. Within his brigade the command of the 12th Illinois went to Lieutenant Colonel Hamilton Bogart Dox, previously the adjutant of the 4th Illinois Cavalry, one of the early Illinois mounted units. Dox appears to have been a totally different sort of man than Davis. The only similarity was that they were both born in the East, Davis in Massachusetts, and Dox in New York. Davis had a college degree and had attempted graduate study in Germany; Dox had little education. Davis was the son of "Honest John" Davis, a U.S. senator who later became governor of Massachusetts; Dox was a bank cashier in Chicago and had few if any political connections.[14]

The civilian population, except for the African Americans, was openly friendly but secretly hostile. Much of their hostility, of course, had to do with the conduct of the war and the unhappiness caused by the occupying army. The citizens hated General Banks, although their hatred for him was never as intense as their hatred for Major General Benjamin Butler, the preceding commander of the Army of the Gulf. Redman wrote home in late

Maj. Gen. George Stoneman (right) and Capt. George A. Custer, 1863.
(From Library of Congress [LC-B8171-7551, 215966])

Sabers and horsetack carried by 1st Lt. Edmund Luff, 12th Illinois Cavalry. Officers'
shoulder scales with fringe were used only on formal occasions.
(From the H. Edmund Luff Collection, courtesy of James M. May III)

Spencer Civil War Repeating Carbine. (From the Milwaukee Public Museum)

Burnside Third Model Carbine. (From the Milwaukee Public Museum)

Colt Model, 1860 Army Revolver. (From the Milwaukee Public Museum)

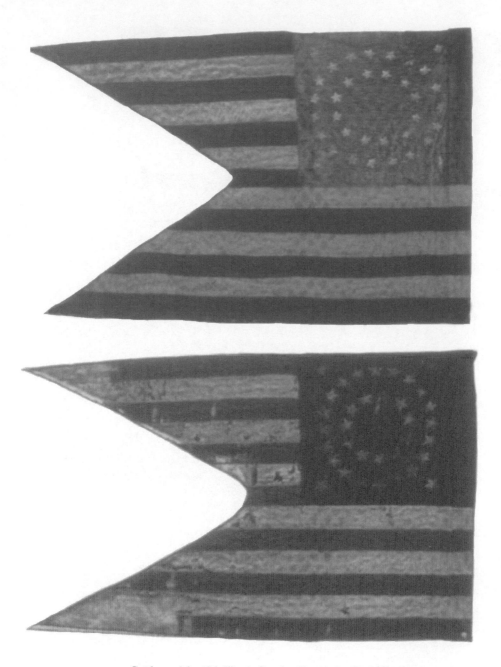

Guidons of the 12th Illinois Cavalry Companies E and F.
(From the Illinois Military Museum, Camp Lincoln, Springfield, Ill.)

12th Illinois Cavalry Regiment flag. (Courtesy of Doug Saloga)

Pontoon bridge crossing the Potomac River at Harpers Ferry,
used by the 12th Illinois, September 1862.
(From Harpers Ferry Association Collection, Harpers Ferry, Va.)

Battle near Upperville, Va., 21 June 1863; Ashbys's group in distance.
(From Library of Congress [LC-US262-15152, 217791])

Kelly's Ford etching. (From *Frank Leslie's Illustrated History of the Civil War*)

Etching of a Union cavalry charge including the 12th Illinois at Upperville, Va., 21 June 1863.
(From Library of Congress [LC-US262-7028, 217791])

May and early June that Banks took good care of the people of New Orleans whereas Butler had taken away from the rich citizens of New Orleans and the surrounding areas to give to the poor, both white and black. The 12th, like almost every other Illinois unit, looked down upon the black populace, in spite of the fact that they kept the Federal troops informed, and therefore alive, during those trying months. Redman indicated that Rebel patrols constantly harassed the outposts of the 12th Illinois and other units and that most Union men were tired of standing by and taking that sort of abuse. The men from northern Illinois had a reputation in the Army of the Gulf for being aggressive and for taking the initiative rather than sitting idly while becoming victims of the heat and rain of the malarial swamps.[15]

In the first week of August the men of the 12th Illinois Volunteer Cavalry had their chance to fight back. With a dozen or so men from Companies L and I Captains Frederick W. Mitchell and R. L. Houck decided to make an unauthorized raid on their own responsibility. They planned to try to penetrate territory far enough north to verify or disprove rumors that Confederate guerrillas were preparing to attack the outposts at Thibodaux and then New Orleans. Davis gave the captains "verbal permission" but nothing more because "the country was said to be full of Texan guerrillas" and he did not wish to lose any more troops.[16]

The men of the two companies "were splendidly mounted on picked horses" and were armed with the new seven-shot Spencer repeating carbines that were until then "unknown in that country." The weapons fired a large-caliber bullet with a heavy powder charge. They rarely jammed, and they gave the two companies of 120 men the firepower of nearly the same firepower as a full regiment of 600 troops firing single-shot breech-loading carbines. The men of Mitchell's detachment moved mostly at night and stayed off the main roads. They visited a plantation about ten miles from their base camp and walked into the middle of a party that members of the local gentry were giving for some Rebel raiders. Upon the arrival of the Federals, the Confederates "abandoned their horses and equipment," everything but their side arms. During the melee, one of the women ran between a man of the 12th Illinois and her husband, a Confederate soldier. A bullet fired from one of the Spencers cut most of her "hair . . . from her head . . . as if by a razor, although she herself was uninjured."[17]

Shortly after the skirmish at the plantation, slaves informed the two Illinois officers that a "Rebel captain was visiting his family" at a nearby plantation. Both Houck and Mitchell brought their entire detachments cross-country in the middle of the night, surrounded the place to prevent the Confederate officer from escaping out doors or windows, and knocked on the front door. A very young woman answered the door and allowed them in to search the house. They found nothing except "a very old woman sitting by the fireplace . . . her head bandaged, and evidently in great pain." Mitchell bade his host good-bye and was about to leave when the young woman made an uncomplimentary remark. As he went out into the night, Mitchell turned and replied:

> "Madam, we are after larger game than guerrilla captains, and have no men to spare to send back a prisoner to our camp, but tell your husband when he next visits you and desires to escape capture not only to cover up his uniform but his spurs as well."
>
> She impulsively held out her hand and said: "God bless you! Yankee captain though you are. Whatever your motives, God bless you. We have been married but a month and he is grievously wounded and he swore he would never be taken alive."[18]

During the expedition, both Mitchell and Houck became concerned about being caught by partisans. At four o'clock one morning, 6 August 1864, after Mitchell's pickets had been harassed all night, Mitchell and his raiders departed and pushed farther into the Teche country. After covering twenty-five miles through the bayous, they stopped for lunch and were nearly ambushed by a party of guerrillas, but the Confederates made the mistake of hitting the front picket, a sergeant and two men, instead of the main body. A brief firefight ensued in which the firepower of the Spencer carbine was the deciding factor. One Rebel was wounded and another, an officer, killed. In the officer's jacket "was a roll of $70,000 in United States greenbacks." The next day, Mitchell was told that the guerrilla party had been raiding the entire county for more than three weeks and collecting all the Federal money available, probably to buy weapons and war materials. That day, Sergeant Richardson of Company H wrote, the expedition got into several skirmishes, including one in which "a miné ball came near enough to scrape the dirt off my fingers, scarcely missing my ring." The 12th Illinois drove the Confederate skirmishers until sundown.[19]

Two days later, on 8 August, the men of the 12th Illinois arrived at Plaquemines Parish, near an artillery base camp close to the Union lines. They had started to unsaddle their mounts for a well-deserved rest when they were told that several members of their regiment who were acting as couriers, and therefore were unarmed, had been ambushed and butchered by Confederate guerrillas. Mitchell rode hard to intercept the foe, but he found that the local inhabitants claimed no knowledge of the deed, and the guilty had taken to the swamp. Mitchell eventually questioned "an old Frenchman," who indicated that he was a member of the Masons (as was Mitchell) and that one of the couriers from the 12th Illinois, also a Mason, had been seriously wounded and had crawled to his home for help. Men in the Union regiments who were Masons often had the fraternal emblem sewn onto the sleeve of their uniform in the hope that if they were wounded or injured in hostile territory, the ancient society's fraternal oaths of faith, hope, and charity would transcend the political differences that caused the war. In this case, the poor soldier did not live to see another day, but at least the guerrillas had not ended his life. After the Confederate guerrillas had shot the courier from his horse, they saw him drag himself to the old man's house, and they pursued him. The old man stepped in and humiliated the Confederates in their effort to kill the mortally wounded man, and he was able to obtain a few hours of relative peace for him. The courier was probably twenty-one-year-old Private Edwin Snow of Company H. Snow was originally from Chicago and had enlisted in December 1863 during the recruiting drive that the 12th Illinois had held after returning from the eastern front that year.[20]

After a few more days of scouting the search-and-destroy mission came to an end, and the men of Mitchell's and Houck's commands returned to their base camp. The mission had ended well for most of the men. Trooper Charles Rose wrote to his father that at the end of Mitchell's foray "every man got a silver 50- or 25-cent piece. Some got Meerschaum pipes, some splendid boots, clothing and razors" from the captured Rebel soldiers. The razors and pipes were not army issue; they had been requisitioned from private citizens.[21]

Then a curious and deadly sequel ensued. A report reached the commanding officer at the Union garrison at Thibodaux that a large guerrilla force hiding in the nearby swamp was about to attack. The commanding officer authorized a preemptive strike. Heading up the mission was a Captain Robert Lawson and a large detachment of more than one hundred men from the 1st Indiana Cavalry. That command clattered into the base camp of the 12th Illinois two days after Mitchell's expedition had returned, and Lawson showed Mitchell the orders that directed him to search the surrounding country for Rebel guerillas. Captain Mitchell said that what they were proposing was a useless and stupid assignment; he and Captain Houck had just returned from "penetrating the rebel lines scouring the country for over a hundred and fifty miles with about a dozen men." They "had used every means in our power to provoke a fight" with the Confederates they had met, but the Rebels had been rather passive. Only a few were what Mitchell described as a "cowardly murdering set," and he would "take ten picked men and camp [overnight] anywhere within that radius" without fear of reprisal.

The Indiana captain replied that his orders were imperative and he was to rout out the Rebels, particularly if there was a Confederate base camp on

Lake Natchez. Mitchell replied, "Why that is but ten miles distant, and we ride down there every few days. We camped there night before last and there isn't a rebel force within a hundred miles."[22]

Captain Mitchell decided to go have a look himself, and he and his command headed to Lake Natchez. At midnight the following day the men of the 12th Illinois were awakened by intruders who proved on close inspection to be members of Lawson's command. They reported that they had been bushwhacked at night while in camp and that many of their number had been killed or taken prisoner. During the day, about twenty or more men came straggling into camp telling the same tale. The men of the 12th immediately made ready, and when "Boots and Saddles" was sounded, about eighty troopers commanded by Captain William J. Steele of Company C started for Lake Natchez. They scattered the Confederate force with little difficulty. Some of the Rebels fled "into the swamps," and others escaped into their boats and rowed for their lives across the lake. The Federals then returned to their own base camp.

The next day, Captain Lawson reached the 12th Illinois in what Mitchell called "a most wretched condition, half starved and completely heart broken" over his loss of men and material. Lawson said that he had been surrounded and overwhelmed. He and a few men had made it into the swamps, and some had been captured. Mitchell later wrote that not one "of the captured has ever been heard from." Lawson said he knew this was the end of his military career, that he had taken "every military precaution" against attack, and yet "no officer could explain away such a disgrace."[23]

Mitchell, who had been entirely wrong about the presence of a Rebel force, said that he felt responsible for the man's fate and that if Lawson was court-martialed, Mitchell would stand in his defense. About a week later, in the middle of August, Mitchell received a letter from Lawson saying that he was indeed under arrest. He wanted Mitchell to act as his counsel at Thibodaux. Mitchell had no legal training, but that did not seem to bother Lawson, who said that Mitchell was the only one who knew all the facts. Mitchell agreed to represent him. He began to interview witnesses and found that Lawson was exceedingly popular with his men. None, including the six men on picket who had somehow survived the Rebel onslaught, blamed their commander for the surprise attack. Lawson had posted fifteen men on guard that night and had given them standing orders to assume that an attack would take place at any time and to conduct themselves accordingly, to "shoot first and inquire afterwards."[24]

During the trial a Confederate prisoner of Captain Steele's expedition made it known to Mitchell that he wanted to see him on a matter of grave importance. Mitchell sent for the Rebel, who commented that he could not stand to see "any man . . . disgraced without cause." Mitchell placed him on the stand, and the Rebel stated that his own command of more than five hundred men had heard tell of a body of enemy soldiers, which may have been the earlier expedition by the 12th Illinois raiding through the Teche. They had organized an expedition not only to apprehend the raiders but also to get the fine-blooded horses that they understood had been given to the Federals by General Banks, who had taken the mounts from the citizens of New Orleans. The Rebel captain had ordered a dozen of his troops to act as scouts and to attempt to find the location of Lawson's troops and pickets, which they did. When the attack came, most of Lawson's command appeared to be surprised. However, the officers of that command were able to "cut their way out, using only their naked sabres." After some searching, Mitchell found other Rebel prisoners who substantiated the story and testified that Captain Lawson had taken every possible precaution.[25]

When Mitchell rested his case, he believed that his client would be fully exonerated. He was distressed to find that the court approved Lawson's sentence of dismissal from the service and "a forfeiture of all pay and allowance." Lawson was forbidden to "again hold a commission" during the war. Also approving the sentence was the commanding general of the cavalry, Albert Lee. Captain Lawson appealed to General Nathaniel Banks, who reviewed the case and overturned the findings in what Mitchell called a "scathing reprimand to the president and members of the court as well as to the commanding general [and] ordered Captain Lawson to be returned to full duty at once, and the proceedings of the court to be set aside."[26]

The men of the 12th Illinois were beginning to be worn down by the harsh Louisiana environment. The notes from the regimental record books at this time detail morale problems arising in the regiment. The problems were visible in two major areas: the care and exercise of horses and the desertion of troops. Many troops in the 12th Illinois appear to have had enough of the war, particularly by the late fall of 1864. Rumor had it that many Federal units had already been sent home. Most of the soldiers seemed to feel that they had made their contribution and deserved to be discharged instead of being sent on pacification missions or getting involved in garrison duties. They began to care less and less about the proper care and maintenance of the mounts on which a horse soldier's life might depend.[27]

As the troops passed the time, elections were one topic of interest. Those who remained in the field voted in the November elections at polling places constructed in rear echelon areas. Redman indicated his preference in a letter he wrote to his mother while he was recovering from malaria. As early as mid-September, he had decided that he would not vote for George B. McClellan, Lincoln's opponent in the 1864 presidential election, "for he is supported by all the Copperheads. . . . I do not approve of all Lincoln has done; but I should prefer him to either of the others." A month later, less than three weeks from the election, Redman wrote that he did not believe that McClellan personally was a traitor and thought "he was loyal to the government." However, he would have to vote for Lincoln and Johnson (on the Union Party ticket) because he believed that the platform of the Democrats was "shrouded with treason." He also felt that if McClellan were elected, the war would be continued; and if that were the case, the men of the 12th Illinois would have to stay in the army.[28]

Back at home in Illinois, McClellan was given his proper due in the newspapers, which printed his acceptance of the 1864 Democratic nomination on the front page. Neither McClellan nor Lincoln, though, was garnering editorial support in northern Illinois that year. As if to marginalize any political impact that McClellan's nomination may have had, the *Waukegan Weekly Gazette* printed a letter from General Ulysses S. Grant on the Virginia front suggesting that what was left of the famed Army of Northern Virginia

> was young boys and old men. A man lost by them cannot be replaced. They have robbed the cradle and the grave equally to get their present force. Besides what they lose in frequent skirmishes and battles, they are losing from desertions and other causes at least one regiment per day. . . . With this drain on them the end is not far distant if we are only true to ourselves. Their only hope is a divided north. This might give them reinforcements from Tennessee, Kentucky, Maryland, and Missouri, while it would weaken us.

The men of the 12th Illinois had no desire to remain in Louisiana, and they saw no reason for being there. After all, it had been almost a year since their last leave. It was true that they appeared to be needed in Louisiana, but the war there was not a cavalry war. What mounted force was needed, as Banks had stated earlier, was being taken from former infantry units.[29]

In late November 1864 the 12th Illinois was involved in its final major combat operation in Louisiana. On 22 November the 12th Illinois and other mounted units received notice that a raid against the Confederates was imminent. The objective was to destroy the Mobile and Ohio Railroad, one of the last of the Confederate railways. The raid commenced on 27 November and lasted until 13 December. According to Redman it did very little damage and was a waste of time.[30]

The journey to Mobile had been long and arduous. The raid had begun at Baton Rouge and had targeted the Mobile and Ohio Railroad. The line of march led the column through eastern Louisiana and southern Mississippi, down the west side of the Pascagoula River to East Pascagoula Bay through very poor country. The men called the expedition their "sweet potato" raid because they ate "sweet potatoes instead of bread." There was little to scavenge, just small patches of corn and sweet potatoes. It rained heavily during the mission, which made the march slow. The column consisted of nearly four thousand men and artillery and included a pontoon bridge train. The raid into the area around Mobile failed, and the army returned west. The southern Mississippi roads, never good in the best of times, were so poor after three years of war that the cavalry troops were pressed into service to build corduroy roads after the wearisome expedition.[31]

On 17 December, the men of the 12th Illinois boarded a steamer on Mississippi's gulf coast for New Orleans, and they fought seasickness and mosquitoes during the voyage. Morale was sagging, and many troopers whose enlistments were expiring were being mustered out and sent home. Redman wrote to his sister Emeline that his company had lost twenty men to mustering out alone—three sergeants, two corporals, and fifteen privates. In Louisiana the regiment had lost twenty-seven men to disability, thirty-seven to desertion, three who had died in action, and forty-five who had died of apparent malarial fevers.

The remaining troops, tired and spent, plainly were not in the mood to return to service in Louisiana, and the horses were exhausted. Colonel Davis appealed to General Banks of the Department of the Gulf to have the regiment transferred to Tennessee. In response to Davis's appeal, Banks ordered the 12th Illinois to Memphis in late 1864. Redman wrote his mother from Memphis, "Hail the distance lessens between us. May it soon diminish to nothing." Many of the members of the 12th Illinois Volunteer Cavalry believed that the transfer would lead to an early end to their service. Maybe they would get back to Illinois in time for the Christmas holidays.[32]

CHAPTER EIGHT

From Tennessee to Texas

When the 12th Illinois Cavalry arrived in Memphis, Tennessee, in January 1865, it was a seasoned veteran unit that had fought in three theaters of the war. Now their experience would be tested, for in these last months of the war the 12th Illinois would again be called on to perform what had become familiar work, counterguerrilla operations. The composition of the 12th Illinois had changed. It had been consolidated from ten companies to eight by Special Order Number 92. Added to the 12th was the remainder of the 4th Illinois Cavalry. The 4th Illinois was a much older organization that had been made up primarily of men who had served in the war much longer than the men in the 12th and who were being discharged and sent home as their enlistments were completed; the remaining men of the 4th no longer qualified as a full regiment.[1]

On 28 January 1865, after they had been in Tennessee for only a few weeks, 260 of the 12th Illinois were involved in a lengthy raid into southeastern Arkansas and northeastern Louisiana. Commanding the expedition was Colonel Embry Ostend of the 3rd U.S. Colored Cavalry. The expedition, composed of 2,600 cavalrymen, was sent into Arkansas and Louisiana to secure the cotton that might otherwise be sold by what was left of the Confederate government in those states. It was also to destroy any property that might be owned by or leased to the Confederate government. The raid was a complete success. The Confederate units that were supposed to confront Ostend's force had either already been stripped of strength or were so lacking in serviceable mounts that meaningful resistance was impossible. The men of the 12th Illinois made no significant contribution to the expedition except to endure the constant rains, overflowing bayous, and intense cold. They returned to Memphis on 12 February 1865.[2]

Southwest Tennessee had been under Federal control for more than three years, a fact that should have been of great comfort to the men of the 12th Illinois. Such was not the case, however. There had been raids all around Memphis throughout the war, a large number of them conducted by the most successful and the most feared of all the Confederate cavalry commanders, Lieutenant General Nathan Bedford Forrest. But no one knew where Forrest was during the early months of 1865. All Federal commands were under a standing order to be in readiness because no one knew when Forrest would strike.

In January 1865 Forrest had moved his headquarters to Verona, Mississippi. In March, he had moved them again, this time to the small town of West Point. He had two cavalry divisions. The first, led by General James Chalmers, numbered 3,648 men organized in three brigades, each led by a veteran commander and a battery of artillery. Forrest's 2nd Division, led by General William H. Jackson, a graduate of the U.S. Military Academy, also was made up of three brigades with combat proven commanders and a battery of artillery. In March Forrest attempted to organize a third Confederate division under Brigadier General Abraham Buford (a cousin of Federal cavalry commander John Buford, who had succumbed to typhoid fever in December 1863), but the unit was never fully formed. Many of the units that were to make up the third brigade either were independent commands or were not assigned to Forrest's command for various reasons. Massed together these Confederate formations probably numbered over five thousand men, more than a match for the detachment to which the 12th Illinois was assigned, which comprised slightly over 2,600 men under John P. C. Shanks.[3]

In addition to Forrest's two divisions, there also were the bushwhackers. Toward the end of the war, with the demise of the Confederate government in the southern states and the dissolution of the Confederate army, massive numbers of former slaves had begun to move toward Union garrisons. The end of the Confederate government and the creation of the Freedmen's Bureau in 1865 had served as the impetus for poor southern whites to create numerous quasi-guerrilla bands. Some of the bands had formal alliances with Confederate commanders, and others, called bushwhackers, were allied with no one. All partisan bands had become increasingly vicious by the spring of 1865, but the bushwhackers were the worst. Forrest did not officially sanction their raids. On the day that he was promoted to lieutenant general, he declared in an order to his brigade commanders that "the illegal organizations of cavalry prowling through the country must be placed regularly and properly in the service or driven from the country. They are, in many instances, nothing more or less than roving bands of robbers, who consume the substance and appropriate the property of citizens without enumeration." Not even the warning from the no-nonsense Forrest, though, could end the continual harassment from the bushwhackers.[4]

During the end of February and the beginning of March, the 1st Iowa Cavalry was detailed to send out a roving patrol of three men beyond the cavalry picket line east of Memphis. The patrol stopped at a house about a mile from the Union line and was rushed by three bushwhackers. A quick firefight ensued, and one of the Iowa men was injured. His fellow troopers tried to help him and all were captured. They were taken to an undisclosed place, stripped of all of their clothing, and shot, once through the mouth and once through the temple. After the bodies were recovered by the morning patrols, they were brought back to Memphis, where the fallen men's comrades viewed the mutilated remains. William Redman observed that all three men were new recruits; veteran soldiers, he thought, never would have allowed themselves to be captured by bushwhackers.[5]

Intelligence reports placing Forrest near Memphis and a desire for vengeance precipitated an order for a reconnaissance in force. A detachment of the Federal Cavalry Division around Memphis would begin the reconnaissance during the first week in March 1865. The members of the 12th Illinois were given orders to be ready to move at a moment's notice. They were to prepare two days worth of rations and be ready to leave Memphis on the morning of 3 March. A rumor was circulating around the 12th Illinois's camp that they were to take no Rebel prisoners, that any Union soldier found taking a Rebel alive would be executed by his own company commander.[6]

The 12th Illinois was involved in the expedition. Since its arrival in Tennessee in February, it had become part of the Post and Defenses Brigade of Memphis under the command of Major General Cadwallader C. Washburn. The cavalry division to which the 12th Illinois was assigned was commanded by Colonel Embry D. Ostend, who had led the 12th into Arkansas and Louisiana in January. There were three full brigades in this cavalry division, and a sizable artillery battalion. The 12th Illinois was assigned to the 2nd Brigade, commanded by Colonel William Thompson. The 1st Iowa also was assigned to the 2nd Brigade, along with the 11th New York, to which the 12th had been attached during the boat ride up the river from Louisiana to Memphis.[7]

As the column prepared to leave Memphis, the overall command of the expedition was given to Colonel John P. C. Shanks of the 7th Indiana Cavalry. The troops of the expedition were organized as the 1st, 2nd, and 3rd

Brigades, which were much smaller than typical brigades. Many of the regiments making up the brigades for this mission were only detachments. The 2nd Brigade, formerly commanded by Thompson and now headed by Colonel Hasbrouck Davis of the 12th Illinois, was what is known as a shell brigade. The total strength was "38 officers and 994 men," about one-third the size of a wartime cavalry brigade. The 12th Illinois Cavalry Regiment was commanded by its executive officer, Major Hamilton B. Dox. Its strength of 228 men on this operation did not represent the regiment's total enrollment; the remaining men had been left as security around Memphis. The 12th Illinois had left New Orleans earlier in the year with more than six hundred officers and men.[8]

Mindful of security and the nearness of Forrest, whose division was thought to be south of Memphis at Verona, Mississippi, the Union cavalry division moved east to Germantown, leaving a small detachment at Whites Station. Patrols were sent out in all directions, paying particular attention to roads leading to or from the Memphis and Charleston Railroad. Once there, using Germantown as the eastern base, the formation encamped at the other points of the compass: the 1st Brigade south of Germantown, the 2nd Brigade north, and the 3rd Brigade west. Every home in Germantown had a military guard. At four o'clock in the afternoon Colonel Ostend arrived with forage for the animals.

On 4 March the command remained in camp because of unrelenting rain. At five o'clock that afternoon Shanks sent a detachment of the 12th Illinois back to Memphis because their horses were in bad shape. He also sent back a detachment of the 3rd U.S. Colored Cavalry, apparently because they feared a repeat of the massacre at Fort Pillow almost a year before. Then, with one day's forage and ten days' rations having been issued, the remaining 2,700 troopers marched southeast from Germantown on the Collierville Road. The division camped one mile southeast of Collierville at the widow Brown's farm that night.[9]

Like the late John Buford in the East more than a year before, Shanks frequently rotated his brigades from front to rear so they would share the responsibility of the advance. On 5 March 1865 the 3rd Brigade was with the 2nd Wisconsin in advance of the entire division. At Mount Pleasant they saw the first Confederates. Major James DeForrest's battalion scattered a small detachment of about ten men, who swam their horses across the Coldwater River to escape. The Union division went into camp early "one mile southeast of Lamar Station on the Mississippi Central Road at six P.M. on the farm of A. C. Treadwell. The distance marched was twenty-four miles." The route taken was southeast by "way of Mount Pleasant and Salem." The division had marched over very muddy roads and had moved quite slowly.[10]

On approaching Ripley, Shanks received information that one of Forrest's subordinates, Colonel Edward Crossland, and his Kentucky Brigade, estimated at five hundred to two thousand men, were in town preparing to move southward to West Point to join Forrest. Shanks moved to intercept Crossland but found Ripley absent of any soldiers except for a recruiting detail; Crossland had left Ripley some thirty hours before with his command, which was re-estimated to number three hundred men. Once he reached Ripley, Shanks was close to the route Major General Samuel D. Sturgis had taken in June 1864 in pursuit of Forrest.

Turning south from Ripley, Shanks continued the march through piney woods that were devoid of any food or fodder. At the end of the day on 6 March, Shanks's raiding column encamped, taking great care to be prepared for attack. Particularly because Forrest's knowledge of the roads was superior to that of any Union detachment, Shanks saw the need for tight security. He placed "the First and Second Brigades in an excellent position on the southwest side of town [Ripley], the Third Brigade on the northwest, controlling roads on which troops would enter from Kentucky or Tennessee." He scattered his scouts across the area. On Oxford Road to Holly Springs Crossing he placed scouts for a distance of fourteen miles. "On Cotton Gin Road to Kelley's Mills and across the Tallahatchie River on the right and left banks for a distance of twelve miles. On Guntown Road to the Junction of Baldwyn Road eighteen miles. On the road north of town, from eight to ten miles I had a guard placed at every house in the town."[11]

On 7 March Shanks detailed a detachment of about fifty men from the 4th Illinois to destroy a section of track on the Mobile and Ohio Railroad from Booneville to Baldwyn, but they learned that Union Major General George H. Thomas and Lieutenant General Forrest had reached a truce, agreeing to let the track be used to carry corn to the citizens of northeast Mississippi. After 8 March the command saw few Rebels, but they kept a tight security detail wherever they camped. They tried to secure enough forage to keep the animals strong enough to return to Memphis. Shanks soon decided that further operations were impossible in the washed-out countryside of northeast Mississippi and that the best thing he could do "was to return his command in the best condition possible."[12]

On 8 March, while they were on their way back to camp, a party of the 12th Illinois Cavalry's Company E, under First Lieutenant Edson D. Pratt of Michigan City, Indiana, swam the Tallahatchie "and drove a party of twenty or thirty Rebels out of New Albany without loss." The entire command recrossed the Wolf River at La Grange, Tennessee, and arrived back in Memphis on 12 March. The northern Illinois men brought back twenty or so prisoners and several animals. Sergeant Redman of the 12th Illinois had been

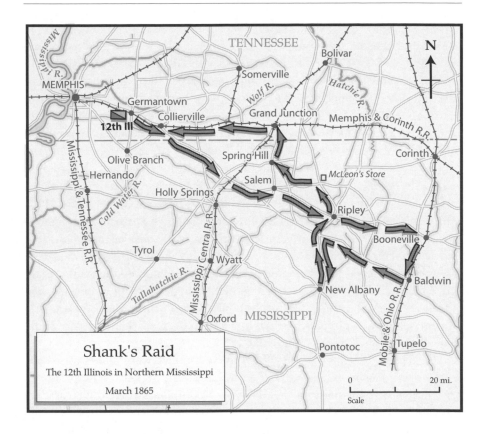

Shank's Raid

The 12th Illinois in Northern Mississippi

March 1865

able to help capture a Confederate officer and had nearly captured one bushwhacker by himself. He had chased him for over a mile, emptying his revolver in the process. Redman was riding a new horse that was not "bridle wise" so he had to give up the chase after the brush became so dense that he had trouble maneuvering his horse through the thicket.[13]

On this mission the 12th Illinois had again dealt with the rigors of a guerrilla conflict. Three men from Company C had been captured on the first day out from Memphis. They were taken twenty miles south of the city and told that they could have a "drink of filthy water" if they wished. The troopers went to a creek to drink, and while they were drinking, two were shot; the third made his escape by running into the woods. The soldier who escaped, only eighteen years old, came into camp before the rest of the command returned from the raid. He had procured "a suit of citizen's clothes" from a black resident and "passed in as a teamster with a load of cotton," happy to make it back alive. During the expedition, the 12th Illinois lost or abandoned fourteen horses and six mules and captured nine horses and ten mules. The regiment also captured five prisoners, one of them a captain.[14]

The 12th Illinois's stay in Memphis was quite short. While the men were in Mississippi chasing Crossland's small Kentucky Brigade, orders had come from Brevet Major General B. H. Grierson at the headquarters of the Military Division of West Mississippi. They were to be relieved of their present duties and to proceed to New Orleans for further duty. During their last few weeks in Memphis, the men received news of Lee's surrender in Virginia and of Lincoln's assassination in Washington. They recognized the death of the president by wearing black crepe on their uniforms, around their saber hilts, and on the bridles of their horses. It seemed to the men that the entire city of Memphis, always strong in Union sympathies, was in a state of shock and mourning.[15]

In May 1865 the 12th Illinois received word of Confederate General Joe Johnston's surrender in North Carolina and finally of Forrest's surrender in Alabama; the last bastion of Confederate resistance east of the Mississippi had fallen. Forrest had chosen not to fight in northeast Mississippi; instead, he had consolidated his forces late in the spring and moved them into southern Alabama. After a house-to-house battle in the town of Selma, he had surrendered, stating that "the further continuation of this war is insane and whomever would pursue the further continuation of this war should be placed in an insane asylum immediately."[16]

The officers and men of the 12th Illinois Cavalry were elated to see the war end and had high hopes that they would return to their homes in northern Illinois without much delay. They had completed their duties as they saw them. "The bright star of peace dawns upon our loved country. We shall all be home soon to enjoy the fruits of our labor—peace—liberty—and all the blessings of the Constitution preserved."

With the official hostilities ended, the men from northern Illinois had varied attitudes toward their former enemies. Many citizens of New Orleans and especially Memphis had been opposed to secession and the war because both cities had been occupied very early in the conflict and had been shipbuilding and refitting areas for the Mississippi River fleets of the U.S. Navy. New Orleans had been a wealthy commercial center for years before the war. Memphis, on the other hand, became a booming center directly as a result of the war, particularly because it was U. S. Grant's supply base for most of the Vicksburg campaign. Even before the war many Northerners had lived in Memphis. By the spring of 1865 the city had become rich from government war supply, and its citizens did not want to bite the hand that fed them. Consequently, the white inhabitants of Memphis were friendlier toward the federal government than the people the 12th had encountered in New Orleans had been. Federal troops faced little hostility in their occupation of Memphis.

The attitudes of the men of the 12th Illinois toward the Confederate leadership were harsh. The men were convinced that those who had led the rebellion needed to be punished. According to Redman, hopes ran rampant in the ranks that the president, Andrew Johnson, "will mete out justice to the Rebels, [and that] all southern leaders should be severely punished and those devilish traitors should never receive the scepter of Power again. . . . It will be enough to give their posterity the privilege of office."[17]

The 12th Illinois Volunteer Cavalry remained in Memphis until 15 June. That day they discovered that instead of being demobilized and sent back to their home state, they were being ordered south once again, this time to Alexandria, Louisiana. There they joined the cavalry division commanded by young Major General George A. Custer. The unit then had a harrowing journey into Texas. Officials in Washington believed that Texas was in a complete state of chaos and disintegration. Too many stories had filtered back to Washington about Federal soldiers that were still in Confederate prisons in the eastern part of the state. Four members of the 12th Illinois Cavalry were imprisoned at Camp Ford near Tyler and Hempstead, Texas. Equally disturbing reports were coming to the U.S. legations in Mexico regarding the French occupation of that country, and there were fears that Indians were pillaging the cattle ranches and white-owned homesteads in western Texas. President Johnson was so concerned that he sent Major General Philip Sheridan to straighten out the mess, not even allowing him to attend the grand review in the capital.

The 12th Illinois was one of the first units to be sent in to occupy Texas in the spring of 1865. They were not ready to go, not acclimatized, and they were led by Custer, an officer to whom training and acclimatization were secondary to his aim of pursuing a military career. A dissatisfied command spent a few days and nights in Newton County, Texas, dealing with the heat, the dust, and "swarms of insects and rattlesnakes that prevented any real sleep." Some of the men of Custer's command were sick, and all of them suffered because they had to march in the summer heat wearing woolen uniforms. One member of the 12th Illinois said that the entire affair was a "very unreasonable undertaking by Major General Custer in attempting to take those men through with the expedition." If anything, this expedition should have given the army brass an idea of the irresponsible character of George Custer, who ten years later, on a hot June day in Montana, would lead another exhausted command too far.[18]

CHAPTER NINE

Reconstruction in a Conquered Land

As Custer's command neared Houston, General Gordon Granger diverted the column northwest. They continued another fifty miles before arriving in the town of Hempstead on 26 August 1865. Granger had chosen the town as a base of operations because he had heard reports of better forage and grass for the animals. In the late summer of 1865 Hempstead was a small village on the Houston and Texas Central Railroad. A junior officer in the 12th Illinois described it as "the sandy desert of Texas," but at least the troops got mail "two or three times a week."[1]

During their brief stay the troops were billeted near a large plantation known as Liendo, the residence of a wealthy planter named Jared Groce. Liendo was near Pond Creek, where only a few months before there had been a prison camp for Union soldiers. The prison, Camp Groce, was rumored to have more than five hundred graves of Federal soldiers who had died there. Custer and his cavalry division were probably sent to Hempstead not only to graze their jaded animals but also to make sure that all former prisoners were released and sent to an army depot for pay and muster out. The men of the 12th Illinois stayed only a few days at Liendo and then were transferred back to Houston by September 19. General Custer remained at Liendo for the rest of the fall, leaving on 1 December.[2]

The men of the 12th Illinois seemed to like Houston. On the Buffalo River not ten miles from Galveston Bay there was a cool breeze blowing, and it was not difficult to sleep. William Redman was promoted to first lieutenant on 19

September. He wrote that the regiment was living "pretty nicely." There was one sorrowful incident at Houston. Corporal Daniel J. Mackey of Mount Carroll, Illinois, who had enlisted with Redman in the spring of 1862 and had been with Company C since the formation and muster of the regiment, died at midnight on 23 September of what then was called congestive fever. He was described as a healthy, robust young man, and Redman thought his early death a mystery. Under orders to leave with an expedition the next day, Redman did not attend the funeral, but he told his mother that Mackey's remains had been "neatly interred in a graveyard near our Camp." Everyone in the company missed Mackey. The men of the 12th Illinois had developed a camaraderie over their years together in combat, and the loss of a fellow soldier this late in the war was deeply felt. On the morning after Mackey's death Redman informed Mackey's father before leaving with Company C.[3]

The 12th Illinois's mission in Texas similar to what its mission had been in Tennessee in the spring and in Louisiana in 1864–pacification. The unit numbered fewer than six hundred men in the fall of 1865. Almost four years of war plus disease and desertion had taken their toll. The men's morale was as high as could be expected, considering that the regiment had been "frozen"–kept in regular service against its will after a national conflict or a rebellion. The army based its right to freeze the 12th Illinois on the reenlistment papers of November 1863. The papers stipulated that the regiment was released from duty in the Virginia theater to come home and reenlist as a veteran regiment for three full years. The 12th could have been ordered to remain in service until November 1866.

The army's rationale for dispatching the 12th Illinois to Texas seems logical enough. In 1863 Napoleon III had decided to use Mexico as a base for reestablishing a French New World empire. He conquered Mexico and installed a puppet government. The puppet government was presided over by Austrian Archduke Maximilian Hapsburg, who had led the French invasion. Lincoln's secretary of state, William Seward, had passionately argued against the French action, but as long as large and potent Confederate armies were still in the field in both Virginia and Georgia, Seward's actions had been limited. When Confederacy ended, Seward decided to push the issue. He began to order thousands of troops to the U.S.-Mexican border. The United States did not really want a war, and there were many diplomatic attempts to end the crisis. The Johnson administration was desperately trying to downsize the U.S. Army while determining how large of a regular army would still be needed. The regular army was to undergo a massive reorganization, and the Act to Increase and Fix the Size of the Military Peace Establishment of the United States increased the army's cavalry from six to ten regiments and its infantry from nineteen to forty-five regiments. The artillery was maintained at five regiments.[4]

Recruits were to be trained and equipped, then sent west to police the citizens of Texas, to fight the French in Mexico, or to contain the Comanches in the western part of the state. Meanwhile, troops whose voluntary enlistments had yet to expire, including the men of the 12th Illinois, were expected to fill the gap. The men from northern Illinois were not sent to the Rio Grande to face the French, or to western Texas to face the Comanches. Instead, the 12th Illinois's mission appears to have been to act as a reserve and to provide a show of force in case relations with the French deteriorated and became explosive; and to perform pacification duty among the unrepentant Rebels, the free blacks, and the white civilians in east-central Texas.

General Charles H. Mower, commander of the Federal cavalry in eastern Texas and Custer's second in command, was a man who would not tolerate any sort of disorder. At any sign of conflict he would send a command to the trouble area. Race relations in particularly were potentially explosive. There were more than two hundred thousand former slaves in Texas, one quarter of the state's population. Some former slaves were native Texans; others were refugees from Arkansas and Louisiana—or had been brought to Texas by their refugee owners from those states during the war. The former slaves stood at the center of the pacification problem because of intense disagreement between white and black and between North and South regarding the precise meaning of emancipation. While most whites agreed that blacks were no longer slave property, many resented the blacks' freedom and continued to treat them in a racist, domineering manner. Whites complained of black theft, impudence, irresponsibility, and refusal to work. Freed slaves were coerced, whipped, cheated, driven off land, and otherwise abused and denied the rights and respect commonly accorded free whites. The federal government sought to make a meaningful reality of emancipation and to restore social and economic stability in the Southern states. It sent in the army to prevent outrageous treatment of the freed blacks while forcing them into a new, but still very exploitative, contract-labor system of agriculture.[5]

There was little order in Texas in those days immediately after the fall of the Confederate government. The provisional administration of Texas under Governor Andrew Jackson Hamilton worked to reestablish civil government, administer loyalty oaths, and bring together a convention to make constitutional changes that would reflect the results of the war. The state was even without its famed Texas rangers. Most of them had entered Confederate cavalry service during the war and had disbanded when the Confederate army surrendered. The ranger units that had remained in state service were sent into the western part of Texas to deal with the Comanches. Even the few remaining forces of the Texas state troops, volunteers who had been in service to the state and had not been called into Confederate service, had been disbanded by the Federal government by the late summer of 1865. In Texas order would be the realm of the Army of Observation—that is, the United States Army.[6]

The entire 12th Illinois Cavalry was assigned to pacification duty of one form or another. The experiences of officers in two companies are illustrative. First Lieutenant William H. Redman was repeatedly detailed to take detachments of Company C into the interior of east-central Texas in search of persons suspected of murdering and mutilating former slaves. In contrast, Captain Edward J. Mann of Oswego, Illinois, formerly an officer in the old 4th Illinois Cavalry and now commander of Company I of the 12th Illinois, enjoyed a very positive experience as an ambassador of goodwill.

On 23 September a special order was issued to William Redman by the provost marshal general of the Military District of Central Texas, Brevet Lieutenant Colonel J. C. Delness. Redman was to proceed with a detail of twenty-five men with six days' rations to Montgomery and Walker Counties. There he was to procure six black men from the Williams plantation who were to appear before the Military Commission and give evidence in the case of a white man accused of murdering a recently freed black man, or freedman. Delness issued a second order on 23 October 1865. Redman and his detail were to proceed to the Houston home of Kenny Bennett and bring Bennett and all of the arms and papers they found in his home to the Military Commission. "If a certain girl Ruthe (Colored) has been taken off the place (Bennet's) you will send a man after her bringing her here, also Adam and Mac (Colored)."[7]

He apprehended Kenny Bennett. Three days after the second order, on 26 October Lieutenant Redman was ordered to arrest and bring to the Military Commission "Julius and Thomas Hutchins, who are charged with murder." Redman was "to bring the most important witnesses" he could find. The provost marshal also ordered Redman to take the body of "the murdered man" (a freedman) "out of his grave and examine his wounds." On 1 November Redman was ordered to lead a detachment into the counties of Harris and Austin for the purpose of

> arresting all parties that have whipped or mutilated the Freedmen. The parties so arrested will be sent to this office. You will also bring witnesses to testify to the outrages committed by the parties that you arrest. You will not allow any of your men to commit any depredations upon citizens. You will also give circulation to the enclosed circulars No. 1 reading them to the Freedmen at every opportunity, advising them to stay with parties from whom they receive good

treatment, but they are free people and have a right to contract with whom they please, but that they must work for somebody to make a living, as the Government cannot support them.

A week later, Redman was doing much the same thing, arresting people guilty of racial violence and investigating allegations of murder. He was sent to a plantation in Austin County to arrest James Wade, Abe Sullivan, Tack Wade, a Mr. Carvius, and a black driver named William. Redman then was to exhume the body of Jerry Wade, a black man, "and hold an inquest over said body to see how Jerry (Wade) died."[8]

Captain Mann of Company I experienced none of the direct police duty through which Redman suffered. Mann was given a detail of fifty men and forty days' provisions and was ordered to leave Houston and proceed to Waco, Texas. His mission was to rescue and secure the records of the state of Missouri, which had been carried there during the war, and to act as a traveling emissary of the army to the planters and the freed men and women. Like all other junior officers in the 12th Illinois, Mann was to "ascertain facts yourself and not act on rumor or ex parte evidence." If Mann or any other commander found that the blacks were being harassed or mutilated, the detachment under his command was to arrest those responsible for the crimes. Mann also was to inform the blacks that lands formerly or presently belonging to white Southerners would not be distributed to the former slaves. Lieutenant Colonel Dox warned Mann, too, that he was not to have anything to do with the making of contracts. Contracts were under the sole direction of the Freedmen's Bureau and were not to be tampered with by the army.[9]

Company I of the 12th Illinois began its mission through Texas on 18 October. Captain Mann was well received by most Texans, but there were those who could not or would not forget the war. Mann had "no particular affection for a rebel, particularly if he is not a repentant one." After the archives of Missouri had been secured, Mann delivered an address to the populace from a stack of cracker boxes at his bivouac site near Waco. Just after the address, Mann was horrified to find that a member of the press had been in the audience taking down his every word in shorthand, but he was surprised and pleased that in the Waco paper the next day the reporter was very complimentary about his address.[10]

The issue of race surfaces throughout Mann's correspondence. The folkways and mores of east-central Texas had been turned upside down, and white Texans had problems dealing with the freed people. Federal agencies, particularly the Freedmen's Bureau, which had been created to guarantee the rights of former slaves, were supposed to help with the situation. But the Freedmen's Bureau was overwhelmed, and many whites did not like what the bureau was trying to do.

The Texas elite's response to emancipation was the establishment of the infamous Black Codes. In Texas the Black Codes were thought by many to be relatively mild because they were repetitious of vagrancy laws that were already in place. Punishments for vagrancy included fines, forced labor, and whipping. However, even the relatively mild Black Codes of Texas constituted an extralegal attempt to reenslave black men and women, a goal that seemed to permeate east-central Texas in late 1865. Captain Edward Mann related that

> no white is guilty of work in this country, he will almost starve to death before he will labor for his living, but if he can rob a black man of his labors he is all right and thinks it no crime. Now that the free labor has been established he is in doubts of getting his living unless he works or pays the laborer his hire which in a great many instances they [the planters] are unwilling to do.[11]

Mann was not alone in his concerns. To most southerners, Texans included, the freed men and women were not to be treated with any respect, politically, socially, or economically. Caleb B. Forshey, a former Confederate colonel, summed up the feelings of his fellow white Texans in testimony before a congressional committee: "I believe that far from the black man's degradation by slavery, he was exalted by it, and that [it was] the best condition he has ever enjoyed, and the best of which, as a race, he is capable." That sentiment was also present in the 12th Illinois. Redman, for instance, opposed slavery, but he certainly never believed that whites and blacks were equal. Black Texans hoping to make something of their freedom faced these prejudices. H. C. Smith, a black man who lived in Galveston, Texas, during Reconstruction, could "speak for every colored man I know, and I say that freedom in poverty and in trials and tribulations, even amidst the most cruel prejudices, is sweeter than the best fed or the best clothed slavery in the world."[12]

The issue of racial equality, and particularly of black suffrage, haunted white Texans as it did most white Southerners during the time of Reconstruction. Local papers recorded great concern that the new president was under the influence of the Radical Republicans and would grant blacks the right to vote. They reported that Johnson entertained the idea of giving the right to vote to former slaves "who have been in the army, and the more intelligent ones who have not." But the president was in no manner a supporter of black suffrage, even thought he was against chattel slavery. When a delegation of blacks visited Johnson in the White House in February 1866, the president proposed that their people emigrate to another country. Members of the old planter class were relieved when the local press reported that Johnson could withhold the right of suffrage from certain classes heretofore exercising it [in those states formerly in rebellion]; but he could not extend it to other classes excluded by State Constitutions. . . . The President, however, is at present clearly of opinion that he has no power to say that the negroes shall vote.[13]

To the sixty men from Company I on this lonely patrol in east Texas in the late fall of 1865, the national policies of the Johnson administration, with all of its inherent racism, were not unlike those of the Texans whom they were trying to pacify. For that matter, the attitudes reflected in those policies were not all that different from their own racist beliefs. Many of the troopers did not support the advancement of black suffrage.[14]

After accomplishing their mission in Waco, Mann and Company I proceeded north to Montgomery County. There Mann did not speak to any community gatherings, but he visited several plantations that he said were well kept and well watered and were properly using the new free labor system. The company then proceeded farther north to Walker County and the county seat of Huntsville, which Mann described as a "pretty little town." Mann did not address the citizenry in Huntsville either because there was an agent of the Freedmen's Bureau in the town who attended to that chore. According to Mann, Huntsville must have been settled by "people of some means," for there were many former large slaveholders who had "pretty planter residences." The people seemed to have been very pro-Confederate during the war but had since taken the oath of allegiance to the Union. Mann did not place much confidence in their loyalty. He wrote that many of the men he talked with in the Huntsville area "would pick out any of the bad consequences of abolishing slavery, but could not see any good in its results."

Mann resented the planters, and he "would like to see them in the field with their coats off—they have a thousand faults to find with the negroes, but not one with themselves, they think the world was made for their special benefit until Uncle Sam's blue coats got among them."[15] He was deep in planter territory not long after the end of the Civil War, and he wondered whether there would be a need for further military action, but most people doubted that the white Southerners still had the will to fight. One Confederate partisan, M. Jeff Thompson of Missouri, had told a Louisville, Kentucky, citizen "that the only persons in the South who wish to do any more fighting are those who didn't do any when they had a chance."[16]

The 12th Illinois again headed north and arrived in the town of Crockett, the seat of Austin County. Cotton, corn, wheat, rye, cattle, and horses were the principal crops and livestock around Crockett. Merchandise was brought up from Houston in wagons, or by train as soon as track for a spur was laid.

The railroads were about the only industry that seemed to grow in Texas after the Civil War. Spurs were built everywhere, often where no tracks had been before. When a train came through, almost the entire population of a town would descend on the depot to gather information that was flowing from the cities. The town of Crockett came to life when Mann's troops arrived.

Almost all day every day that he was in Crockett, Mann's camp was overcrowded with people of both races complaining about the injustices of each to the other. Mann became convinced that he was acting in the capacity of both military provost marshal and Freedmen's Bureau agent. In the latter role he had to tread lightly; regimental commander Hamilton Dox, acting on orders from Major General Mower, who was commanding the Union cavalry in east-central Texas, had specifically forbidden army officers to make contracts of any kind. It appears that Mann was able to settle disputes and arguments between whites and blacks in accord with existing contracts. He talked to the freed men and women of a number of large plantations and "advised them to go to work and earn a living for themselves, which they promised to do, and did in many instances before I left." Mann did find a few instances of abuse to the freed people, which were "corrected by summoning the parties before me at my camp and either fining them or giving them advise according to the nature of the offense."[17]

One of the more interesting meetings that Mann and the men of the Company I attended while they were in Crockett was held at the plantation of Thomas Reagan, brother of the former postmaster general of the Confederacy. In the true fashion of upper-class Southern gentlemen, Reagan arranged a fox hunt. Mann allowed members of his company to attend the hunt, but he himself declined. He preferred instead to spend his time by the campfire with an old frontiersman he had met along the way, hearing his tales of the Texas of an earlier time. There is no evidence of much interaction between Mann and Reagan, but Mann was quite progressive in his attitude toward blacks, and Reagan's brother John, recently returned from detention in the North, repeatedly urged the Texas constitutional convention to take a small step toward equal rights for blacks, such as giving the ballot to those who could read and write.[18]

The village of Rusk, "a beautiful place with more than a few orchards of apple, peach, and pear trees," was Mann's destination after Crockett. The troops had to explain their presence to a delegation of Rusk's citizens, and Mann made it clear to them that "U.S. Troops had a right to go where they had a mind to without being questioned as to the object." The community evidently had appointed a leader, a local lawyer, who tried to engage Mann in a political discourse about who had started the late war and why. Mann would say only that he was a United States Army officer acting under orders, and that if the lawyer would come to Illinois after the 12th was mustered out, he would be glad to talk to him as long as he pleased. Satisfied, the man apologized for his bad manners.

At Rusk Mann was approached by a Mexican-American family by the name of Felico, well-to-do planters who invited him to their house for dinner. Mann commented that, unlike other Texas planters, the Felicos had a well-kept garden, lots of shrubbery, and a very nice house. He indicated that he was well treated and would not forget their hospitality. Mann left a lieutenant and fifteen men to keep a close eye on the Felico plantation, for he thought that some of the "mean set of inhabitants" might seek revenge against a family that had befriended a Union Army officer.

Upon leaving Rusk Mann took up a line of march westward to Palestine, which he described as "a well-watered prairie skirted with timber principally oak, mixed with a few scattering pines." It was the most beautiful town that Mann had seen during his forty-day tour. As the men of Company I neared Palestine, freed men and women began to line the route. They had heard a great deal about the Yankees and were ecstatic that they had come at last. Mann wrote that

> one old black man looked at me for some time, to see whether his eyes did not deceive him, at last he exclaimed "he is a Yankee! Yessir Ise glad yous come. I did recond I would never see you no how." I met them in large numbers all along the road and at night our camp would be full of them, they would come twelve to fifteen miles to see us. It is strange how the news of our coming would pop ahead of us among them, they would hear of our last camping place and then meet us at our next camp.

Mann believed that he had done something positive in this area of central Texas. The planters complained to Mann that "the black men had got an idea that after Christmas the Government was going to give them all homes and consequently they would not hire for a longer period than next Christmas." This organized resistance by the black population seemed to Mann to be a threat to the entire economy of east-central Texas because in that part of the country planters began planting the cotton crop in January and the wheat and rye crops in December.

Mann stated that most of the blacks believed the government was not only going to give them a home but also would give "them each 40 acres and a mule and a year's provisions." He told the blacks that "the Government had done all it could for them by giving them their freedom and that they did not show much gratitude for what had been done for them. Some of them seemed quite disappointed and could hardly credit what I said to them, 'but there,' they said, 'he is a Yankee Officer, we is bound to believe him.'" The word of a U.S. Army officer, Mann noted, "is all gospel to them." The captain of Company I told them to go to work and purchase a home while things were still cheap.

Mann would describe a day's work on a farm near Oswego, Illinois, to the planters and the freed slaves. The planters would invariably say that if Mann could get their people to work like that, they could soon get rich. The response of the blacks, of course, was a little different. If they worked that hard, they would not even have time to attend Sunday meeting.

Company I moved from Palestine to Fairfield, where their commander spoke once again to a large crowd. Then they went to Springfield, which in 1865 was in Limestone County. Here, for the only time in his assignment, Mann accepted indoor accomodations for his sixty men, who appreciated the invitation of the clerk of the circuit court of Limestone County to use the courthouse as a barracks. The heavy rain was the first they had seen in twenty-three days. The people of Springfield received the men of Company I well.

After addressing the populace in the Springfield courthouse the next day, Mann and his command departed for Waco. The country from Springfield to Waco is flat prairie, and the soil is so black that Mann felt that he was back in northern Illinois. Wildlife was plentiful. Wild geese, jack rabbits, and deer were in such great numbers that the commanding officer allowed the men to break ranks and shoot at the geese with their carbines. As they crossed the Trinity River, the men of Company I encountered an orchard of almost one hundred acres of pecan trees, where both blacks and whites were gathering nuts with some level of harmony. Mann ordered a halt, and the sixty troopers of Company I helped themselves to as many pecans as they could carry.

Once they were in Waco, the men of Company I camped by the Brazos River. Captain Mann addressed about two thousand people who had come to see him. Waco was on the edge of the wheat-growing country of Texas, and most of the white people Mann encountered seemed to be prosperous. Waco's economy was built on farming, cotton, railroads, and a college, Baylor University, which was established there in 1840. Waco was the first town in the central part of the state where almost everyone had a garden and where black and white citizens appeared to be tolerant of one another.

The men of Company I were now at the western end of their radius of operations. They turned southeast back toward Houston. They followed the Brazos for most of the ride back and observed that the surrounding land was the best in the state. While bivouacking at the Fortune plantation, Captain Mann learned that another Federal column, under the command of Brevet Brigadier General Henry Wells Perkins, was about ten miles southeast at a town called Marlin. Mann rode into the Marlin camp and spent the night, undoubtedly

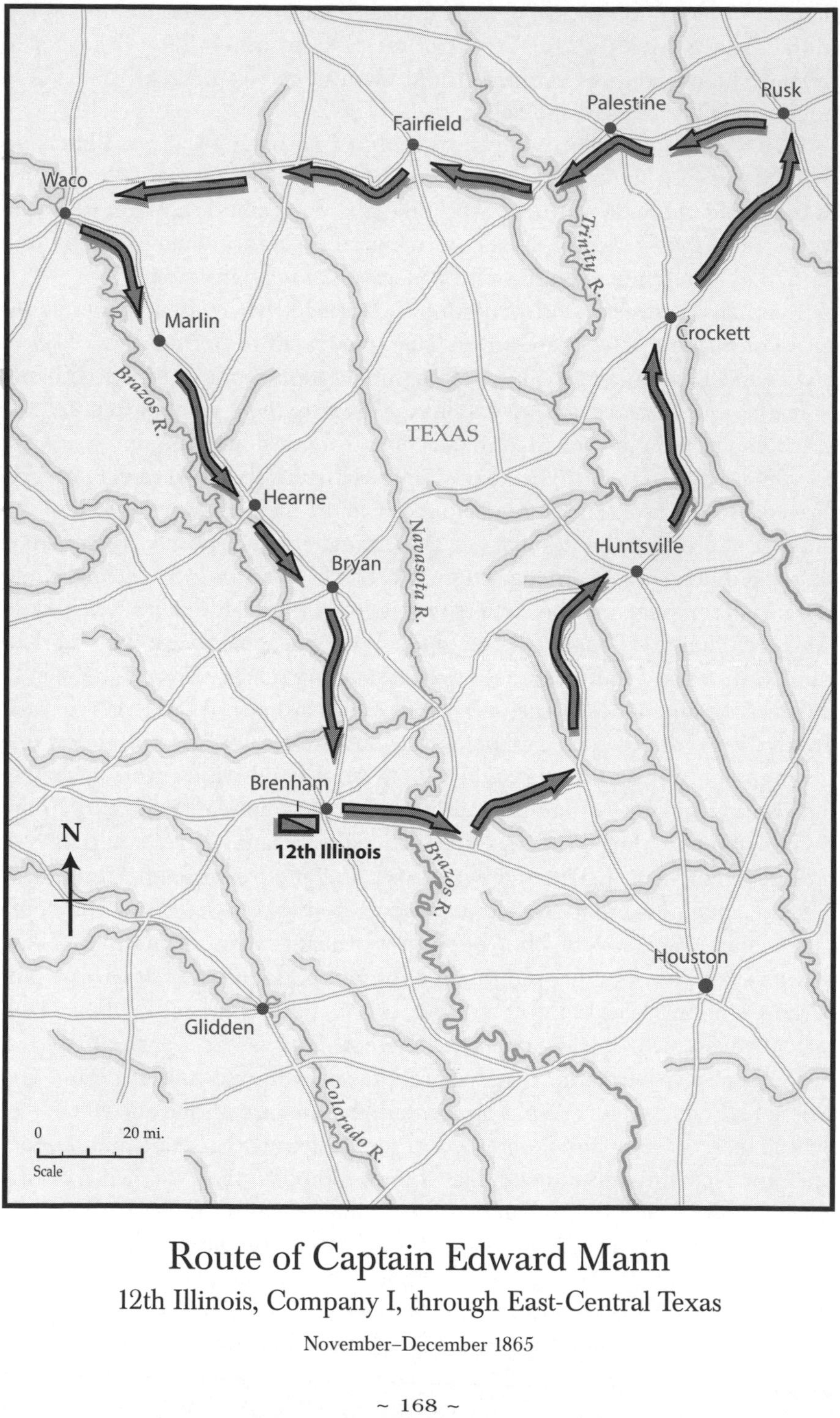
Rusk
Palestine
Fairfield
Waco
Trinity R.
Marlin
Crockett
Brazos R.
TEXAS
Hearne
Navasota R.
Huntsville
Bryan
Brenham
12th Illinois
Brazos R.
N
Houston
Glidden
Colorado R.
0
20 mi.
Scale

Route of Captain Edward Mann

12th Illinois, Company I, through East-Central Texas

November–December 1865

enjoying the better rations of a camp of general officers. Perkins was supposed to address the local populace, but because Captain Mann, with his splendid speaking ability, was present, the general and his headquarters escort left Marlin early the next morning after the general instructed Mann to deliver one of his famous speeches. This was Mann's last speech on the trip, and he was glad of it because "he had become pretty tired of talking so much."

After leaving Marlin, Company I proceeded through Brenham to Hempstead, where they once again spent the night at Liendo. Here Mann left the company in charge of his second in command, First Lieutenant Andrew Norton, and returned to Houston via the railroad. He arrived at the main camp of the 12th Illinois Volunteer Cavalry forty days after he had set out on his trek through eastern Texas. Edward Mann wrote his wife that the trip was tiring but had been a great success. He had learned more about "the inhabitants both white and black than if I had resided here a year." He thought he would be sent out again, but instead he received a telegram from General Mower's staff informing him that he had been appointed judge advocate of a court-martial. Mann was a farmer, not an attorney, and he had great misgivings about the assignment, but he accepted anyway. He probably had no choice. His fellow officers taunted him, hoping "to see Mann take a job" he could not accomplish.[19]

In December 1865 General Mower ordered the commander of the 12th Illinois, Lieutenant Colonel Hamilton B. Dox, to proceed to the area of the Brazos River in Huntsville, Walker County, and to prepare to control any rebellion by blacks or whites. Mower warned Dox not to become overeager in dealing with the blacks, for the "rumors of intended insurrection of the negroes may be a ruse on the part of persons who are badly affected toward them, thereby furnishing an excuse for an attack upon the freedman." While there seems to have been a serious attempt to bring transgressors to justice, especially for capital crimes, President Andrew Johnson's federal government showed more concern toward the cotton economy of Texas. According to Captain Edward Mann, there was an obvious interest in supplying the planters with labor, but little or no federal concern regarding the question of fair compensation for labor provided. The men of the 12th Illinois were, quite simply, the enforcers of policies that reflected these interests.[20]

From the time they returned to Houston to their mustering out in the late spring of 1866, the men of the 12th Illinois served in various areas in east-central Texas and were almost always assigned to control, and at times police, the population of Texas, the largest state in the South and a conquered province. The officers and men continued to display pride and patriotism during their Reconstruction duty, but at times internal troubles surfaced. Company F was ordered dismounted, disarmed, and confined to the cavalry camp at Houston for attempting to foster a mutiny. The records are sketchy. The report of the adjutant general of Illinois indicates that Company F, under the command of First Lieutenant Charles A. Amet, was composed of troops mostly from Chicago and at one time numbered around one hundred officers and men. Most of the men in the company had served for the entire war, and it appears that they just wanted out of the service. The tedium of recent duty had strained Company F to the breaking point. During the Texas tour, nine of its men had deserted and one had committed suicide; this represented 10 percent of the company's original number.[21]

Life in Houston had become monotonous for the men of the 12th Illinois and was enlivened only by a few social get-togethers. At the end of January the officers of the regiment were invited to a Union party. It was evidently a strained affair; one officer wrote his sister that he would have enjoyed a party in northern Illinois much better. The single women in attendance constantly referred to themselves as "young Texans," a criticism of their forced United States citizenship. The young gentlemen, always called "Union officers," could feel the tension.[22]

It was almost impossible for people on either side to forgive and forget the fratricidal conflict that had lasted more than four years and consumed more than a half million lives. To the troopers of the 12th Illinois the Texans were still Rebels, and the men had little patience for those who had attempted to destroy the Union. Lieutenant Redman did not hide his pleasure when he told his family that the

> U.S. Tax Collectors are here to collect the taxes of 1861. It hurts the rebels to pay taxes for the time of the Rebellion but they have to do it and let them growl as much as they please. The taxes will be collected. It pleases me to see the Government striking so earnestly at the purse of these Southern Rebels. . . . I do hope the Government will collect taxes for every year since the commencement of the Rebellion. I am in favor of making them pay their share of the war debt of the United States. I believe that they should help pay the debt incurred to support those very Armies that whipped them so completely. . . . Illinois Copperheads used to blow so much that the South could not be subjected. If ever a people was subjugated it is the South at the present time. A soldier can do almost anything in Texas and citizens dare not say a word to them. But I must say the soldiers in nearly every case . . . treat the Citizens with courtesy and respect while at the same time they are frowned upon by the ladies of every household. Ladies can do as they please and their insults are overlooked but the men must walk a straight line.[23]

The men of the 12th Illinois would not have to deal with the Texas populace much longer. Their service was almost completed. Lieutenant George

R. Stowe, Jr., second in command of Company C, returned to Houston from his home in Chicago in the winter of 1866. He had been on a short leave, and he was mustered out of the service shortly after this return to Texas. Stowe was a veteran of the escape at Harpers Ferry; of the capture of Longstreet's wagon train at Sharpsburg in 1862; of the Stoneman Raid in May of 1863; of the battles of Aldie, Middleburg, and Upperville in June 1863; and of Gettysburg and the actions that followed. Stowe had been only fourteen years old when he enlisted as a private with William Redman in February 1862 at Camp Butler near Springfield, Illinois. He was promoted over his superiors, receiving a commission as a first lieutenant in early 1866 at age eighteen. Captain A. D. Mauer, who served as second in command of the company in Stowe's absence, had also enlisted with Redman in Springfield in 1862 at the age of fourteen and had shared the cold, miserable training days at Camp Butler outside the state capital.[24]

In the waning days of February 1866 the men began to get wind of a possible move to establish a military post in Livingston County, Texas. William Redman arrived at Livingston on 18 March 1866 to assume the command of Company C. He had only recently returned from Houston, where he had been promoted and remustered into the army as a captain. He was justifiably proud of his accomplishment after four years of service. He wrote to his mother on March 12: "Yes, Mother, Hank now wears the two bars instead of one and you can address one of your sons as Captain. It is a rank I never expected to have conferred on me although I cannot say that I never desired the position, for I did and soldiered four long years to obtain." He later wrote that his pay had increased to 175 dollars per month after six dollars in taxes.[25]

Redman was becoming affluent by the standards of the time. He wrote home that he would try to bring a string of horses when he was mustered out. He expressed indignation when he learned that his sister Jane was "working out" of their home in Lanark as a domestic. In order to ensure she stop working and would remain at home, he sent her four hundred dollars. Redman was so incensed by Jane's willingness to work as a maid that he commented in a letter to his brothers that he would pay her the same amount to stay at home that she would have earned by working outside the home.[26]

Easter Sunday in 1866 found the men of Company C at their leisure in Livingston, Texas. They were about a month from muster out, and it was beginning to show. Some officers were being considered for commissions in the peacetime army, but almost no one accepted. They usually wanted to leave that honor to men who liked the army, for they did not. The men began to refer to their service as "short." Redman said he had "been a slave too long [and] wanted to know how it would seem to be free once more." On 15 April 1866, the men of Company C at Livingston and the rest of the

12th Illinois in Houston began to hear rumors that they were going home. Redman was ordered to Galveston to draw pay for Company C, and he was to prepare them for transit from Livingston back to Houston. Many of the officers were getting their affairs in order. Not all of them would return to northern Illinois after their discharge. No less than five of those on the regimental staff, including the temporary commander, Major Andrew Langholtz, had purchased plantations in Texas and intended to remain there after muster out.[27]

On 8 May 1866 Company C arrived in Houston to end its service. The men of the 12th Illinois would be on their way back to Illinois by the end of the month. Until that time most of them were kept busy cleaning and turning in weapons and equipment. The officers were occupied with endless paperwork chores. Redman, writing his mother for the last time from Texas, said that he was required to give a full history of each man since he had entered the service. "It takes much time and patience in searching the old records of the Company as some of the Company enlisted so far back as in November 1861–before I joined the Company." He reported that of the 102 men on the final muster-out roll, two officers and forty-two other men were still members of Company C. The rest of the 102 had been discharged since the 12th Illinois had left Memphis in 1865. Redman thought that he had a good clerk, but he would "superintend the work myself, to assure myself of its correctness." Nine days after they arrived in Houston the 12th was mustered out of the U.S. Army and left Texas for Illinois. The men arrived at Camp Butler in Springfield on 14 June 1866. Five days after their arrival at the camp where they had started more than four years before, they received their final pay and were discharged from the service of Illinois.[28]

Epilogue *Sound Taps*

In August 1891 the men of the 12th Illinois Cavalry attended a regimental reunion in Detroit, Michigan, their third reunion in the twenty-five years since the end of the war. As is the case with so many of these gatherings, the veterans' emphasis was on the camaraderie produced by the military experience, not on the horrors of combat.

At most military reunions, officers of the association (which was usually named after the military organization) were elected, business was conducted, and friendships were renewed. Few, if any, controversies or personality clashes were discussed. There was frequently a banquet at which members of the regiment presented their wives. In some cases the soldier's wife was "the girl he had left behind" when he had gone to war. Toward the end of the evening, there was usually a recounting of the military service record of the organization, a roll call of those who had died, a time of prayer, and promises to attend the next reunion. Quite often a written history of the regiment would be proposed, and costs of publication and plans for distribution would be discussed. The newly elected officers would see to it that all would receive word of the time and location of the next reunion.

There was, however, an interesting twist to the agenda of the third reunion of the 12th Illinois Cavalry. Major Stephen Bronson presided over the small convention at which Captain William Henry Redman was "chosen as Secretary pro-temps." Bronson had been the controversial second in command of the 12th Illinois, which often referred to itself as the "Horse Thieves," and he had finished the war with a brevet as a brigadier general. Bronson and Redman had apparently had very little personal contact when they served together from the spring of 1862 to November 1863. Bronson had been a field-grade officer while Redman, at the time of the reenlistment leave, was a sergeant. By the time Redman was commissioned during the 12th's last year of service, Bronson had resigned under the heat of the court of inquiry of Hasbrouck Davis and had gone on to command an infantry regiment from Wisconsin.[1]

One internal association committee took on the responsibility of restoring the good name of Captain George Washington Shears. Shears had been allowed to resign in the spring of 1864 after his charges that Lieutenant Colonel Hasbrouck Davis had abandoned his command in the field were found to be groundless. Shears had left the service, never to return, and had moved to New York. In 1891 a monument to the 12th Illinois Cavalry was nearing completion. It would be placed on McPherson's Ridge, where the 12th Illinois had fought on the first day of the Battle of Gettysburg. The committee "requested to have suitable engraved upon the Gettysburg monument the name of Captain George W. Shears, showing the fact that he was the officer who gallantly commanded the 12th Illinois Cavalry (the four companies who were on line that day) at the Battle of Gettysburg. Also to be engraved was the name of Private Fred Usher [Ferdinand Ushuer] of Company C of the 12th as the first Union soldier killed in that battle."[2]

The monument stands today on McPherson's Ridge at the Gettysburg National Battlefield. It is similar to other monuments of regiments of the 1st Cavalry Division that opened the engagement on 1 July 1863. The monument is made of granite and features a McClellan saddle, two saddle rolls, two crossed steel sabers, and a bronze regimental crest. At the bottom of the monument are the names of the five men of the 12th Illinois who died on the morning of July 1. Private Ferdinand Ushuer's name is on the scroll. On the back of the monument is a short synopsis of the role 12th Illinois played on the first day at Gettysburg. Shears's name does not appear there either. In 1891 the group of veterans had not been able to resolve the conflict between Hasbrouck Davis, the de facto commander of the 12th Illinois during most of the Civil War, and Shears, one of his better company commanders. The monument at Gettysburg reflects the lingering controversy.

The 12th Illinois held its fourth reunion at the World's Fair in Chicago in 1893, but the event was not well planned. Association president Redman and his fellow officers scheduled the gathering for four days in mid-September 1893. Those who came for the first day could not stay over,

This monument to the 12th Illinois Cavalry's role in the
Battle of Gettysburg is placed on McPherson's Ridge on the
Chambersburg Pike northwest of Gettysburg.
The battle opened a few yards from the site of this
monument on 1 July 1863.

while those who came for the last day were not able to "meet some of their dearest friends who had been there but were gone." Between seventy and eighty members of the regiment attended the fourth reunion. One member, William Luff, read an academic paper that he had written about his adventures as a young lieutenant in the 12th Illinois Cavalry. This was undoubtedly a Military Order of the Loyal Legion of the United States (MOLLUS) paper that Luff had given elsewhere. He interlaced his address with warm patriotic references and a word of thanks to the members of the 12th Illinois for asking him to speak. Luff, who was paid for making his remarks that day, had been seriously wounded in the face in an action in Louisiana in 1864 and had undergone numerous facial reconstructive surgeries to correct the disfigurement.[3]

T. Benton Kelly of Company E of the 8th Illinois, the 12th Illinois's sister regiment, was present at the fourth reunion, and there was a sharp but friendly discussion about who had fired the first shot at the Battle of Gettysburg. Most believed then, as now, that the first shot had been fired by Lieutenant Marcellus Jones of the 8th Illinois. There was no disagreement that Private Ferdinand Ushuer of Company C of the 12th Illinois "was the first Union soldier to baptize that field with his blood."[4]

Some of the members were concerned about the fate of one of the 12th Illinois's battle flags. William Luff notes in the roster of the fourth reunion that the "Battle Flag of the Twelfth bore a horse's head in gold 'rampant in a blue field.' The battle flag also bore a greeting, 'I like your style!' All was surrounded by heavy gold fringe." The flag had been created during the regiment's furlough in Illinois in late 1863 after their sixteen months in the East. The men had returned to Illinois on a chartered train on a bitterly cold November day. They had been taken to the Chicago armory, where the governor of Illinois, Richard Yates, had welcomed them with an army band and a banquet. Yates had spoke of the many actions the regiment had participated in, and he had concluded his remarks by declaring, "I like your style!" During the furlough period, a group of citizens had made the flag for the men of the 12th, and it was presented to them before they left for the Department of the Gulf in early 1864.

The Illinois Military Museum at Camp Lincoln in Springfield, Illinois, has charge of the original regimental colors that were turned in by the Illinois regiments as they mustered out at the end of the war. Members wondered what had happened to their colors. The report of the adjutant general of Illinois states that the 12th Illinois turned in one flag to the Illinois secretary of state's office when they were demobilized in 1866, but it was not the horse's head flag Luff described in his remarks at the 1893 reunion. The flag with the "I like your style!" inscription was the one the men had served under, but it was simply not regulation. The flag that was turned in following the war was a blue field trimmed with gold fringe. It had a gold eagle with wings spread and a scroll in its talons, and on the scroll was the name of the regiment. The flag was a regulation regimental standard that denoted the combat arms of the cavalry. A couple of swallow-tailed company-level flags were turned in at the same time, but there is no way to positively identify them as having been carried by companies of the 12th Illinois.

The unique flag praising the style of the men of the 12th had never been turned in. It appeared to be lost to history, to exist only in the memories of the old soldiers. But recently a flag reappeared, well preserved and up for sale in Little Rock, Arkansas. It has the "I like your style!" inscription, but no horse's head. Perhaps a third flag existed, or perhaps the recollection of the soldiers at the 1893 reunion was not quite perfect.[5]

Fifteen years later, in October 1918, the reunion of the 12th Illinois coincided with the dedication of the Lincoln and Douglas statues on what is known as the "new" state capitol grounds in Springfield. The Illinois National Guard, the descendant organization of the Illinois Volunteer Militia, of which the 12th had been a part, had been on active duty since the spring of 1917 in response to President Woodrow Wilson's declaration of war that April. The Illinois National Guard, which was organized as the 33rd Infantry Division, would see bloody combat in the fall of 1918. No doubt many members of the 12th Illinois wondered if their grandchildren in the trenches of France were experiencing what they had experienced on the fields of Virginia, Louisiana, and Mississippi. According to the press reports of October 1918, the war would soon be over. Possibly the old gentlemen of the 12th Illinois wondered if their grandsons would be frozen in their enlistments as occupation troops in France or Germany, just as they had been frozen in Texas some fifty years earlier.[6]

Despite the shadow of another war, the reunion in 1918 appears to have been a gala affair. Most of the ceremony was held at the grand coliseum at the state fair grounds. As the stage was set up a band played out of view, a low, easy marching step, and the members of the 12th Illinois and members of other regiments marched across the stage in front of an audience of more than three thousand people. Many dignitaries were present, including President Woodrow Wilson's secretary of the navy, Josephus Daniels, and Illinois Governor Frank O. Lowden. A special guest was Lord Charnwood of England, one of the better-known biographers of Abraham Lincoln. Each dignitary gave an informative and rousing speech, but more interesting than the speeches of the elites in attendance were the quiet commentaries of the aged veterans of the 12th Illinois, who talked of their experiences in the great War of the Rebellion. Their comments were captured for posterity by the pen of Homer Calkins, who prepared a historical sketch of the command, and by Zora Custer, who elaborated on the capture of Rooney Lee after the Stoneman Raid.

At the dedication of the Lincoln statue on the capitol lawn, several members of the 12th Illinois spoke of encounters they had had with President Lincoln during the war. Homer Calkins, who usually acted as the scribe for the unit at its reunions, spoke of being in Washington, D.C., on a special assignment. He was on Pennsylvania Avenue on 4 July 1863 when Lincoln happened by and met with the young soldiers.

> Together, they watched the upper windows of the War Department from which bulletins with news from the battlefield at Gettysburg were displayed every few minutes. After each report, the President made a short, hopeful remark. Not a cabinet officer or any one but "us" spoke with him for more than half an hour. We were alone with Lincoln! When the final route of Lee's Army came, then the great throng in the street as far as one could see shouted "Victory!" Lincoln's face dropped nearly to his immaculate shirt front, showing a great change in appearance— especially his features became pallid. On that hot July of 1863, he murmured to himself, "Yes, Victory, Victory; but, oh, the cost! Homes, all American homes—north, south, east, and west—are draped in mourning this day." As we backed away from the President's presence, we never saw that face again.[7]

The members of the 12th Illinois who were in Springfield at the time of the reunion were in attendance at the laying of the cornerstone of the Centennial Building, which contains most of the regimental flags of Illinois from four wars. They then visited the Logan Memorial, where the regimental flags of the Civil War were on display. There they saw the standard of the 12th Illinois (the official that was flag turned in in May 1866). According to Calkins, it appeared as it had in April of 1865 when he carried it at memorial services for Lincoln in Memphis, Tennessee. The rest of the reunion consisted of religious services for people of all faiths and trips to Lincoln's grave at Oak Lawn Cemetery. Several well-meaning citizens offered to take the members of the 12th to Camp Butler, but offers to visit the basic training center were refused. The next reunion was scheduled for one year later in 1919 in Kansas City. Although detailed records do not exist, many probably attended just as they had in 1918.

The 1913 reunion was held at Gettysburg. J. N. Baker, who had served in Company A of the 12th Illinois at Gettysburg, attended the reunion, traveling the entire distance from Woodstock, Minnesota, by train. According to his great-granddaughter, Diane Baker Orgler of Crystal Lake, Illinois, he enjoyed the entire experience.[8] Not everyone felt this way. To many soldiers and maybe to most of the 12th Illinois, the Civil War was a horrible experience from which they never recovered, and they did not want a reunion to recall the nightmare. They wanted to honor the camaraderie and friendship that developed over four years of wartime service. There were many other memories of which they did not speak, reliving them only in their deepest thoughts and their worst dreams.

Appendix

12th Illinois Volunteer Cavalry

A G E S

	15–19	20–29	30–39	40–over
	23%	55%	15%	6%

H E I G H T S

	5'0"–5'4"*	5'5"–5'10"	5'11"–above
	7%	81%	12%

* The shortest man, not included in this count, was four feet, eight inches tall.

P E R C E N T   F O R E I G N   B O R N

Company A	31%
Company B	4%
Company C	25%
Company D	32%
Company E	26%
Company F	17%
Company G	5%
Company H*	5%
Company I*	5%
Company K	43%
Company L	—
Company M	12%

* McClellan's Dragoons

12th Illinois Volunteer Cavalry

NUMBER OF MEN

Company	Officers	Enlisted Men
A	5	64
B	6	61
C	6	65
D	6	57
E	7	47
F	6	68
G	6	67
H (already in the East–no numbers available)		
I	8	91
K	4	40
L	3	30
M	3	88
Regimental Headquarters	25	22
totals	86	674

12th Illinois Volunteer Cavalry

ILLINOIS COUNTIES OF ENLISTMENT BY COMPANY

A Boone
Cook
DeKalb
DuPage
Perry
Winnebago

B Champaign
Cook
DeWitt
DuPage
Jersey
Jo Daviess
LaSalle
Madison
Monroe
St. Clair
Sangamon
Stephenson

C Carroll
DeKalb
Lee
Ogle
Stephenson
Winnebago

D Carroll
Cook
Kankakee
Pulaski
Sangamon

E Adams
Clark
Cook
Hancock
Kankakee
Lake

F Adams
Christian
Cook
Greene
Jersey
Kane
Lake
Macoupin
Madison
Morgan
Sangamon

G Brown
Cass
Champaign
Cook
Fulton
Hancock
Knox
Livingston
McDonough
McHenry
Macoupin
Pike
Sangamon
Schuyler
Whiteside

H Cook
Hancock
Whiteside

I Carroll
Cook
Edgar
Henry
Kankakee
Lee
Whiteside

K Carroll
Cook
DeWitt
Effingham
Fulton
Jackson
McHenry
Menard
Montgomery
Ogle
Randolph
St. Clair
Sangamon
Shelby
Vermilion
Will
Winnebago

L Cook
Fulton
Hancock
Henderson
Knox
McDonough
McLean
Mercer
Warren

M Adams
Boone
Brown
Carroll
Clay
Cook
Grundy
Hancock
Kankakee
Kendall
Lee
McDonough
Madison
Pike
Sangamon
Vermilion
Whiteside
Will
Winnebago

SOURCE: Roster of the survivors of the 12th Illinois Veteran Volunteer Cavalry, March 1894, 1–26, n.p., n.d., Illinois State Historical Society, Springfield; Dyer's Compendium, available at <http://www.rootsweb.com/~ilcivilw/reg_htmlcav_012.htm>.

Notes

1: "Rally 'round the Flag"

1. John K. Mahon, *History of the Militia and the National Guard*, vol. 2 of *The Macmillan Wars of the United States*, gen. ed. Louis Morton (New York: Macmillan, 1983), 97.

2. Ibid.

3. Ibid.

4. Stephen Z. Starr, *From Fort Sumter to Gettysburg, 1861–1863,* vol. 1 of *The Union Cavalry in the Civil War* (Baton Rouge: Louisiana State University Press, 1979), 88; Old State Capitol Square Historical Marker, Illinois State Monument Commission, Springfield; Brigadier General J. N. Reece, *Report of the Adjutant General of the State of Illinois,* 8:332–405 (Springfield, Ill.: Journal Company Printers and Binders, 1900).

5. Reece, *Report of the Adjutant General,* 8:332–405; Starr, *From Fort Sumter to Gettysburg,* 211.

6. Jack Coggins, *Arms and Equipment of the Civil War* (New York: Doubleday, 1962), 46–60.

7. Starr, *From Fort Sumter to Gettysburg,* 63; James L. Morrison Jr., *The Best School in the World: West Point, the Pre–Civil War Years, 1833–1866* (Kent, Ohio: Kent State University Press, 1986), 98; Russell F. Weigley, *The American Way of War: A History of United States Military Strategy and Policy* (Bloomington: Indiana University Press, 1973), 71.

8. John W. Thomason Jr., *Jeb Stuart* (New York: Charles Scribner's Sons, 1930), 25.

9. Starr, *From Fort Sumter to Gettysburg,* 58–59

10. Reece, *Report of the Adjutant General,* 8:332–405.

11. Lieutenant Colonel Hasbrouck E. Davis, Regimental Commander, 12th Illinois Volunteer Cavalry, to Major General Steven A. Hurlbut, Commanding General, Department of the Gulf, 26 December 1864, Administrative Files of Civil War Companies and Regiments, 12th Illinois Volunteer Cavalry, Records of the Illinois Adjutant General, Archives and Records Group 301.18, Illinois State Archives, Springfield (hereafter cited as Administrative Files #301.18); Frederick H. Dyer, *Regimental Histories,* vol. 2 of *A Compendium of the War of the Rebellion* (New York: Thomas Yoseloff, 1959).

12. Camp Atterbury, Indiana, during the Korean conflict would be a rough modern analogy.

13. Ashley K. Alexander to his sisters from Camp Butler, Springfield, Illinois, 3 March 1862, Alexander-Ackerly Family Papers, Manuscripts Division, Illinois

State Historical Library, Springfield; Davis to Hurlbut, 26 December 1864, Administrative Files #301.18, Headquarters Folder.

14. Davis to Hurlbut, 26 December 1864, Administrative Files #301.18, Headquarters Folder.

15. Victor Hicken, *Illinois in the Civil War* (Urbana: University of Illinois Press, 1986), 6–7; Camp Butler National Military Cemetery brochure, Department of the Interior, Illinois State Historical Society, Springfield; Alexander to his sisters from Camp Butler, Springfield, Illinois, 3 March 1862, Alexander-Ackerly Family Papers.

16. Alexander to his sisters from Camp Butler, Springfield, Illinois, 13 March 1862, Alexander-Ackerly Family Papers.

17. Pension Record of Major John D. Fonda, Pension Records of Union Army Volunteer Veterans, Microfilm roll T/289, Record group 94, National Archives, Washington, D.C. (hereafter cited as Pension Records); G. V. Rolph and Noel Clark, *The Civil War Soldier* (Washington, D.C.: Historical Impressions, 1961), 4.

18. Alexander to his sisters from Camp Butler, Springfield, Illinois, 13 March 1862, Alexander-Ackerly Family Papers.

19. Winthrop S. G. Allen to his sister, 13 November 1861, Winthrop S. G. Allen Collection, Manuscripts Division, Illinois State Historical Library, Springfield.

20. Administrative Files #301.18, Headquarters Folder; Starr, *From Fort Sumter to Gettysburg,* 119; William F. Scott, *The Story of a Cavalry Regiment: The Career of the Fourth Iowa Veteran Volunteers* (New York, G.P. Putman, 1893), 26–27.

21. Alexander to his brothers and sisters from Camp Butler, Springfield, Illinois, 24 June 1862, Alexander-Ackerly Papers; Thomas I. Cogley, *History of the Seventh Indiana Cavalry Volunteers* (Laporte, Ind.: Herald Steam Printers, 1876), 64–65.

22. Alexander to his brothers and sisters, 24 June 1862; Robert P. Howard, *Illinois: A History of the Prairie State* (Grand Rapids, Mich.: Eerdmans, 1972), 306.

23. Alexander to his brothers and sisters, 24 June 1862; Allen to his sister Jane from Camp Butler, Springfield, Illinois, 8 June 1862, Allen Collection.

24. William H. Kooser, "Barker's and McClellan's Dragoons" (paper presented at the Illinois State Historical Society, Springfield, 5 December 1998); Administrative Files #301.18, Regimental Headquarters Muster Roll; Harold Holzer, ed., *The Lincoln-Douglas Debates* (New York: HarperCollins, 1993), 164–65.

25. Hasbrouck Davis to Adjutant General A. C. Fuller, Illinois State Militia, October 1863, and Governor Richard Yates to Adjutant General A. C. Fuller, 28 September 1861, both in Administrative Files #301.18; Reece, *Report of the Adjutant General,* 7:333; Herbert B. Enderton, ed., *The Private Journal of Abraham Joseph Warner* (San Diego: Colonel Herbert B. Enderton, 1973).

26. Administrative Files #301.18.

27. Starr, *From Fort Sumter to Gettysburg,* 139.

28. Reece, *Report of the Adjutant General of the State of Illinois,* 1:333.

2: "Drop Carbines! . . . Draw Sabers! . . . Charge!"

1. Alexander to his brothers and sisters from Camp Wool, Martinsburg, Virginia, 2 July 1862, Alexander-Ackerly Papers.

2. Enderton, *Private Journal of Abraham Joseph Warner,* 144.

3. Alexander to his sisters from Camp Wool, Martinsburg, Virginia, 12 July 1862, Alexander-Ackerly Papers.

4. Alexander to his sisters, 12 July 1862.

5. Enderton, *Private Journal of Abraham Joseph Warner,* 145.

6. Ibid., 145–46; James Lee McDonough, *Shiloh: In Hell before Night* (Knoxville: University of Tennessee Press, 1977), 4.

7. Enderton, *Private Journal of Abraham Joseph Warner,* 146.

8. Douglas Southall Freeman, *Cedar Mountain to Chancellorsville,* vol. 2 of *Lee's Lieutenants: A Study in Command* (New York: Charles Scribner's Sons, 1942), 405–6.

9. Patricia L. Faust, ed., *Historical Times Illustrated Encyclopedia of the Civil War* (New York: Harper & Row, 1986), 97; Allen to W. A. Tunnell, 17 September 1862, Allen Collection.

10. Starr, *From Fort Sumter to Gettysburg,* 245.

11. Allen to his brother and sister from Greencastle, Pennsylvania, 21 September 1862, Allen Collection.

12. Freeman, *Cedar Mountain,* 156–65; Champ Clark, *Decoying the Yanks: Jackson's Valley Campaign,* The Civil War Series, vol. 4 (Alexandria, Va.: Time-Life Books, 1984), 90–91.

13. Faust, *Encyclopedia of the Civil War,* 27; Freeman, *Cedar Mountain,* 433; Enderton, *Private Journal of Abraham Joseph,* 179.

14. Stephen W. Sears, *Landscape Turned Red: The Battle of Antietam* (New Haven, Conn.: Ticknor & Fields, 1983), 59–63, 65.

15. Grady McWhiney and Perry D. Jamieson, *Attack and Die: Civil War Military Tactics and the Southern Heritage* (University, Ala.: University of Alabama Press, 1982), 8.

16. Sears, *Landscape Turned Red,* 65.

17. Ibid.; Vincent J. Esposito, ed., *1689–1900,* vol. 1 of *The West Point Atlas of American Wars* (New York: Praeger Publishers, 1978), map 65.

18. Esposito, *1689–1900,* map 65; Sears, *Landscape Turned Red,* 65; Starr, *From Fort Sumter to Gettysburg,* 305; Jay Luvaas and Howard W. Nelson, *The U.S. Army War College Guide to the Battle of Antietam: The Maryland Campaign of 1862* (Carlisle, Pa.: South Mountain Press, 1987), 94–95; Isaac W. Heysinger, "The Cavalry Column from Harpers Ferry in the Antietam Campaign," in *Civil War Catalog Number Twenty-Two,* ed. Dennis E. Frye (Dayton, Ohio: Morningside Press, 1987), 6. Corporal Heysinger was a member of Company B, 7th Squadron of the Rhode Island Cavalry.

19. Thomason, *Jeb Stuart,* 260–62; Esposito, *1689–1900,* map 69.

20. Brigadier General Julius White, "The First Sabre Charge of the War," in *Military Essays and Recollections, Papers Read before the Commandery of the State of Illinois,* vol. 3 of *Military Order of the Loyal Legion of the United States* (Chicago: Dial Press, 1899), 3:26. The paper was read on 12 January 1888.

21. Ibid.; Enderton, *Private Journal of Abraham Joseph Warner,* 179–80.

22. Clement A. Evans, ed., *Confederate Military History,* vol. 3 of *Virginia* (Atlanta, Ga.: Confederate Publishing Company, 1899), 241.

23. Enderton, *Private Journal of Abraham Joseph Warner,* 179–82.

24. White, "First Sabre Charge," 27.

25. Ibid.

26. Ibid., 28.

27. George Baylor, *Bull Run to Bull Run; or, Four Years in the Army of Northern Virginia* (Richmond, Va.: B. F. Johnson, 1900), 71. Captain Baylor was commander of the Baylor Light Horse, Company B, 12th Virginia Cavalry, C.S.A. Allan L. Tischler, *The History of the Harpers Ferry Cavalry Expedition, September 14 and 15, 1862* (Winchester, Va.: Five Cedars Press, 1993), 22.

28. Tischler, *History of the Harpers Ferry Cavalry Expedition,* 22; Enderton, *Private Journal of Abraham Joseph Warner,* 191–92. Warner's journal includes a copy of the Official Report of Colonel Voss, Operations of the Twelfth Cavalry, Camp Wool, Near Martinsburg, Va., 9 September 1862.

29. Enderton, *Private Journal of Abraham Joseph Warner,* 184, 191–92.

30. Declaration for an original invalid pension by his mother for John McCarthy, M.D., R.G. 91, Pension No. 302.614, National Archives, Washington, D.C.

31. Declaration of original invalid pension, Pension No. 574.996, National Archives, Washington, D.C. See also Army of the United States, Certificate of Disability for Discharge, 21 March 1863. Application for an invalid pension for George Banghart, National Archives, Washington, D.C.; Carded Medical Records of George Banghart, Company B, 12th Illinois Cavalry, National Archives, Washington, D.C.

32. Enderton, *Private Journal of Abraham Joseph Warner,* 188

33. Ibid., 190.

34. Ibid., 193.

35. A. P. Hill quoted in James I. Robertson Jr., *General A. P. Hill: The Story of a Confederate Warrior* (New York: Random House, 1987), 138.

36. Dennis E. Frye, "The Siege of Harpers Ferry," *Blue & Gray Magazine* (September 1987): 12.

37. Ibid.; Robertson, *General A. P. Hill,* 135.

38. Luvaas and Nelson, *Guide to the Battle of Antietam,* 94–95; Frye, "Siege of Harpers Ferry," 20; George B. Davis, Leslie J. Perry, and Joseph W. Kirkley, *The Official Military Atlas of the Civil War,* comp. Captain Calvin D. Cowles (New York: Fairfax Press, 1983), plate 29, #1.

39. Robertson, *General A. P. Hill,* 135.

40. Ibid., 135–36; Enderton, *Private Journal of Abraham Joseph Warner,* 195; Frye, "Siege of Harpers Ferry," 51.

41. Frye, "Siege of Harpers Ferry," 51; Robertson, *General A. P. Hill,* 137.

42. Captain William M. Luff, "The March of the Cavalry from Harpers Ferry, September 14th, 1862," in *Military Order of the Loyal Legion of the United States* (Chicago: Barnard & Gunthrop, Law Printers, 1887), 5. Paper read 13 January 1887 before the Illinois Commandery. Luff was a captain in the 12th Illinois Volunteer Cavalry.

43. Ibid., 6. There were, of course, some casualties in the shelling. First Lieutenant Frederick Blaidsell, for instance, was thrown from his horse, landing on his left arm. The arm never healed correctly. On 1 December 1862, Blaidsell resigned his commission. He stayed on with his command until he was wounded in his right arm at Upperville, Virginia, in June 1863. See Request of 1st Lieutenant Frederick Blaidsell, Company A, 12th Illinois Cavalry, Pension Record No. 310.078, National

Archives, Washington, D.C.; Carded Medical Records of 1st Lieutenant Frederick Blaidsell, National Archives, Washington, D.C.

44. Alexander to his friend from Williamsport, Maryland, 30 September 1862, Alexander-Ackerly Papers.

45. Luff, "March of the Cavalry," 7.

46. Ibid.; Frye, "Siege of Harpers Ferry," 27.

47. Luff, "March of the Cavalry," 8.

48. Ibid., 8–9.

49. Ibid., 9.

50. Ibid., 9–10; Frye, "Siege of Harpers Ferry," 49.

51. Frye, "Siege of Harpers Ferry," 47; Heysinger, "Cavalry Column," 6.

52. Luff, "March of the Cavalry," 10.

53. Ibid., 10–11; Frye, "Siege of Harpers Ferry," 47; Heysinger, "Cavalry Column," 11.

54. Luff, "March of the Cavalry," 12–13. There is some disagreement about the number of wagons captured, with Luff reporting ninety-seven, Voss ninety-one, and Heysinger seventy-five. Whatever the number in the train, only thirty-seven wagons actually made it to Chambersburg, the train's final stop. Heysinger reported that sixteen wagons were blown up by the Federals on the way to Greencastle because they broke down after being captured.

55. Ibid., 11.

56. Ibid., 15.

57. Heysinger, "Cavalry Column," 6.

3: "Picket and Reconnaissance Duty"

1. James M. McPherson, *Battle Cry of Freedom: The Civil War Era* (New York: Oxford University Press, 1988), 544.

2. Esposito, *1689–1900,* map 70; W. W. Blackford, *The War Years with Jeb Stuart* (New York: Charles Scribner's Sons, 1945), 153.

3. Report of Brigadier General John Kenly, attached to Report of Captain Thomas Logan on the Chambersburg Raid, U.S. War Department, *The War of the Rebellion: A Compilation of the Official Records of the Union and Confederate Armies* (Washington, D.C.: Government Printing Office, 1880–1901), ser. 1, vol. 19, pt. 2, 37–38 (hereafter cited as *OR*).

4. William Henry Redman to his sisters from Clear Spring, Maryland, 21 September 1862, William Henry Redman Papers (#7415-a), Special Collections Department, Manuscript Division, Alderman Library, University of Virginia, Charlottesville; "Letter from Company A," *Rock River Democrat* 18 February 1863, Illinois State Historical Library, Illinois State Archives, Springfield; McPherson, *Battle Cry of Freedom,* 544. To further underscore the casualties of Antietam, it is interesting to note that the bodies of three more Union soldiers killed at Antietam were discovered in 1988. See Stephen R. Potter, *Initial Report of Irish Brigade Remains at Antietam National Battlefield* (Washington, D.C.: National Capitol Region, U.S. National Park Service, 1988).

5. Redman to the *Rock River Democrat,* 12 November 1862; Blackford, *War Years with Jeb Stuart,* 146.

6. Charles W. Ramsdell, "General Robert E. Lee's Horse Supply, 1862–1865," *American Historical Review* 35 (1930): 758–77.

7. Redman to his sisters from Williamsport, Maryland, 9 October 1862.

8. Editorial, *Rock River Democrat,* 12 November 1862.

9. Lincoln and Halleck quoted in McPherson, *Battle Cry of Freedom,* 568–69.

10. Heroes von Borcke, *Memoirs of the Confederate War for Independence* (New York: Peter Smith, 1938), 322–323.

11. Starr, *From Fort Sumter to Gettysburg,* 309 n. 62; Ramsdell, "Lee's Horse Supply." Greased heel is a chronic inflammation of a horse's fetlocks and pasterns, marked by an oily secretion, sores, and sometimes a general swelling of the legs accompanied by a smelly discharge. Incidentally, owing to bad feelings between Professor Thaddeus Lowe and the high command of the Army of the Potomac, observation balloons were not in use after Antietam.

12. Thomason, *Jeb Stuart,* 197, 297–98; Emory Thomas, *Bold Dragoon* (New York: Harper & Row, 1986), 175; J. David Truby, "Pesky Ships of the Air," *Military History* 4 (February 1988): 8, 58–61.

13. Stuart's Expedition into Maryland and Pennsylvania, Captain Thomas Logan report, *OR,* ser. 1, vol. 19, pt. 2, 37–38.

14. Ibid.; U.S. War Department, *Atlas* to accompany *The War of the Rebellion: A Compilation of the Official Records of the Union and Confederate Armies* (Washington, D.C.: Government Printing Office, 1891–1895), plate 27. Hereafter referred to as *OR Atlas.*

15. Logan report, *OR,* ser. 1, vol. 19, pt. 2, 37–38; *OR Atlas,* plate 25, map 5.

16. Sears, *Landscape Turned Red,* 331.

17. Thomason, *Jeb Stuart,* 300–1.

18. Logan report, *OR,* ser. 1, vol. 19, pt. 2, 37.

19. Ibid., 38.

20. Ibid.; Blackford, *War Years with Jeb Stuart,* 178–79. The highest Federal signal station, on Sugarloaf Mountain in Maryland, did not pick up the Confederate column until 12 October, but watched it every step of the way in the final phases of the raid.

21. Thomas, *Bold Dragoon,* 175.

22. Report of Major General J. E. B. Stuart, CS Army, Commanding Cavalry Division, Headquarters Cavalry Division, 14 October 1862, to Colonel R. H. Chilton, Assistant Adjutant General, Army of Northern Virginia, *OR,* ser. 1, vol. 19, pt. 2, 57; Freeman, *Cedar Mountain,* 288; Blackford, *The War Years with Jeb Stuart,* 165–166.

23. Freeman, *Cedar Mountain,* 304–5.

24. Ibid.; Blackford, *War Years with Jeb Stuart,* 172; Captain Thomas Logan's Report of Actions near McCoy's Ford, *OR,* ser. 1, vol. 19, pt. 2, 36–38. In addition to having good guides, Stuart was fortunate enough to have detailed maps. "[Captain W. W. Blackford] learned at Mercersburg that a map of Franklin County [Pennsylvania] was in a private home and he rode there promptly and procured it. As this map had on it all the roads, Stuart could consider alternative routes and could check readily the information that his guides gave him" (Freeman, *Cedar Mountain,* 304).

25. Herman Hattaway and Archer Jones, *How the North Won* (Urbana: Univer-

sity of Illinois Press, 1983), 103–4.

26. *OR Atlas,* plate 37; Redman to his father from Hancock, Maryland, 21 October 1862.

27. Starr, *From Fort Sumter to Gettysburg,* 321 n.97; Jay Luvaas and Harold W. Nelson, eds., *The U.S. Army War College Guide to the Battles of Chancellorsville and Fredericksburg* (Carlisle, Pa.: South Mountain Press, 1987), x.

28. Luvaas and Nelson, *Guide to the Battles of Chancellorsville and Fredericksburg,* x; James Longstreet, "The Battle of Fredericksburg," in *Battles and Leaders of the Civil War,* ed. R. U. Johnson (New York: Century, 1887–1888), 3:76; Allen Nevins, *A House Dividing,* vol. 2 of *The War for the Union* (New York: Scribner, 1960), 43, 343.

29. Thomason, *Jeb Stuart,* 319; H. B. McClellan, *I Rode with Jeb Stuart: The Life and Campaigns of Major General J.E.B. Stuart* (Bloomington: Indiana University Press, 1958), 167. For an account of the elections, see *Rock River Democrat,* 12 November 1862.

30. Howard, *Illinois: A History,* 304

31. *OR,* ser. 1, vol. 19, pt. 2, 545; Gallagher, *Fighting for the Confederacy: The Personal Recollections of General Edward Porter Alexander* (Durham: University of North Carolina Press, 1989), 166; Redman to his sisters from Williamsport, Maryland, 27 October 1862. The Confederate high command did not know about Burnside's appointment as commander of the Army of the Potomac for a couple of days after it happened and only found out about it via the soldier "trade and rumor route," not as a matter of official courtesy. See Longstreet, "Battle of Fredericksburg," 3:76.

32. *OR,* ser. 1, vol. 19, pt. 2, 57; Starr, *From Fort Sumter to Gettysburg,* 324–25; Reece, *Report of the Adjutant General,* 8:187.

33. Esposito, *1689–1900,* map 71; Correspondence from Lincoln to Burnside, 14 November 1862, *OR,* ser. 1, vol. 19, pt. 2, 545.

34. John MacDonald, *Great Battles* (New York: Macmillan, 1988), 68–69; Esposito, *1689–1900,* map 71.

35. Esposito, *1689–1900,* map 71; MacDonald, *Great Battles,* 68; Shelby Foote, *The Civil War: A Narrative,* vol. 2, *Fredericksburg to Meridian* (New York: Random House, 1963), 21.

36. Reports, *OR,* ser. 1, vol. 19, pt. 2, 790; Ramsdell, "Lee's Horse Supply," 759.

37. Faust, *Encyclopedia of the Civil War,* 202.

38. Ibid.

39. MacDonald, *Great Battles,* 71; Luvaas and Nelson, *Guide to the Battles of Chancellorsville and Fredericksburg,* 95; Gallagher, *Fighting for the Confederacy,* 169.

40. Starr, *From Fort Sumter to Gettysburg,* 325.

41. Gallagher, *Fighting for the Confederacy,* 169; Alexander to his sister, 17 January 1863, quoted in Hicken, *Illinois in the Civil War,* 334.

42. Lee quoted in McPherson, *Battle Cry of Freedom,* 572 n. 9.

43. "Letter from Company A," *Rock River Democrat,* 18 February 1863; Reece, *Report of the Adjutant General,* 8:376–79.

44. Redman to his mother from Fairfax Courthouse, 14 December 1862, on paper that has a picture of George Washington and the inscription, "A Southern Man with Union Principles." Confederate Major White's report from the Official Records states that he had been following Company C of the 12th Illinois since it passed

Hillsboro. White until the 12th Illinois had cleared Leesburg, then ordered his advance company to push on. They caught the 12th about three miles below Leesburg and drove them into the rear guard of their infantry. (Redman does not mention Federal infantry.) White's report agrees with Redman's letter that the 12th Illinois captured two men and wounded three. He does not refer specifically to the wagons but adds them to another capture of Federal supplies that occurred the following day during a raid on Poolesville, Maryland. See Report of Major E. V. White, Commanding 35th Maryland Battalion, *OR,* ser. 1, vol. 21, 691.

45. Redman to his mother from Clear Spring, Maryland, 14 and 18 December 1862; Pension Records.

46. Redman to his mother from Clear Spring, Maryland, 14 December 1862; "Letter from Company A," *Rock River Democrat,* 18 February 1863.

47. "Letter from Company A," *Rock River Democrat,* 18 February 1863; Redman to his mother from Clear Spring, Maryland, 14 December 1862.

48. Thomas, *Bold Dragoon,* 195; General U. S. Grant's map of the armies under his command, 1864–1865, *OR Atlas,* map of Central Virginia.

49. Thomas, *Bold Dragoon,* 195; Report from Gen. Robert E. Lee to Gen. Samuel Cooper, Inspector General of the Confederate Armies, 13 December 1862; Report from Hampton to J. E. B. Stuart, 15 December 1862; Report of J. E. B. Stuart, 19 December 1862, all in *OR,* ser. 1, vol. 21, pt. 2, 689–91. Hampton reported only seventeen wagons captured, two destroyed in the center of the town, and one broken down on the way to the Confederate lines on the south side of the Rappahannock.

50. Thomas, *Bold Dragoon,* 195–96; Thomason, *Jeb Stuart,* 347; Stuart report, *OR,* ser. 1, vol. 21, pt. 2, 691; Report of Lt. Col. Hasbrouck Davis, Commanding the 12th Illinois Cavalry, 28 December 1862, *OR,* ser. 1, vol. 21, pt. 2, 728–30.

51. Hasbrouck Davis report, *OR,* ser. 1, vol. 21, pt. 2, 728–30.

52. Ibid.; Redman to his mother from Camp Dumfries, Virginia, 30 December 1862.

53. Hasbrouck Davis report, *OR,* ser. 1, vol. 21, pt. 2, 728–30; Reports of Lt. Col. Eugene Powell, 66th Ohio Volunteers; Col. W. R. Creighton, 7th Ohio, and 1st Lt. William Rodgers, 6th Maine Artillery, *OR,* ser. 1, vol. 21, pt. 2, 727–31.

54. Report of J. E. B. Stuart, 19 Dec. 1862, *OR,* ser. 1, vol. 21, pt. 2, 731–32; Hasbrouck Davis report, *OR,* ser. 1, vol. 21, pt. 2, 729. The glancing shell caused a severe contusion of Hayden's right hip. He was admitted to the hospital on 27 December 1862. Carded Medical Records of Captain R. N. Hayden, National Archives, Washington, D.C.

55. Hasbrouck Davis report, *OR,* ser. 1, vol. 21, pt. 2, 729; Redman to his mother from Dumfries, Virginia, 30 December 1862.

56. Redman to his mother from Dumfries, Virginia, 30 December 1862; Hasbrouck Davis report, *OR,* ser. 1, vol. 21, pt. 2, 730.

57. Redman to his mother from Dumfries, Virginia, 30 December 1862.

4: Raids

1. Luvaas and Nelson, *Guide to the Battles of Chancellorsville and Fredericksburg,* 119; Redman to the *Rock River Democrat,* 18 February 1863.

2. Redman to his mother from Dumfries, Virginia, 12 January 1863; Redman to his brothers from Dumfries, Virginia, 15 January 1863; William C. Davis, *The Fighting Men of the Civil War* (New York: Salamander Books, 1989), 180–81.

3. Defenses of the Upper Potomac, Organization of the Railroad Division, *OR,* ser. 1, vol. 31, pt. 2, 963.

4. Correspondence, *OR,* ser. 1, vol. 31, pt. 1, 1005.

5. Robert K. Krick, "Lee's Greatest Victory," *American Heritage Civil War Chronicles* (Summer 1991), 82; Hattaway and Jones, *How the North Won,* 350.

6. Hattaway and Jones, *How the North Won,* 350; Starr, *From Fort Sumter to Gettysburg,* 339.

7. Starr, *From Fort Sumter to Gettysburg,* 339.

8. Abner B. Frank, *The Civil War Diary of Abner B. Frank,* transcribed by Larry D. Smith, vol. 1 (Carlisle Barracks, Pa.: Institute of Military History, U.S. Army War College, 1982), 7 April 1863. Hereafter cited as Frank diary.

9. E. B. Long, *The Civil War Day by Day: An Almanac, 1861–1865* (Garden City, N.Y.: Doubleday, 1971), 311; Redman to his sister from Dumfries, Virginia, 13 March 1863; Dudley Taylor Cornish, *The Sable Arm* (New York: W. W. Norton, 1966), 163; Brian C. Pohanka, "Carnival of Death," *America's Civil War* (September 1991): 30–36; John T. Glatthaar, *Forged in Battles* (New York: Macmillan, 1990), 140.

10. Allen to his sister, April 1863, quoted in Henry E. Pratt, "Civil War Letters of Winthrop S. G. Allen," *Journal of the Illinois State Historical Society* (October 1931): 573; Frank diary, 3–9, April 1863.

11. Redman to his mother from Dumfries, Virginia, 13 February 1863; Robert Lanier and Theo F. Rodenbough, *Photographic History of the Civil War* (New York: Fairfax Press, 1989), 33; John Bigelow Jr., *The Campaign of Chancellorsville: A Strategic and Tactical Study* (New Haven: Yale University Press, 1910), 23.

12. Bigelow, *Campaign of Chancellorsville,* 49; McPherson, *Battle Cry of Freedom,* 639.

13. Luvaas and Nelson, *Guide to the Battles of Chancellorsville and Fredericksburg,* 137; Hooker quoted in Foote, *Civil War,* 2:262.

14. Faust, *Encyclopedia of the Civil War,* 325, 728.

15. Starr, *From Fort Sumter to Gettysburg,* 95; Garry James, "The Reliable Remington," *Civil War Times Illustrated* (September–October 1990): 18–20; Ken Bauman, *Arming the Suckers* (Dayton, Ohio: Morningside Press, 1988), 61.

16. Adjutant General's Office, *The Volunteer Force General Orders, 1862* (Washington, D.C.: National Archives), 46–47, 154–55; Administrative Files #301.18.

17. Redman to his mother from Belle Plain, Virginia, 17 April 1863; Silas D. Wesson, 3 October 1862, Silas D. Wesson diary, Batavia, Ill.: Kane County Historical Society.

18. Hattaway and Jones, *How the North Won,* 151; Report of Brigadier General David M. Gregg, Commanding the Third Cavalry Division, 15 May 1863, *OR,* ser. 1, vol. 25, pt. 1, 1081–83; Longacre, "The Raid That Failed," *Civil War Times Illustrated* (January 1988): 16; Frank diary, 15 April 1863.

19. Gregg report, 15 May 1863, *OR,* ser. 1, vol. 25, pt. 1, 1082; Frank diary, 29–30, April 1863.

20. Redman to the *Mount Carroll Weekly Mirror,* 8 June 1863; Bigelow, *Campaign of Chancellorsville,* 441–42.

21. Longacre, "Raid That Failed," 18; Krick, "Lee's Greatest Victory," 24.

22. Robert Krick, *The 9th Virginia Cavalry* (Lynchburg, Va.: H. E. Howard Publishing, 1988), 17; McClellan, *I Rode with Jeb Stuart,* 227; Report of Maj. Gen. George Stoneman, *OR,* ser. 1, vol. 25, pt. 1, 1061; William Sturtevant Nye, *Here Come the Rebels!* (Baton Rouge: Louisiana State University Press, 1965), 15.

23. Gregg report, *OR,* ser. 1, vol. 25, pt. 1, 1082; Redman to the *Mount Carroll Weekly Mirror,* 8 June 1863; Longacre, "Raid That Failed," 44; Bigelow, *Campaign of Chancellorsville,* 443.

24. Frank diary, 2 May 1863; Bigelow, *Campaign of Chancellorsville,* 444–45.

25. Bigelow, *Campaign of Chancellorsville,* 444 45; Stoneman report, *OR,* ser. 1, vol. 25, pt. 1, 1061.

26. Report of Lt. Col. Hasbrouck Davis to Brig. Gen. Rufus King, *OR,* ser. 1, vol. 28, pt. 1, 708; Frank diary, 3 May 1863; Redman to the *Mount Carroll Weekly Mirror,* 8 June 1863; Report of Lt. Col. Hasbrouck Davis, *OR,* ser. 1, vol. 25, pt. 1, 1085–87.

27. Davis report, *OR,* ser. 1, vol. 25, pt. 1, 1085–87.

28. Ibid.; Frank diary, 3 May 1863; Redman to the *Mount Carroll Weekly Mirror,* 8 June 1863.

29. Longacre, "Raid That Failed," 21.

30. Frank diary, 3–4 May 1863; Davis report, *OR,* ser. 1, vol. 25, pt. 1, 1085–87; Redman to the *Mount Carroll Weekly Mirror,* 8 June 1863.

31. Davis report, *OR,* ser. 1, vol. 25, pt. 1, 1087; Redman to the *Mount Carroll Weekly Mirror,* 8 June 1863; Personal Service Records of William A. Arter, Sergeant, 12th Illinois Cavalry, Prisoner of War Record Copy, National Archives, Washington, D.C.

32. Coggins, *Arms and Equipment,* 38–39, 76–77.

33. Davis report, *OR,* ser. 1, vol. 25, pt. 1, 1087.

34. John B. Jones, *A Rebel War Clerk's Diary* (Philadelphia: J. B. Lippincott, 1866), 1:300, 307.

35. Redman to the *Mount Carroll Weekly Mirror,* 8 June 1863; Betsey Fleet and John D. P. Fuller, eds., *Green Mount: A Virginia Plantation Family during the Civil War: Being the Journal of Benjamin Robert Fleet and Letters of His Family* (Lexington: University of Kentucky Press, 1962), 224; Jones, *Rebel War Clerk's Diary,* 307; Capt. Frederick W. Mitchell, "A Personal Episode of the First Stoneman Raid," in *Military Order of the Loyal Legion of the United States,* War Papers 56 (Washington, D.C.: Commandery of the District of Columbia, 7 December 1904); Davis report, *OR,* ser. 1, vol. 25, pt. 1, 1087.

36. Davis report, *OR,* ser. 1, vol. 25, pt. 1, 1087; Frank Moore, ed., *The Rebellion Record, The Diary of Events* (New York: G. P. Putnam, 1864), 6:71; Redman to the *Mount Carroll Weekly Mirror,* 8 June 1863.

37. Longacre, "Raid That Failed," 49; Historical Sketch of the Command, *Reunion of the 12th Illinois Cavalry, Springfield, Illinois* (Chicago: 12th Illinois Volunteer Cavalry Association, 1918), 16.

38. Redman to his mother from Gloucester Point, Virginia, 9 May 1863; Longacre, "Raid That Failed," 45; Davis report, *OR,* ser. 1, vol. 25, pt. 1, 1087; Redman to the *Mount Carroll Weekly Mirror,* 8 June 1863.

39. Redman to the *Mount Carroll Weekly Mirror,* 8 June 1863; Jones, *Rebel War Clerk's Diary,* 302; Longacre, "Raid That Failed," 21, 44.

40. Reece, *Report of the Adjutant General,* 8:378.

41. Correspondence, *OR,* ser. 1, vol. 25, pt. 2, 477, Special Orders No. 30 by the Command of Maj. Gen. Hooker, Assistant Adjutant General B. Williams; Frank diary, 20 May 1863.

42. Correspondence, *OR,* ser. 1, vol. 25, pt. 2, 477, Special Orders No. 30 by the Command of Maj. Gen. Hooker, Assistant Adjutant General B. Williams; Frank diary, 20 May 1863; Redman to his brothers from Gloucester Point, Virginia, 23 May 1863.

43. Samuel B. Rice, "Letters of Samuel B. Rice, Company D, 9th Virginia Cavalry," *Bulletin of the Northumberland County Historical Society* 26 (1989): 39–41.

44. Redman to his mother, sisters, and brothers from Potomac Creek, Virginia, 6 June 1863.

45. Redman to his brothers from camp near Belle Plain, Virginia, 9 June 1863.

46. Rice, "Letters of Samuel B. Rice"; Redman to his brothers, 23 May 1863; Frank diary, 20–30 May 1863; Robert Krick, ed., *Lee's Colonels: A Biographical Register of the Field Officers of the Army of Northern Virginia,* 2nd ed. (Dayton, Ohio: Morningside Press, 1984), 279.

5: Forcing the Rebels to Deploy

1. Jay Luvaas and Harold W. Nelson, *The U.S. Army War College Guide to the Battle of Gettysburg* (New York: Harper & Row, 1986), 222.

2. Thomas, *Bold Dragoon,* 224; Historical Sketch of the Command and Dedication of the Lincoln and Douglas Statues and article by Homer Calkens, *Reunion of the 12th Illinois Cavalry* (1918), 15; Thomason, *Jeb Stuart,* 411; Report of Col. Samuel P. Spears, 11th Pennsylvania Cavalry, Commanding Expedition, 28 June 1863, *OR,* ser. 1, vol. 27, pt. 2, Reports, 796–97.

3. Thomason, *Jeb Stuart,* 411.

4. Faust, *Encyclopedia of the Civil War,* 89; Edwin C. Bearss, *Forrest at Brice's Crossroads* (Dayton, Ohio: Morningside Press, 1979), 337–38.

5. Faust, *Encyclopedia of the Civil War,* 89, 269–70; Bearss, *Forrest,* 338; Glen Sunderland, *Wilder's Lightning Brigade* (Washington, Ill.: Book Works, 1984), 181.

6. Foote, *Civil War,* 2:436–37. The 12th Illinois joined Buford sometime between 10 and 15 June. John Buford quoted in Edward Longacre, *The Cavalry at Gettysburg* (Lincoln: University of Nebraska Press, 1993), 168–69.

7. Ray P. Stonesifer Jr., "The Union Cavalry Comes of Age," *Civil War History* (September 1965), 275–76.

8. Luvaas and Nelson, *Guide to the Battle of Gettysburg,* 222.

9. Starr, *From Fort Sumter to Gettysburg,* 399; advertisement placed by James Fry, Acting Provost Marshall of the U.S. Army, *Mount Carroll Weekly Mirror,* 3 June 1863.

10. Frank Diary, 11 June 1863; Redman to his brothers from Belle Plain, Virginia, 9 June 1863; Report No. 10, Return of Casualties in the Union forces at Brandy Station (Fleetwood), Beverly Ford, and Stevensburg, Va., 9 June 1863, *OR,* ser. 1, vol. 27, pt. 1, Reports, 168–70.

11. Hooker quoted in Starr, *From Fort Sumter to Gettysburg,* 400.

12. Frank diary, 18 June 1863.

13. Ibid.

14. Ibid., 21 June 1863; Nye, *Here Come the Rebels!* 180–81; Report of Lt. Col. Thomas Marshall, 7th Virginia Cavalry, 9 August 1863, *OR,* ser. 1, vol. 27, pt. 2, 759.

15. Marshall report, *OR,* ser. 1, vol. 27, pt. 2, 759; Nye, *Here Come the Rebels!* 195–96; Krick, *Lee's Colonels,* 226; Frank diary, 19–20 June 1863.

16. Redman to the *Mount Carroll Weekly Mirror,* 8 July 1863.

17. Stephen Z. Starr, *The War in the East, from Gettysburg to Appomattox, 1863–1865,* vol. 2 of *The Union Cavalry in the Civil War* (Baton Rouge: Louisiana State University Press, 1980), 8; Reports of Colonel William Gamble, 8th Illinois Cavalry, Commanding 1st Brigade, *OR,* ser. 1, vol. 27, pt. 1, 932–33 (22 June 1863). Hereafter cited as Gamble reports.

18. Reports of Brigadier General John Buford, *OR,* ser. 1, vol. 27, pt. 1, 921 (24 June 1863) [hereafter cited as Buford reports]; Gamble reports, *OR,* ser. 1, vol. 27, pt. 1, 932–33.

19. Buford reports, *OR,* ser. 1, vol. 27, pt. 1, 932–33.

20. Buford reports, *OR,* ser. 1, vol. 27, pt. 1, 921.

21. Robert F. O'Neill Jr., *The Cavalry Battles of Aldie, Middleburg, and Upperville, June 10–27, 1863* (Lynchburg, Va.: H. E. Howard, 1993); Krick, *9th Virginia Cavalry,* 138.

22. Buford reports, *OR,* ser. 1, vol. 27, pt. 1, 921; Eugene M. Scheel, *Map of the Civil War in Fauquier* (Warrenton, Va.: The Fauquier National Bank, June 1985), 10. Interestingly, part of the Laurel Brigade was formed before the war to ensure that Irish railroad workers in Fauquier County would not form a labor union.

23. Buford reports, *OR,* ser. 1, vol. 27, pt. 1, 921; Gamble reports, *OR,* ser. 1, vol. 27, pt. 1, 932–33; Redman to his mother from near Aldie, Virginia, 24 June 1863.

24. Nye, *Here Come the Rebels!* 204; Return of Casualties in the Union Forces at Upperville, Va., 21 June 1863, *OR,* ser. 1, vol. 27, pt. 1, Reports, 171.

25. Von Borcke, *Memoirs,* 294–95; Scheel, *Civil War in Fauquier,* 59.

26. McClellan, *I Rode with Jeb Stuart,* 314.

27. Redman to his mother from near Aldie, Virginia, 24 June 1863; Frank diary, 21 June 1863.

28. Report of Major General Alfred Pleasonton, *OR,* ser. 1, vol. 27, pt. 3, 913; Starr, *From Fort Sumter to Gettysburg,* 411.

29. R. F. S. Starr, "Lest We Forget, A Confederate Memorial, Ivy Hill Cemetery, Upperville, Virginia," *Virginia Country Civil War Quarterly* 7 (1987): 72–73.

30. Frank diary, 25 June 1863; Mark Nesbitt, *Saber and Scapegoat: J. E. B. Stuart and the Gettysburg Controversy* (Mechanicsburg, Pa.: Stackpole Books, 1994); Report of Maj. Gen. J. E. B. Stuart, 30 August 1863, *OR,* ser. 1, vol. 27, pt. 2, 687–710; Foote, *Civil War,* 2:462.

31. Frank diary, 26 June 1863; Report of Lt. John H. Calef, Battery A, Second U.S. Artillery, 27 July 1863, *OR,* ser. 1, vol. 27, pt. 1, Reports, pp. 1029–34.

32. Buford reports, *OR,* ser. 1, vol. 27, pt. 1, 921.

33. Frank diary, 6 June 1863; Starr, *From Fort Sumter to Gettysburg,* 418, 422; Henry P. Moyer, *History of the 17th Regiment Pennsylvania Volunteer Cavalry* (Lebanon, Pa.: Sowers Printing, 1911), 58, quoted in Starr, *From Fort Sumter to Gettysburg,* 422.

34. Buford reports, *OR,* ser. 1, vol. 27, pt. 1, 926; Longacre, *Cavalry at Gettysburg,* 181.

35. Buford reports, *OR,* ser. 1, vol. 27, pt. 1, 926–27; McPherson, *Battle Cry of Freedom,* 653; Luvaas and Nelson, *Guide to the Battle of Gettysburg,* 50–51; Allen Nevins, *The Organized War 1863–1864,* vol. 3 of *The War for the Union* (New York: Scribner, 1971), 97.

36. Buford reports, *OR,* ser. 1, vol. 27, pt. 1, 922–24; Foote, *Civil War,* 2:467.

37. Redman to his mother from Gettysburg, Pennsylvania, 1 July 1863.

38. Gamble reports, *OR,* ser. 1, vol. 27, pt. 1, 934.

39. Redman to his mother from Gettysburg, Pennsylvania, 1 July 1863.

40. Hill quoted in Foote, *Civil War,* 2:465; Buford reports, *OR,* ser. 1, vol. 27, pt. 1, 924.

41. Samuel M. Blackwell, Jr., "Illinois at Gettysburg," *Illinois Magazine* (July–August 1984), 33–37; Richard A. Sauers, "Gettysburg Controversies," *Gettysburg Magazine* (January 1991): 115; Buford reports, *OR,* ser. 1, vol. 27, pt. 1, 924.

42. Gamble reports, *OR,* ser. 1, vol. 27, pt. 1, 934; Foote, *Civil War,* 2:468. The flank regiments, too, were fighting with a quarter of their men out of the line. During the nineteenth century, horse cavalry units fighting dismounted placed one out of every four troopers behind the line holding four to six horses. The horses were held with their heads toward the center to keep them under control.

43. Sauers, "Gettysburg Controversies," 116; Gamble reports, *OR,* ser. 1, vol. 27, pt. 1, 934.

44. Gamble reports, *OR,* ser. 1, vol. 27, pt. 1, 934.

45. E. P. Halsted, "Incidents of the First Day at Gettysburg," in Johnson, ed., *Battles and Leaders of the Civil War,* 3:284–85.

46. John L. Beveridge, "The First Gun at Gettysburg," in Ken Bandy and Florence Freeland, eds., *The Gettysburg Papers,* vol. 1 (Dayton, Ohio: Morningside Press, 1978), 97. See also David G. Martin, *Gettysburg, July 1* (Conshohocken, Pa.: Combined Books, 1995), 420.

47. Gamble reports, *OR,* ser. 1, vol. 27, pt. 1, 937; Martin, *Gettysburg,* 420–22.

48. Varina D. Brown, *A Colonel at Gettysburg and Spotsylvania* (Columbia, S.C.: State Company, 1931), 80–81, 208–9; Bandy and Freeland, *Gettysburg Papers,* 97; Church Papers, 935.

49. Martin, *Gettysburg,* 86; Letter of Mrs. Maria Raney to Adjutant General Fuller, Belvidere, Illinois, 28 July 1863, Positive Working Copy, #309-1463, Civil War Companies and Regiments, 12th Illinois Cavalry, Company A, Illinois State Archives, Springfield; Surgeon's Certificate for Willet S. Haight, Company A, 12th Illinois Cavalry, 21 May 1888, Pension Claim, 23-203, Soldiers Pension Record, National Archives, Washington, D.C., 1891.

50. Letter from William Gamble, Col., 8th Illinois Cavalry, at Gettysburg, to W. L. Church, March 10, 1864, William L. Church Papers, Archives and Manuscripts Division, Chicago Historical Society; Gamble reports, *OR,* ser. 1, vol. 27, pt. 1, 935.

51. M. F. Steele, *American Campaigns* (Washington, D.C.: U.S. Infantry Assoc., 1922), 392, quoted in Starr, *From Fort Sumter to Gettysburg,* 426 n.38; Starr, *From Fort Sumter to Gettysburg,* 426; Gallagher, *Fighting for the Confederacy,* 232.

52. Third Reunion of the 12th Illinois Cavalry held at Detroit, Michigan, 5 August 1891, Illinois State Historical Library, Springfield (n.p., n.d.), 28; Frank diary, 1 July 1863.

53. Redman to his sisters from Westminster, Maryland, 3 July 1863.

54. Buford reports, *OR,* ser. 1, vol. 27, pt. 1, 927.

6: "Fighting the Rebs for Seven Days"

1. Buford reports, *OR,* ser. 1, vol. 27, pt. 1, 927–28; Reece, *Report of the Adjutant General,* 8:378; Marshall D. Krolick, "Forgotten Field: The Cavalry Battle East of Gettysburg on July 3, 1863," *Gettysburg Magazine* (January 1991): 75.

2. Gallagher, *Fighting for the Confederacy,* 267; John D. Imboden, "The Confederate Retreat from Gettysburg," in Johnson, ed., *Battles and Leaders of the Civil War,* 3:426.

3. Starr, *From Fort Sumter to Gettysburg,* 444–47, 450.

4. Ibid., 451; Krolick, "Forgotten Field," 76.

5. Reece, *Report of the Adjutant General,* 8:378; Buford reports, *OR,* ser. 1, vol. 27, pt. 1, 928; Starr, *From Fort Sumter to Gettysburg,* 443.

6. Redman to his mother from Frederick City, Maryland, 6 July 1863.

7. Buford reports, *OR,* ser. 1, vol. 27, pt. 1, 928; Gamble reports, *OR,* ser. 1, vol. 27, pt. 1, 935.

8. Imboden, "Confederate Retreat," 426; Gamble reports, *OR,* ser. 1, vol. 27, pt. 1, 935; Buford reports, *OR,* ser. 1, vol. 27, pt. 1, 928.

9. Gamble reports, *OR,* ser. 1, vol. 27, pt. 1, 936; Redman to his mother from Boonsboro, Maryland, 10 July 1863; Longacre, *Cavalry at Gettysburg,* quotation on 265.

10. Redman to his mother from camp near Berlin, Maryland, 16 July 1863. Murat, Napoleon's cavalryman, was disposed to gallant, headlong cavalry charges. These were largely successful in the days before rifled muskets, which could empty the saddles of charging cavalrymen before the soldiers reached their objectives.

11. Starr, *From Fort Sumter to Gettysburg,* 458.

12. Gamble reports, *OR,* ser. 1, vol. 27, pt. 1, 935.

13. Ibid., 936–37.

14. Ibid., 937; Redman to his sister Emeline from camp near Berlin, Virginia, 16 July 1863.

15. Frank diary, 18 July 1863.

16. Frank diary, 20 July 1863.

17. Buford reports, *OR,* ser. 1, vol. 27, pt. 1, 929; Gamble reports, *OR,* ser. 1, vol. 27, pt. 1, 937; the correspondence of Colonel William Gamble to Brigadier General John Buford, *OR,* ser. 1, vol. 27, pt. 3, 741. Hereafter cited as Gamble correspondence.

18. Report of Brigadier General John Buford to Major General Alfred Pleasonton, *OR,* ser. 1, vol. 27, pt. 3, 742.

19. Ibid.; Luvaas and Nelson, *Guide to the Battle of Gettysburg,* 207.

20. Frank diary, 22 July 1863; Redman to his sister Emeline from camp near Chester Gap, Virginia, 25 July 1863; Redman to his mother from Chester Gap, Virginia, 2 July 1863.

21. Gamble correspondence, *OR,* ser. 1, vol. 27, pt. 3, 937.

22. Report of Brig. Gen. W. E. Jones, Army of Northern Virginia, Commanding Jones's Brigade, Stuart's Cavalry, 30 July 1863, *OR,* ser. 1, vol. 27, pt. 2, 751–54; Lt. Col. Thomas Marshall, Seventh Virginia Cavalry, 9 August 1863, *OR,* ser. 1, vol. 27, pt. 2, 758–62; Major C. E. Flournoy, Sixth Virginia Cavalry, 18 July 1863, *OR,* ser. 1, vol. 27, pt. 2, 755–56; Col. Lunsford L. Lomax, Eleventh Virginia Cavalry, Commanding, 30 July 1863, *OR,* ser. 1, vol. 27, pt. 2, 763–65 (Stuart included no casualty listing for the six actions that would contradict with those by Gamble); Carded Medical Records, 12th Illinois Cavalry, National Archives, Washington, D.C.

23. Correspondence and report of Brig. Gen. George Gordon Meade, 31 July 1863, *OR,* ser. 1, vol. 27, pt. 3, 804; Starr, *War in the East,* 19–20.

24. Frank diary, 31 July 1863; Report of Brig. Gen. Rufus King, 7 August 1863, *OR,* ser. 1, vol. 29, pt. 1, 66.

25. King report, *OR,* ser. 1, vol. 29, pt. 1, 66.

26. Redman to his mother from 1st Division Cavalry Corps headquarters near Kelly's Ford, Virginia, 14 August 1863.

27. Charges against Capt. G. W. Shears, Company H, 12th Illinois Volunteer Cavalry, Administrative Files #301.18. Court Martial 936, Military Records Division, National Archives, Washington, D.C.

28. Major S. F. Bronson to the Adjutant General of Illinois, 14 May 1863, enclosure in the personnel file of Lt. Col. Hasbrouck Davis, Compilation of Records of Union Volunteer Army Soldiers, Record Group 94, Military Records Division, National Archives, Washington, D.C. (hereafter cited as Compilation); Court of Inquiry of Lieutenant Colonel Hasbrook Davis, Court of Inquiry 936, Compilation, RG 94; Court of Inquiry of Captain George W. Shears, Company H, 12th Illinois Volunteer Cavalry, File S2315, Military Records Division, National Archives, Washington, D.C.; Records of the Court of Inquiry of Captain George W. Shears, Administrative Files #301.18; Roger D. Hunt, *Brevet Brigadier Generals in Blue* (New York: Olde Soldier Books, 1991), 149.

29. Hunt, *Brevet Brigadier Generals,* 149; Court of Inquiry 936, Compilation, RG 94-1.

30. Redman to his mother from Warrentown Junction, Virginia, 25 August 1863.

31. Redman to his brothers from Kelly's Ford, Virginia, 28 August 1863.

32. *Mount Carroll Weekly Mirror,* 19 August 1863; Redman to his mother from Bealton Station, Virginia, 2 November 1863.

33. Long, *Civil War Day by Day,* 408–9; Meade quoted in Starr, *War in the East,* 21; McClellan, *I Rode with Jeb Stuart,* 373.

34. T. M. Eddy, *The Patriotism of Illinois: A Record of the Civil and Military History of the State in the War for the Union,* vol. 1 (Chicago: Clarke & Co., 1865), 565. See also Pension Records of Napoleon B. and Thomas J. Kemper, Pension No. 305970, Company F, 12th Illinois Cavalry, Pension Records of Union Army Volunteer Veterans, Microfilm roll T/289, Record group 94. National Archives, Washington, D.C.

35. Starr, *War in the East,* 22–23; Frank diary, 22 September 1863.

36. McClellan, *I Rode with Jeb Stuart,* 375; Frank diary, 22 September 1863.

37. Starr, *War in the East,* 23.

38. McClellan, *I Rode with Jeb Stuart,* 379–80; Buford reports (14 November

1863), *OR,* ser. 1, vol. 29, pt. 1, 347–49.

    39. Buford reports, *OR,* ser. 1, vol. 29, pt. 1, 347–49.

    40. Starr, *War in the East,* 24.

    41. Frank diary, 12 October 1863.

    42. Buford reports, *OR,* ser. 1, vol. 29, pt. 1, 351.

    43. Casualty Report of Maj. Gen. Fitzhugh Lee, *OR,* ser. 1, vol. 29, pt. 1, 464; Starr, *War in the East,* 28–29.

    44. Frank diary, 27 October 1863; Report of Major John S. Mosby, Commanding the 43rd Ranger Battalion, *OR,* ser. 1, vol. 29, pt. 1, 495.

    45. Frank diary, 12 November 1863; Reece, *Report of the Adjutant General,* 8:378.

7: Search and Destroy

    1. Frank diary, 25–30 November 1863; Reece, *Report of the Adjutant General,* 8:378; Redman to his sister from Camp Fry, Illinois, 20 January 1864.

    2. Redman to his friends from Camp Fry, Illinois, 31 January 1864.

    3. Ibid., 8 February 1864.

    4. Reece, *Report of the Adjutant General,* 8:378; Correspondence, Maj. Gen. N. P. Banks from Headquarters, Department of the Gulf, New Orleans, to Maj. Gen. H. W. Halleck, General in Chief, U.S. Army, Washington, D.C., 8 March 1864, 527–28; Maj. Gen. and Chief of Staff H. W. Halleck from Washington, D.C. to Lt. Gen. Grant, Nashville, Tennessee, 17 March 1864, 634–35; U. S. Grant, Lt. Gen., Commanding from Nashville to Gen. Davidson, Cavalry Depot, Saint Louis, Missouri, 17 March 1864, 638, all in *OR,* ser. 1, vol. 34, pt. 2; Redman to his mother from Cairo, Illinois, 2 April 1864.

    5. Redman to his sisters from on board the Edward Walsh near Fort Pillow, Tennessee, 4 April 1864; Richard E. Beringer et al., *Why the South Lost the Civil War* (Athens: University of Georgia Press, 1986), 24; Stephen Z. Starr, *The War in the West, 1861–1865,* vol. 3 of *The Union Cavalry in the Civil War* (Baton Rouge: Louisiana State University Press, 1985), 324–25. The wharf from which the Edward Walsh departed is still in Cairo, as is almost the entire river-wharf complex that was built in that city during the Civil War. See David C. Roth, "The War at the Confluence," *Blue and Gray Magazine* (Spring 1991): 17.

    6. Redman to his mother from New Orleans, Louisiana, 15 April 1864; Redman to his brothers from Camp Parapet, Louisiana, 19 April 1864; Starr, *War in the West,* 324.

    7. Redman to his brothers from New Orleans, Louisiana, 19 April 1864.

    8. Redman to his mother from on board the *Jennie Rogers* near Port Hudson, 21 April 1864; Redman to his mother from camp near Alexandria, Louisiana, 25 April 1864.

    9. Ludwell Harrison Johnson, *Red River Campaign: Politics and Cotton in the Civil War* (Baltimore: Johns Hopkins University Press, 1958), 258–59.

    10. Redman to his mother from camp near Alexandria, Louisiana, 8 May 1864; Carded Medical Records, Pension Record of Captain William M. Luff, Company I, 12th Illinois Cavalry, National Archives, Washington, D.C.

    11. Redman to his mother from camp near Alexandria, Louisiana, 8 May

1864; Redman to his mother from Napoleonville, Louisiana, 8 May 1864; Redman to his mother from Napoleonville, Louisiana, 16 June 1864.

12. Johnson, *Red River Campaign.*

13. Redman to his sisters from Napoleonville, Louisiana, 1 August 1864; Letter from Henry Richardson to Miss Jemina Robertson, Wyoming, New York, 6 June 1864, Noel Reen Collection, Lafayette, Indiana.

14. Faust, *Encyclopedia of the Civil War,* 89; Reece, *Report of the Adjutant General,* 8:381; Hunt, *Brevet Brigadier Generals,* 170.

15. Redman to his mother from camp near Carrollton, Louisiana, 30 May 1864; Frederick W. Mitchell, "Fighting Guerrillas on the La Fourche," In *Military Order of the Loyal Legion of the United States,* War Papers 56 (Washington, D.C.: Commandery of the District of Columbia, 7 December 1904).

16. Mitchell, "Fighting Guerrillas."

17. Ibid., 3–4.

18. Ibid., 5–6.

19. Ibid., 9; Letter from Henry Richardson to Miss Jemina Robertson, Wyoming, New York, 6 June 1864.

20. Ibid., 11; Reece, *Report of the Adjutant General,* 8:359.

21. Charles Rose to his father, 23 August 1864, printed in the *Waukegan Weekly Gazette,* 17 September 1864, Illinois State Historical Society, Springfield.

22. Mitchell, "Fighting Guerrillas," 11–12.

23. Ibid., 11–13.

24. Ibid.

25. Ibid., 14–15.

26. Ibid., 15–16.

27. *Regimental Order Books, 12th Illinois Volunteer Cavalry,* Record Group 94, Military Records Division, National Archives, Washington, D.C.

28. Redman to his mother from the post hospital in Donaldsonville, Louisiana, 15 September 1864; Redman to his mother from Baton Rouge, Louisiana, 5 October 1864.

29. U. S. Grant to Congressman E. H. Washburn, 2 September 1864, printed in the *Waukegan Weekly Gazette,* 17 September 1864.

30. Redman to his mother, 22 and 27 November 1864.

31. Long, *Civil War Day by Day,* 601; Redman to his mother from Greenville, Louisiana, 21 December 1864.

32. Redman to his sister from Greenville, Louisiana, 24 December 1864; Redman to his mother from Memphis, Tennessee, 12 February 1865.

8: From Tennessee to Texas

1. Reece, *Report of the Adjutant General,* 8:378–80. Special Order No. 92, Memphis, Tennessee, March 2, 1865: "1. In pursuance of Circular No. 36, paragraph III, section 2 from the War Department A.G.O. of 1864, the Twelfth Illinois Cavalry will be consolidated into an eight company organization."

2. Reports of Col. Embry Ostend, Third U.S. Colored Cavalry, Memphis, Tenn., 25 February 1865, *OR,* ser. 1, vol. 48, pt. 1, 68–71.

3. James Pickett Jones, *Yankee Blitzkrieg: Wilson's Raid through Alabama and Georgia* (Athens: University of Georgia Press, 1987), 44–45; Report of Col. John P. C. Shanks, 7th Indiana Cavalry, *OR,* ser. 1, vol. 49, pt. 1, 77. Hereafter cited as Shanks report.

4. Forrest quoted in J. P. Jones, *Yankee Blitzkrieg,* 43.

5. Redman to his sister Emeline from the Christian Commissions Rooms in Memphis, Tennessee, 11 March 1865.

6. Ibid.

7. Correspondence between Col. Hasbrouck Davis and Col. John P. C. Shanks, *OR,* ser. 1, vol. 49, pt. 2, 539.

8. Shanks report, *OR,* ser. 1, vol. 49, pt. 1, 76, 78–79.

9. Ibid., 76–77.

10. Ibid.; Redman to his mother from Memphis, Tennessee, 13 March 1865.

11. Shanks report, *OR,* ser. 1, vol. 49, pt. 1, 77.

12. Ibid., 78.

13. Report of Col. Hasbrouck Davis, 13 March 1865, *OR,* ser. 1, vol. 49, pt. 1, 82.

14. Redman to his mother from Memphis, Tennessee, 13 March 1865; Reports of Capt. Oliver Grosvenor, Twelfth Illinois Cavalry, Memphis, Tenn., 12 March 1865, *OR,* ser. 1, vol. 49, pt. 1, 83.

15. Order of Bvt. Maj. Gen. B. H. Grierson, Military Division of the West, 15 March 1865, *OR,* ser. 1, vol. 49, pt. 1, 839–40; Redman to his sister Jane from Memphis, Tennessee, 19 April 1865.

16. Forrest quoted in Brian Steel Wills, *A Battle from the Start: The Life of Nathan Bedford Forrest* (New York: HarperCollins, 1992), 316.

17. Redman to his sister Jane from Memphis, Tennessee, 19 April 1865; Redman to his mother from Memphis, Tennessee, 25 April and 2 May 1865.

18. Redman to his mother from Newton County, Texas, April 1865; William Richter, *The United States Army in Texas during Reconstruction* (College Station: Texas A & M University Press, 1987), 19.

9: Reconstruction in a Conquered Land

1. Dyer, *Regimental Histories;* Richter, *U.S. Army in Texas,* 19; Redman to his mother from Hempstead, Texas, August 1865.

2. Carrie B. Coss, *Liendo Plantation,* Historic Homes, series 3 (Hempstead, Tex.: Waller County Historical Commission, 1979).

3. Redman to his brother Nelson from Hempstead, Texas, 2 September 1865; Redman to his mother from Houston, Texas, 19 September 1865; Redman to his mother from Houston, Texas, 29 September 1865.

4. Walter LaFeber, *The American Age* (New York: W. W. Norton, 1989), 144; Robert Utley, *Frontier Regulars* (New York: Macmillan, 1973), 12.

5. Eric Foner, *Reconstruction: America's Unfinished Revolution, 1863–1877* (New York: Harper & Row, 1988), 294; Walter Buenger and Robert A. Calvert, eds., *Texas through Time: Evolving Interpretations* (College Station: Texas A & M University Press, 1991), 169; Barry A. Crouch and L. J. Schultz, "Crisis in Color, Racial Separation in Texas during Reconstruction," *Civil War History* (March 1970): 37.

6. Richter, *U.S. Army in Texas,* 19–20; David Paul Smith, *Frontier Defense in the Civil War: Texas Rangers and Rebels,* (College Station: Texas A & M University Press, 1992), 163.

7. Orders from the Office of the Provost Marshal General, District of East Texas, 23 September, 23 October 1865, Redman Papers.

8. Ibid., 26 October, 1 November, 8 November 1865 (orders issued by both the Office of the Provost Marshal General and the Bureau of Freedmen and Abandoned Lands).

9. Special Order No. 66, Extract, from Bvt. Maj. Gen. Charles H. Mower, Commanding Cavalry Forces Headquarters, East District of Texas, Houston, 8 December 1865, to Lt. Col. Hamilton B. Dox, Commanding Twelfth Illinois Cavalry, Personnel Records file of Lt. Col. Hamilton B. Dox, Compilation, RG 94; Captain Edward Mann, 12th Illinois Cavalry, to his wife, 2 December 1865, Adolphus Skinner Hubbard Collection, Chicago Historical Society.

10. Mann to his wife from Houston, Texas, 2 December 1865.

11. Crouch and Schultz, "Crisis in Color," 39; Mann to his wife from Houston, Texas, 2 December 1865.

12. Crouch and Schultz, "Crisis in Color," 38, Forshey quoted on p. 40; *San Antonio Express,* 23 September 1867, quoted in Crouch and Schultz, "Crisis in Color," 40 n. 9.

13. *Crockett Quid Nunce,* 25 July 1865, Texas Newspaper Collection, Center of American History, University of Texas at Austin.

14. Johnson quoted in Foner, *Reconstruction,* 181.

15. Mann to his wife from Houston, Texas, 2 December 1865.

16. *Tri-Weekly Telegraph,* 24 October 1865, 2, Texas Newspaper Collection, Center of American History, University of Texas at Austin.

17. Mann to his wife from Houston, Texas, 2 December 1865; Special Order No. 66 from Mower to Dox, Redman Papers.

18. Mann to his wife from Houston, Texas, 2 December 1865; T. R. Fehrenbach, *Lone Star,* (New York: Macmillan, 1968), 399.

19. Mann to his wife from Houston, Texas, 2 December 1865.

20. Special Order No. 66 from Mower to Dox, Redman Papers.

21. Redman to his brother Nelson from Houston, Texas, 15 March 1866; Report of the Adjutant General, State of Illinois, Administrative Files #301.18.

22. Redman to his sister Jane from Houston, Texas, 1 February 1866.

23. Redman to his mother from Livingston, Texas, 13 February 1866.

24. Ibid.; Redman to his brother Nelson, 16 March 1866; *Chicago Typographical,* Redman Papers.

25. Redman to his mother from Livingston, Texas, 12 March 1866; Redman to his brother Nelson from Livingston, Texas.

26. Redman to friends from Livingston, Texas, 19 March 1866; Redman to his brothers Nelson and Mark from Livingston, Texas, 25 March 1866.

27. Redman to his mother from Livingston, Texas, Easter Sunday, 1 April 1866; Redman to his mother from Livingston, Texas, 12 March 1866.

28. Redman to his mother from Cavalry Headquarters, Houston, Texas, 20

May 1866; Reece, *Report of the Adjutant General,* 8:379.

Epilogue: Sound Taps

1. Roster of the Third Reunion of the 12th Illinois Cavalry, held at Detroit, Michigan, August 5, 1891, Illinois State Historical Society, Springfield, 27. This roster appears to have been printed by the *National Tribune,* a newspaper.

2. Ibid.

3. Roster of the Fourth Reunion of the 12th Illinois Cavalry, held at the World's Fair in Chicago, 1893, Illinois State Historical Society, Springfield, 32.

4. Ibid.

5. Ibid., 34.

6. John K. Mahon, *History of the Militia.*

7. Reunion of the 12th Illinois Cavalry, 5–7 October 1918, Historical Sketch of the Command and of the Dedication of the Lincoln and Douglas Statues, Illinois State Historical Society, Springfield, 6.

8. *Pipestone County Star,* 1 July 1913, p. 4, col. 4. Courtesy of Diane Baker Orgler of Crystal Lake, Illinois.

Bibliography

Primary Sources

Adjutant General's Office. *The Volunteer Force General Orders, 1862.* National Archives, Washington, D.C.

Administrative Files of Civil War Companies and Regiments, 12th Illinois Volunteer Cavalry. Records of the Illinois Adjutant General. Archives and Records Group 301.18. Illinois State Archives, Springfield.

——. Records of the Court of Inquiry of Captain George W. Shears. Illinois State Archives, Springfield.

Alexander-Ackerly Family Papers. Manuscripts Division, Illinois State Historical Library, Springfield.

Allen, Winthrop S. G., Collection. Manuscripts Division, Illinois State Historical Library, Springfield.

Alumni Records, 12th Illinois Cavalry. Williams College, Williamstown, Mass.

Arter, William A., 12th Illinois Cavalry. Personal Service Records. Prisoner of War Record Copy, National Archives, Washington, D.C.

Artlip, John V., Company M, 12th Illinois Cavalry. Diary. Illinois State Historical Library and Preservation Agency, Springfield.

Bandy, Ken, and Florence Freeland, eds., *The Gettysburg Papers.* Vol. 1. Dayton, Ohio: Morningside Press, 1978.

Baylor, George. *Bull Run to Bull Run; or, Four Years in the Army of Northern Virginia.* Richmond, Va.: B. F. Johnson, 1900.

Blackford, W. W. *The War Years with Jeb Stuart.* New York: Charles Scribner's Sons, 1945.

Brown, Varina D. *A Colonel at Gettysburg and Spotsylvania.* Columbia, S.C.: State Company, 1931.

Bureau of Freedmen and Abandoned Lands. Record Group 308. National Archives, Washington, D.C.

Carded Medical Records, 12th Illinois Volunteer Cavalry. Record Group 94. The National Archives, Washington, D.C.

Church, William L. Papers. Archives and Manuscript Division, Chicago Historical Society.

Civil War Companies and Regiments, 12th Illinois Cavalry, Company A, Illinois State Archives, Springfield.

Compilation of Records of Union Volunteer Army Soldiers. Record Group 94. Military Records Division, National Archives, Washington, D.C.

Compiled Records Showing Service of Military Units in Volunteer Union Organizations. Microfilm roll 12: Illinois Seventh Cavalry through Twelfth Cavalry (Microcopy No. 594). National Archives, Washington, D.C.

Court of Inquiry of Lieutenant Colonel Hasbrouck Davis, 12th Illinois Cavalry, 23 July 1863. Special Order No. 142. Extract. Court Martial NN 937, Record Group 153, Box 1610. Department of Old Military Records, National Archives, Washington, D.C.

Court of Inquiry of Captain George W. Shears, Company H, 12th Illinois Volunteer Cavalry. File S2315. Military Records Division, National Archives, Washington, D.C.

Crockett Quid Nunce. Texas Newspaper Collection. Center of American History, University of Texas at Austin.

Department of the Interior. Brochure about Camp Butler National Military Cemetery. Illinois State Historical Society, Springfield.

Eddy, T. M. *The Patriotism of Illinois: A Record of the Civil and Military History of the State in the War for the Union.* 2 vols. Chicago: Clarke & Co., 1865–1866.

Enderton, Herbert B., ed. *The Private Journal of Abraham Joseph Warner.* San Diego: Colonel Herbert B. Enderton, 1973.

Evans, Clement A., ed. *Virginia.* Vol. 3, *Confederate Military History.* Atlanta: Confederate Publishing Company, 1899.

Fleet, Betsey, and John D. P. Fuller, eds. *Green Mount: A Virginia Plantation Family during the Civil War: Being the Journal of Benjamin Robert Fleet and Letters of His Family.* Lexington: University of Kentucky Press, 1962.

Frank, Abner B. *The Civil War Diary of Abner B. Frank.* Transcribed by Larry D. Smith. Vols. 1 and 2. Carlisle Barracks, Pa.: Institute of Military History, U.S. Army War College, 1982.

Gallagher, Gary W., ed. *Fighting for the Confederacy: The Personal Recollections of General Edward Porter Alexander.* Durham: University of North Carolina Press, 1989.

Hamilton, Andrew Jackson. Introduction to *The Papers of Andrew Jackson Hamilton, June 17, 1865 to August 9, 1866.* Governor's Records, RG 101. Archives and Manuscripts Division, Texas State Library and Archives, Austin.

Hardee, William J. *Rifle and Light Infantry Tactics.* Washington, D.C.: J. B. Lippincott, 1861.

Holzer, Harold, ed. *The Lincoln-Douglas Debates.* New York: HarperCollins, 1993.

Hubbard, Adolphus Skinner, Collection. Chicago Historical Society.

Imboden, John D. "The Confederate Retreat from Gettysburg." In *Battles and Leaders of the Civil War.* Edited by R. U. Johnson. 3 vols. New York: Century, 1887–1888.

Johnson, R. U., ed. *Battles and Leaders of the Civil War.* 3 vols. New York: Century, 1887–1888.

Jones, John B. *A Rebel War Clerk's Diary.* Vol. 1. Philadelphia: J. B. Lippincott, 1866.

Longstreet, James. "The Battle of Fredericksburg." In *Battles and Leaders of the Civil War.* Edited by R. U. Johnson. 3 vols. New York: Century, 1887–1888.

Luff, William M., Capt. "The March of the Cavalry from Harpers Ferry, September 14th, 1862." In *Military Order of the Loyal Legion of the United States.* Chicago: Barnard & Gunthrop, Law Printers, 1887.

McClellan, H. B. *I Rode with Jeb Stuart: The Life and Campaigns of Major General J.E.B. Stuart.* Bloomington: Indiana University Press, 1958.

Military Order of the Loyal Legion of the United States. Manuscripts Division, Illinois State Historical Library, Springfield.

Military Order of the Loyal Legion of the United States. National Archives, Washington, D.C.

Mitchell, Frederick W., Capt. "Fighting Guerrillas on the La Fourche." In *Military Order of the Loyal Legion of the United States.* War Papers 56. Washington, D.C.: Commandery of the District of Columbia, 7 December 1904.

——. "A Personal Episode of the First Stoneman Raid." In *Military Order of the Loyal Legion of the United States.* War Papers 56. Washington, D.C.: Commandery of the District of Columbia, 7 December 1904.

Moore, Frank, ed. *The Rebellion Record: The Diary of Events.* 11 vols. New York: G. P. Putnam, 1864.

Pension Records of Union Army Volunteer Veterans. Microfilm roll T/289. Record group 94. National Archives, Washington, D.C.

Portrait and Biographical Record of Winnebago and Boone Counties, Illinois. Chicago: Biographical Publishing Co., 1892.

Redman, William Henry. Papers (#7415-a). Special Collections Department, Manuscripts Division, Alderman Library, University of Virginia Library, Charlottesville.

Reece, J. N., Brig. Gen. *Report of the Adjutant General of the State of Illinois.* Vols. 1–15. Springfield, Ill.: Journal Company Printers and Binders, 1900.

Regimental Order Books, 12th Illinois Volunteer Cavalry. Record Group 94. Military Records Division, National Archives, Washington, D.C.

Reunion of the 12th Illinois Cavalry, Springfield, Illinois. Chicago: 12th Illinois Volunteer Cavalry Association, 1893, 1894, 1918. Illinois State Historical Library and Preservation Agency, Springfield.

Rice, Samuel B. "Letters of Samuel B. Rice, Company D, 9th Virginia Cavalry." *Bulletin of the Northumberland County Historical Society* 26 (1989): 39–41.

Richardson, Henry, First Lieutenant, 12th Illinois Cavalry. Letter to his fiancée, Miss Jemina Robertson. Wyoming, New York, 6 June 1864. Noel Reen Collection, Lafayette, Indiana.

Rock River Democrat. Illinois State Historical Library, Illinois State Archives, Springfield.

Roster of the Survivors of the 12th Illinois Veteran Volunteer Cavalry, March 18, 1894. Illinois State Historical Library and Preservation Agency, Springfield.

Soldiers Pension Records. National Archives, Washington, D.C.

Sterling County Republican. Illinois State Historical Library, Springfield.

Tri-Weekly Telegraph. Texas Newspaper Collection. Center of American History. University of Texas at Austin.

U.S. Army Military History Institute. *Photos of the Men of the 12th Illinois.* Carlisle Barracks, Carlisle, Penn.

U.S. War Department. *Atlas* to accompany *The War of the Rebellion: A Compilation of the Official Records of the Union and Confederate Armies.* Washington, D.C.: Government Printing Office, 1891–1895.

U.S. War Department. *The War of the Rebellion: A Compilation of the Official Records of the Union and Confederate Armies.* 128 vols. Washington, D.C.: Government Printing Office, 1880–1901.

von Borcke, Heroes. *Memoirs of the Confederate War for Independence.* New York: Peter Smith, 1938.

Waukegan Weekly Gazette. Illinois State Historical Library, Springfield.

Wesson, Silas D. Diary. Kane County Historical Society, Batavia, Ill.

White, Julius, Brig. Gen. "The First Sabre Charge of the War." In *Military Essays and Recollections, Papers Read before the Commandery of the State of Illinois.* Vol. 3, *Military Order of the Loyal Legion of the United States.* Chicago: Dial Press, 1899.

Secondary Sources

Bauman, Ken. *Arming the Suckers.* Dayton, Ohio: Morningside Press, 1988.

Bearss, Edwin C. *Forrest at Brice's Crossroads.* Dayton, Ohio: Morningside Press, 1979.

Beringer, Richard E., et al. *Why the South Lost the Civil War.* Athens: University of Georgia Press, 1986.

Bigelow, John, Jr. *The Campaign of Chancellorsville: A Strategic and Tactical Study.* New Haven: Yale University Press, 1910.

Blackwell, Samuel M., Jr. "Illinois at Gettysburg." *Illinois Magazine* (July–August 1984): 33–37.

——. "An Illinois Regiment at Chickamauga." *Illinois Magazine* (September–October 1981): 10–19.

Boatner, Mark M., III. *Civil War Dictionary.* New York: Random House, 1987.

Boyd, Belle. *Belle Boyd in Camp and Prison.* Baton Rouge: Louisiana State University Press, 1998.

Bragg, Jefferson Davis. *Louisiana in the Confederacy.* Baton Rouge: Louisiana State University Press, 1941.

Brownlee, Richard S. *Gray Ghosts of the Confederacy: Guerrilla Warfare in the West, 1861–1865.* Baton Rouge: Louisiana State University Press, 1958.

Buenger, Walter, and Robert A. Calvert, eds. *Texas through Time: Evolving Interpretations.* College Station: Texas A & M University Press, 1991.

Clark, Champ. *Decoying the Yanks: Jackson's Valley Campaign.* The Civil War Series, vol. 4. Alexandria, Va.: Time-Life Books, 1984.

Coggins, Jack. *Arms and Equipment of the Civil War.* New York: Doubleday, 1962.

——. *Brother against Brother.* New York: Time-Life Books, 1990.

Cogley, Thomas I. *History of the Seventh Indiana Cavalry Volunteers.* Laporte, Ind.: Herald Steam Printers, 1876.

Cornish, Dudley Taylor. *The Sable Arm.* New York: W. W. Norton, 1966.

Coss, Carrie B. *Liendo Plantation.* Historic Homes, series 3. Hempstead, Tex.: Waller County Historical Commission, 1979.

Crouch, Barry A., and L. J. Schultz. "Crisis in Color, Racial Separation in Texas during Reconstruction." *Civil War History* (March 1970): 37–49.

Davis, George B., Leslie J. Perry, and Joseph W. Kirkley. *The Official Military Atlas of the Civil War,* comp. Captain Calvin D. Cowles. New York: Fairfax Press, 1983.

Davis, William C. *The Fighting Men of the Civil War.* New York: Salamander Books, 1989.

Dyer, Frederick H. *Regimental Histories.* Vol. 2 of *A Compendium of the War of the Rebellion.* New York: Thomas Yoseloff, 1959.

Esposito, Vincent J., ed. *1689–1900.* Vol. 1 of *The West Point Atlas of American Wars.* New York: Praeger Publishers, 1978.

Faust, Patricia L., ed. *Historical Times Illustrated Encyclopedia of the Civil War.* New York: Harper & Row, 1986.

Fehrenbach, T. R. *Lone Star.* New York: Macmillan, 1968.

Foner, Eric. *Reconstruction: America's Unfinished Revolution, 1863–1877.* New York: Harper & Row, 1988.

Foote, Shelby. *The Civil War, A Narrative.* 3 vols. New York: Random House, 1963.

Freeman, Douglas Southall. *Cedar Mountain to Chancellorsville.* Vol. 2 of *Lee's Lieutenants: A Study in Command.* New York: Charles Scribner's Sons, 1942.

Frye, Dennis E. "The Siege of Harpers Ferry." *Blue & Gray Magazine* (September 1987): 12–24.

——, ed. *Civil War Catalogue Number Twenty-Two.* Dayton, Ohio: Morningside Press, 1987.

Glatthaar, John T. *Forged in Battles.* New York: Macmillan, 1990.

Grimsley, Mark. *The Hard Hand of War: Union Military Policy toward Southern Civilians, 1861–1865.* Melbourne: University of Cambridge, 1995.

Hale, Douglas. *The Third Texas Cavalry in the Civil War.* Norman: University of Oklahoma Press, 1993.

Hall, Clark B. "Brandy Station, 9 June 1863." In *The Civil War Battlefield Guide,* edited by Frances H. Kennedy. New York: Houghton Mifflin, 1990.

Hartwig, D. Scott. "The Defense of McPherson's Ridge." *Gettysburg: Historical Articles of Lasting Interest,* no. 1 (1 July 1980): 15–24.

Hattaway, Herman, and Archer Jones. *How the North Won.* Urbana: University of Illinois Press, 1983.

Hearn, Chester G. *Six Years of Hell: Harpers Ferry during the Civil War.* Baton Rouge: Louisiana State University Press, 1996.

Hess, Earl J. *The Union Soldier in Battle: Enduring the Ordeal of Combat.* Lawrence: University Press of Kansas, 1997.

Heysinger, Isaac W. "The Cavalry Column from Harpers Ferry in the Antietam Campaign." In *Civil War Catalogue Number Twenty-Two.* ed. Dennis E. Frye. Dayton, Ohio: Morningside Press, 1987.

Hicken, Victor. *Illinois in the Civil War.* Urbana: University of Illinois Press, 1986.

Hildenbrand, William F. *Guide to Research Collections of Former United States Senators, 1789–1982.* U.S. Senate Bicentennial Publication #1. Washington, D.C.: U.S. Senate Historical Office, 1983.

Holzer, Harold, ed. *The Lincoln-Douglas Debates.* New York: HarperCollins, 1993.

Howard, Robert P. *Illinois: A History of the Prairie State.* Grand Rapids, Mich.: Eerdmans, 1972.

Hunt, Roger D. *Brevet Brigadier Generals in Blue.* New York: Olde Soldier Books, 1991.

Illinois State Monument Commission. Old State Capitol Square Historical Marker, Springfield, Ill.

James, Garry. "The Reliable Remington." *Civil War Times Illustrated* (September–October 1990): 18–20.

Johnson, Ludwell Harrison. *Red River Campaign: Politics and Cotton in the Civil War.* Baltimore: Johns Hopkins University Press, 1958.

Jones, James Pickett. *Yankee Blitzkrieg: Wilson's Raid through Alabama and Georgia.* Athens: University of Georgia Press, 1987.

Kooser, William H. "Barker's and McClellan's Dragoons." Paper presented at Illinois State Historical Society, Springfield, Ill., 5 December 1998.

Krick, Robert. *The 9th Virginia Cavalry.* Lynchburg, Va.: H. E. Howard Publishing, 1988.

——. "Lee's Greatest Victory." *American Heritage Civil War Chronicles* (Summer 1991): 62–85.

——, ed. *Lee's Colonels: A Biographical Register of the Field Officers of the Army of Northern Virginia,* 2nd ed. Dayton, Ohio: Morningside Press, 1984.

Krolick, Marshall D. "Forgotten Field: The Cavalry Battle East of Gettysburg on July 3, 1863." *Gettysburg Magazine* (January 1991): 61–75.

LaFeber, Walter. *The American Age.* New York: W. W. Norton, 1989.

Lanier, Robert, and Theo F. Rodenbough. *Photographic History of the Civil War.* New York: Fairfax Press, 1989.

Long, E. B. *The Civil War Day by Day: An Almanac, 1861–1865.* Garden City, N.Y.: Doubleday, 1971.

Longacre, Edward. *The Cavalry at Gettysburg.* Lincoln: University of Nebraska Press, 1993.

——. *Lincoln's Cavalrymen: A History of the Mounted Forces of the Army of the Potomac.* Mechanicsburg, Penn.: Stackpole Books, 2000.

——. *Mounted Raids of the Civil War.* Lincoln: University of Nebraska Press, 1975.

——. "The Raid That Failed." *Civil War Times Illustrated* (January 1988): 15–21.

Lowry, Thomas P. *Tarnished Eagles: The Court-Martial of Fifty Union Colonels and Lieutenant Colonels.* Mechanicsburg, Pa.: Stackpole Books, 1997.

Luvaas, Jay, and Harold W. Nelson. *The U.S. Army War College Guide to the Battle of Gettysburg.* New York: Harper & Row, 1986.

——. *The U.S. Army War College Guide to the Battle of Antietam: The Maryland Campaign of 1862.* Carlisle, Pa.: South Mountain Press, 1987.

——. *The U.S. Army War College Guide to the Battles of Chancellorsville and Fredericksburg.* Carlisle, Pa.: South Mountain Press, 1987.

MacDonald, John. *Great Battles.* New York: Macmillan, 1988.

McDonough, James Lee. *Shiloh: In Hell before Night.* Knoxville: University of Tennessee Press, 1977.

McPherson, James M. *Battle Cry of Freedom: The Civil War Era.* New York: Oxford University Press, 1988.

——. *For Cause and Comrades: Why Men Fought in the Civil War.* New York: Oxford University Press, 1997.

McWhiney, Grady, and Perry D. Jamieson. *Attack and Die: Civil War Military Tactics and the Southern Heritage.* University, Ala.: University of Alabama Press, 1982.

Mahon, John K. *History of the Militia and the National Guard.* Vol. 2 of *The Macmillan*

Wars of the United States, gen. ed. Louis Morton. New York: Macmillan, 1983.

Martin, David G. *Gettysburg, July 1.* Conshohocken, Pa.: Combined Books, 1995.

Morrison, James L., Jr. *The Best School in the World: West Point, The Pre–Civil War Years, 1833–1866.* Kent, Ohio: Kent State University Press, 1986.

National Park Service. Harpers Ferry brochure. Washington, D.C.: U.S. Department of the Interior, n.d.

Nesbitt, Mark. *Saber and Scapegoat: J. E. B. Stuart and the Gettysburg Controversy.* Mechanicsburg, Pa.: Stackpole Books, 1994.

Nevins, Allen. *A House Dividing.* Vol. 2 of *The War for the Union.* New York: Scribner, 1960.

———. *The Organized War 1863–1864.* Vol. 3 of *The War for the Union.* New York: Scribner, 1971.

Nye, William Sturtevant. *Here Come the Rebels!* Baton Rouge: Louisiana State University Press, 1965.

O'Neill, Robert F., Jr. *The Cavalry Battles of Aldie, Middleburg, and Upperville, June 10–27, 1863.* Lynchburg, Va.: H. E. Howard, 1993.

Pohanka, Brian C. "Carnival of Death." *America's Civil War* (September 1991): 30–36.

Potter, Stephen R. *Initial Report of Irish Brigade Remains at Antietam National Battlefield.* Washington, D.C.: National Capitol Region, U.S. National Park Service, 1988.

Pratt, Henry E. "Civil War Letters of Winthrop S. G. Allen." *Journal of the Illinois State Historical Society* (October 1931): 553–74.

Ramsdell, Charles W. "General Robert E. Lee's Horse Supply, 1862–1865." *American Historical Review* 35 (1930): 758–77.

Richter, William. *The United States Army in Texas during Reconstruction.* College Station: Texas A & M University Press, 1987.

Robertson, James I., Jr. *General A. P. Hill: The Story of a Confederate Warrior.* New York: Random House, 1987.

Rolph, G. V., and Noel Clark. *The Civil War Soldier.* Washington, D.C.: Historical Impressions, 1961.

Roth, David C. "The War at the Confluence." *Blue and Gray Magazine* (Spring 1991): 17–64.

Sauers, Richard A. "Gettysburg Controversies." *Gettysburg Magazine* (January 1991): 115.

Scheel, Eugene M. *Map of the Civil War in Fauquier.* Warrenton, Va.: The Fauquier National Bank, 1985.

Scott, William F. *The Story of a Cavalry Regiment: The Career of the Fourth Iowa Veteran Volunteers.* New York: G.P. Putnam, 1893.

Sears, Stephen W. *Landscape Turned Red: The Battle of Antietam.* New Haven, Conn.: Ticknor & Fields, 1983.

Shue, Richard S. *Morning at Willoughby Run: July 1, 1863.* Gettysburg, Pa.: Thomas Publications, 1995.

Smith, David Paul. *Frontier Defense in the Civil War: Texas Rangers and Rebels.* College Station: Texas A & M University Press, 1992.

Starr, R. F. S. "Lest We Forget, A Confederate Memorial, Ivy Hill Cemetery, Upperville, Virginia." *Virginia Country Civil War Quarterly* 7 (1987): 72–73.

Starr, Stephen Z. *From Fort Sumter to Gettysburg, 1861–1863.* Vol. 1 of *The Union Cavalry in the Civil War.* Baton Rouge: Louisiana State University Press, 1979.
——. *The War in the East, from Gettysburg to Appomattox, 1863–1865.* Vol. 2 of *The Union Cavalry in the Civil War.* Baton Rouge: Louisiana State University Press, 1980.
——. *The War in the West, 1861–1865.* Vol. 3 of *The Union Cavalry in the Civil War.* Baton Rouge: Louisiana State University Press, 1985.
——. *Jennison's Jayhawkers: A Civil War Cavalry Regiment and Its Commander.* Baton Rouge: Louisiana State University Press, 1973.
Stonesifer, Ray P., Jr. "The Union Cavalry Comes of Age." *Civil War History* (September 1965): 275–76.
Sunderland, Glen. *Wilder's Lightning Brigade.* Washington, Ill.: Book Works, 1984.
Thomas, Emory. *Bold Dragoon.* New York: Harper & Row, 1986.
Thomason, John W., Jr. *Jeb Stuart.* New York: Charles Scribner's Sons, 1930.
Tischler, Allan L. *The History of the Harpers Ferry Cavalry Expedition, September 14 and 15, 1862.* Winchester, Va.: Five Cedars Press, 1993.
Truby, J. David. "Pesky Ships of the Air." *Military History* 4 (February 1988): 8, 58–61.
Tyler, E. H. "A Cavalryman's Legacy: The Story of a Burnside Carbine." *North South Traders Civil War* 18 (1991): 35–40.
Utley, Robert. *Frontier Regulars.* New York: Macmillan, 1973.
Weigley, Russell F. *The American Way of War: A History of United States Military Strategy and Policy.* Bloomington: Indiana University Press, 1973.
Wert, Jeffry D. *Mosby's Rangers.* New York: Simon & Schuster, 1990.
Wills, Brian Steel. *A Battle from the Start: The Life of Nathan Bedford Forrest.* New York: HarperCollins, 1992.
Winters, John D. *The Civil War in Louisiana.* Baton Rouge: Louisiana University Press, 1963.

Index